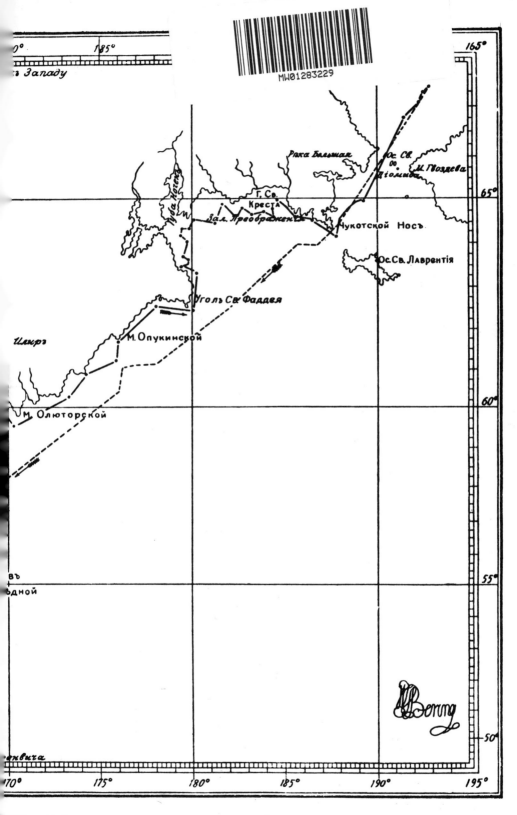

0° | 185° | 165°

къ Западу

Рѣка Большая | Ос. Св.
Діомида | М. Гвоздева
65°
г. Св.
Креста
Зал. Преображенія | Чукотской Носъ
Уба Пенжи
Ос.Св. Лаврентія
Уголъ Св Фаддея
Илиръ | М. Опукинской
М. Олюторской
60°
55°
въ
дной
Bering
50°
жвича
170° | 175° | 180° | 185° | 190° | 195°

1728—1729 гг. (Опубликована В. Берхом).

BERING'S SEARCH FOR THE STRAIT

Vitus Bering was known to declaim,

Sailor,

beware,

lest ye become

the sport of the winds.

(from Horace, *Odes* 1.14, vv. 15-16, translated from Latin)

BERING'S SEARCH FOR THE STRAIT

*The First
Kamchatka
Expedition
1725–1730*

EVGENII G. KUSHNAREV

Edited & Translated by
E.A.P. CROWNHART-VAUGHAN

OREGON HISTORICAL SOCIETY PRESS

Endpapers: Bering's precise signature is reproduced on a scale map later compiled from the expedition's sketch map by Vasilii Berkh, designed to show the track of Vitus Bering's vessel *Sv. Gavriil*, 1728–1729. From D.M. Lebedev, *Plavanie A. I. Chirikova*, opposite p. 20.

Originally published as *V. Poiskakh Proliva: Pervaia Kamchatskaia Ekspeditsiia, 1725–1730*. © 1976 Gidrometeoizdat, Leningrad.

This edition was designed and produced by the Oregon Historical Society Press.

Kushnarev, E.G. (Evgeniĭ Grigor' evich)
    (V poiskakh proliva. English)
    Bering's Search for the Strait: the first Kamchatka
Expedition, 1725–1730 / Evgenii G. Kushnarev; edited and
translated by E.A.P. Crownhart-Vaughan.
        p. cm. -- (North Pacific studies series; 15)
    Translation of: V poiskakh proliva.
    Includes bibliographical references.
    ISBN 0-87595-224-0
    1. Bering, Vitus Jonassen, 1681–1741. I.
Kamchatskaia ekspeditsiia (1st: 1725–1730) II.
Crownhart-Vaughan, E.A.P. III. Title. IV. Series: North
Pacific studies series; no. 15.
G700.1725.B47K8713 1990
910'.92—dc20
                                                     89-26626
                                                        CIP

The paper used in this publication conforms to all significant criteria for archival quality.

Copyright © 1990 Oregon Historical Society,
1230 S.W. Park Avenue, Portland, Oregon 97205
United States of America

Printed in the United States of America.

For all
who dare explore
lands,
seas,
heavens,
&
knowledge.

Publication of this book was assisted financially by the Bureau of Educational and Cultural Affairs of the United States Information Agency, Bruce S. Gelb, Director, under the authority of the Fulbright-Hays Act of 1961, as amended.

In 1988 the importance of the Oregon Historical Society's North Pacific Studies program was recognized at the Federal level. With the support of Senators Mark O. Hatfield and Robert Packwood, and Congressman Les AuCoin, legislation was signed by President Ronald Reagan establishing the North Pacific Studies Center at the Oregon Historical Center in Portland, as an integral department of the Oregon Historical Society.

Permission to publish in English has been granted by VAAP, the All-Union Agency for Authors' Rights, Moscow, V. Tverdovsky, Deputy Chief, Export and Import Department, Scientific and Technical Books.

Contents

BERING'S SEARCH FOR THE STRAIT

Preface
to the
First English Edition

IN THE SPRING AND SUMMER of 1968, Thomas Vaughan, then Executive Director of the Oregon Historical Society, and I made an extended journey within the USSR and the then Soviet bloc for the purpose of establishing research ties with learned societies. Our successes in that initial year were in Khabarovsk, Irkutsk, Novosibirsk, Leningrad, and Moscow. It was far from easy. Cold War attitudes were intensified by competition for the moon race, but through weeks of concentrated effort we gradually instituted a significant group of exchange programs with academic colleagues. Many have been mutually productive for more than two decades.

During that first journey one of the most memorable meetings occurred in a great landmark in Leningrad on the Neva River, the former Bourse, which has long served as Russia's Central Naval Museum. The director, Captain I. M. Kuleshov, received us there with the scientific secretary, the author of this present study, Evgenii Grigorevich Kushnarev. Undaunted by the loss of an arm, this energetic naval scholar had just discovered archival materials pertaining to the great First Kamchatka Expedition of Vitus Bering, which, since the documents had not been brought to light for two hundred years, had never received the attention it deserved, nor its proper place in the history of exploration. Kushnarev was in a state of feverish excitement so familiar to any person engrossed in historical research.

When we returned to the Soviet Union two years later, much had happened. The American moon landings had taken place, with results dismaying to the Soviets. Astronaut Neil Armstrong had just paid an official visit to the Naval Museum, and our hosts there felt we should see everything he had been privileged to see. It was a great opportunity to view all the holdings of the museum. Kushnarev by then had completed his research and was just finishing the manuscript for the present book. It was obvious to us that this work would be an important link in the annals of voyages of exploration in the North Pacific, and might well fit into the proposed North Pacific Studies Series Vaughan was planning to publish through the Oregon Historical Society Press.

In 1976, Kushnarev's work was published in Leningrad. A handshake agreement for OHS to publish an English language edition was followed by a formal official agreement.

Through the years a number of meetings with the author resolved translation queries and provided a most felicitous working relationship and collaborative friendship. Kushnarev's death in January of 1986 deprived him of the pleasure he so much anticipated of seeing the OHS publication of his work, but he was most grateful, as are Thomas Vaughan and I, to all who have made this production possible.

Earliest support for the Russian venture came from an enthusiastic and loyal group of benefactors who, under the aegis of OHS, in 1967–68 established the Irkutsk Archival Research Group. This group has for the past two decades provided support for the scholarship of the Russian sources published in the North Pacific Studies Series. John Youell first headed this vanguard group; he was succeeded by Samuel S. Johnson, Jane West Youell, James B. Thayer, and Noydena L. Brix. Support for research and publication of the series has also come from the National Endowment for the Humanities; Northwest Area Foundation; Westland Foundation; and the S.S. Johnson Foundation. In recent years, the Academy of Sciences of the USSR has evinced special interest in three other North Pacific Studies Series books, the multi-volume documentary history *To Siberia and Russian America: Three Centuries of Russian Eastward Expansion, 1558–1867.*

The publication of this study, *Bering's Search for the Strait,* has been made possible by funds provided by the United States Information Agency; within that agency we especially wish to thank Bruce S. Gelb, Director, and Dr. Raymond H. Harvey, Division of Private Sector Programs. President Ronald Reagan, Senators Mark O. Hatfield and Bob Packwood, and Congressman Les AuCoin have been of significant assistance to this program.

For scholarly assistance we wish to thank Colonel M.J. Poniatowski-d'Ermengard and Daniel Olds.

As with all North Pacific Studies Series publications, this volume was edited, designed, and produced by the Oregon Historical Society Press, under the leadership of Director Bruce Taylor Hamilton. His associates in this endeavor were Kim L. Carlson, George T. Resch, Susan Applegate, and Virginia Linnman. Indexing was done by our longtime expert, Jean Brownell. Volunteers Tessa Hinrichs and Jeffrey Klausmann were instrumental in preparing the manuscript.

Finally, we share with Aleksandra A. Alekseeva-Kushnareva pleasure in the knowledge that her husband's work is hereby made available to English-reading scholars everywhere.

E.A.P. Crownhart-Vaughan
Director, North Pacific Studies Center
Oregon Historical Society

Editorial
Principles
for the
First English Edition

THE TRANSLATION of this study, Number 15 in the Oregon Historical Society Press North Pacific Studies Series, has been an especially rewarding experience, for the author was a twentieth-century scholar, and was not only very much alive in every sense of the word during the time his work was being translated into English, but indeed actively cooperated by consulting with the translator on a number of occasions until his death in 1986.

Evgenii Grigorevich Kushnarev was thus able to correct typographical errors from the Russian publication, restore material excised from his manuscript by the Russian editor, and make a number of brief additions to the text to clarify or enlarge upon a point for readers of the English language edition. We have included these corrections and additions without comment.

We have followed Kushnarev's system of bibliographic reference and citation exactly as he used it; at his request we have added nine titles that were inadvertantly omitted from the Russian publication, or were published subsequently. The superior numbers (e.g.,[14]) refer to the author's notes; archival materials and other sources consulted are indicated in the following manner: |14, p. 19|. Sources have been translated into English in most cases; however, if the source is included in a periodical or anthology, only the title of the piece is translated.

In transliterating Russian words into English we use the Library of Congress system, slightly modified; we omit ligatures and terminal soft signs but retain certain internal soft signs: *zimov'e*. We anglicize plurals of words that have no exact English equivalent: *ostrogs*. Given names of Russian rulers are anglicized: *Peter the Great*.

Dates are given in accordance with the Julian calendar, which was in official use in Russia from 1700 until 1918. In the eighteenth century the calendar was eleven days behind the Gregorian calendar.

As in our previous publications, we have placed the Glossary at the front of the book, where we feel it will be of greatest use to the reader.

Our constant aim in translation is to attempt to render the original into English as the author would have done if he had written in English. A literal, word-for-word translation from Russian to English would resemble a misassembled jigsaw puzzle. In this volume our aim has been immeasurably aided by the many hours spent consulting with Evgenii Grigorevich Kushnarev, hours treasured as well for the special friendship afforded the translator and her husband with the author.

Archival Acronyms Used in This Text

TsGADA: Tsentralnyi gosudarstvennyi arkhiv drevnikh aktov [Central
      State Archive of Ancient Arts]
TsGAVMF: Tsentralnyi gosudarstvennyi arkhiv Voenno-Morskogo Flota
      [Central State Archive of the Navy]
TsGVIA: Tsentralnyi gosudarstrennyi voenno-istoricheskii arkhiv
      [Central State Military History Archive]

Archival abbreviations:
    Ch.:   *chernovik,* draft version
    d.:   *delo,* item or unit
    f.:   *fond,* basic unit group of archival records
    kn.:   *kniga,* book
    op.:   *opis,* list, schedule, inventory
    otd.: *otdel,* section, department
    t.:   *tom,* volume
    vyp.: *vypusk,* issue number

Glossary

Ataman.   A word of Ukrainian origin (*otoman*) applied to various ranks of elected and self-appointed cossack military commanders. From the Ukraine the term spread among the Don and Volga cossacks, and later among the Siberian cossacks.

Baidara.   A large open boat with a wooden framework, covered with cured sea-mammal hides fastened with thongs. Similar to the Eskimo *umiak*. Used by Aleutian Island natives for hunting at sea. It could hold as many as forty persons. Also adapted for use by the Russians, sometimes with a mast, sail, and rudder.

Balagan.   A Tatar word for a stable, barracks, or a temporary shelter for storing goods or equipment; also a summer hut.

Bata.   A river or coastal boat, often made from a single log.

Byk.   A swift current along one shore of a river.

Chetvert.   An old Russian unit of measure. In linear measurement, seven inches; as a unit of dry measure it varied, according to the substance being weighed, from two to four *puds*.

Cossack.   A word of Tatar origin (Kazak) that originally denoted a free frontiersman. In the period of Russian expansion to the North Pacific the term referred to a member of a garrison in a fortified *ostrog* who performed military service under the jurisdiction of Siberian officials.

Desiatnik.   A Russian term for a low-ranking leader of ten cossacks or other armed men.

Doshchanik.   A flat-bottomed river boat about 150 feet long, constructed of pine and fir planks. Used by the Russians for river and coastal transport, it could carry several hundred tons of cargo and forty to fifty people.

Gramota.   A word of Greek origin that referred to a letter, deed, will, charter, or any other official or private written document.

Hieromonk.   In the Russian Orthodox Church, a monk who has been ordained as a priest.

Iasak.   A Mongol-Tatar term meaning tribute paid by the conquered to the conqueror; in this study it refers to a tribute paid in furs. The practice was widespread in Siberia, and introduced briefly in the Aleutian Islands, but officially terminated by tsarist ukaz in 1768. Unofficially it continued throughout the eighteenth and early nineteenth centuries in Russia's American colonies.

Iukola.   Dried meat or fish, especially salmon, used widely in Siberia for winter provisions. The head and backbone were given to sled dogs, and the rest was eaten by natives and by Russians.

Iurt.   A Turkic word for a settlement, camp, or dwelling. In Siberia it referred to a dwelling dug into the earth, or to a semi-excavated dwelling covered with hides.

Izba.   A cottage, cabin, hut, or peasant dwelling; also, any structure housing a wilderness station or post.

Kaiur.   A Kamchadal word for a post or dogsled driver; also a word used to refer to a native taken captive by a rival tribe, who later worked for the Russians in eastern Siberia and Russian America.

Kamerir.   An official whose duties pertained to accounting and other financial matters.

Koch.   A small flat-bottomed sailing vessel used by seventeenth century Russians on Siberian rivers and along the sea coast. Generally the koch had a small deck and could carry a crew of about ten men as well as their equipment and provisions.

Kokura.   The lower part of a tree trunk along with the major perpendicular roots.

Lodka.   A river boat about two hundred feet long capable of transporting up to 1,200 tons of cargo and seventy persons.

Oblast.   A Russian term for a province, region, or administrative district.

Osmina.   A Russian term for two units of measure: (1) a dry measure equal to three bushels; and (2) a measure of land equal to approximately 0.7 acres.

Ostrog.   A Russian term for a fort, fortification, blockhouse, settlement, or town.

Peredovshchik.   A foreman, experienced seaman, or pilot of a vessel, especially one engaged in the fur trade; also, an experienced hunting guide.

Prikashchik.   A low-ranking official or agent; a town or village administrator; a steward; a merchant's agent.

Promyshlennik.   A hunter of fur-bearing animals, fish, or birds. Also, an individual Russian hunter, trader, or trapper who worked for himself, in a group, or for a wealthy merchant; or government officials on assignments such as exploration, conquest, and pacification of natives.

Pud.   A Russian unit of weight equal to 36 pounds or 16.38 kilograms.

Purga.   A Siberian blizzard; a blinding snowstorm with high winds and intense cold.

Raznochintsy.   Intellectuals not belonging to the gentry.

Sazhen.   A unit of linear measure equal to seven feet or 2.134 meters.

Shitik.   Literally, a "sewed" seagoing vessel, whose planking was fastened together with twisted willow and fir withes.

Shivera.   A swift current that pulses from rocks all across a river.

Skazka.   An oral account.

Sluzhitel.   A servant or attendant; a civil or military servitor.

Sotnik.   A Russian term for a commander of a military unit of one hundred men, cossacks, or streltsy.

Syn boiarskii.   An impoverished member of Russian nobility; in Siberia such persons played a prominent role as middle-rank military commanders and civil administrators.

Telega.   A cart or wagon, with shafts, used for peasant or post transport.

Ulus.   A Mongol term for a settlement, an area inhabited by a native tribe, or a domain or realm belonging to a Tatar, Mongol, Kalmyk, or Uzbek ruler.

Uezd.   A Russian term for a district administrative unit that included a settlement and the surrounding rural area; also, a subdivision of a diocese.

Ukaz.   A Russian term for a decree, edict, or order issued by the Tsar.

Vedro.   A Russian unit of measure equal to twenty-one pints; more generally, a bucketful or pailful.

Vershok.   A Russian unit of linear measure equal to 1.75 inches.

Verst.   A Russian unit of linear measure equal to 3,500 feet or 1.06 kilometers.

Voevoda.   An old Slavic term for a military commander. A Tsar-appointed administrator holding military, civil, and judicial powers over a region.

Volokush.   A piece of heavy webbing dragged by men or horses to transport bulky cargo.

Zakazchik.   An overseer or foreman.

Zimov'e.   A Russian term for a small winter outpost in a newly conquered region.

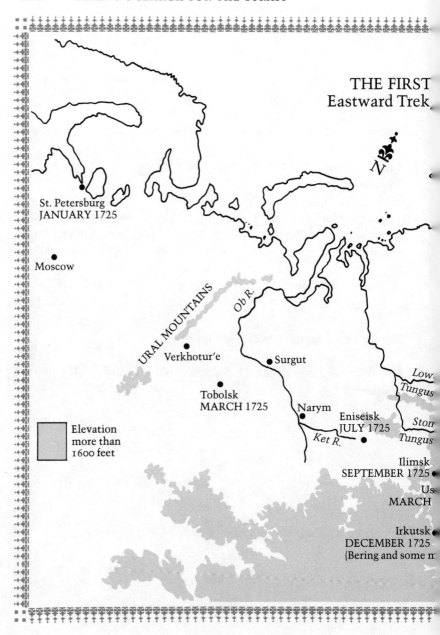

THE FIRST
Eastward Trek

N

St. Petersburg
JANUARY 1725

Moscow

URAL MOUNTAINS

Ob R.

Verkhotur'e

Surgut

Low
Tungus

Tobolsk
MARCH 1725

Narym

Eniseisk
JULY 1725

Ston

Ket R.

Tungus

Elevation
more than
1600 feet

Ilimsk
SEPTEMBER 1725

Us
MARCH

Irkutsk
DECEMBER 1725
(Bering and some m

KAMCHATKA EXPEDITION
January 1725–August 1728

North
America
(Alaska)

Diomede Is.

AUGUST
1728

Cape
Chukotskii

Holy Cross Bay

Chukotsk Peninsula

*Anadyrskii
Bay*

Anadyr R.

Indigirka R.

Kolyma R.

Oliutorskii

Komandorskie Is.

Kamchatka

JULY
1728

iberia

Lena R.

Okhotsk
OCTOBER 1726

Kamchatka R.

Iakutsk
JUNE 1726

Sea of Okhotsk
AUGUST 1727

Bolsheretsk
SEPTEMBER
1727

Iudoma R.

Kuril Is.

dan R.

STANOVOI MOUNTAINS

Sakhalin I.

*Sea of
Japan*

BERING'S SEARCH FOR THE STRAIT
The First Kamchatka Expedition, 1725–1730

[*V Poiskakh Proliva:*
Pervaia Kamchatskaia Ekspeditsiia, 1725–1730]

EVGENII G. KUSHNAREV

Translation of the Russian edition,
originally published in 1976

Introduction

I N OUR TIME every Russian school child knows that Asia and
America are separated by a strait that was discovered by
Semen Dezhnev in 1648. But why did Peter the Great send out
an expedition, led by Vitus Bering, to search for this strait in 1725,
seventy-seven years after Dezhnev had already discovered it?
How and why was the idea conceived to outfit such an expedition, how was it made ready, who took part in it, and what ob-
stacles did the expedition members surmount during the course
of the three and a half years in order to reach the shores of
Chukotka? What did the expedition accomplish, and what was it
unable to achieve? What place does it occupy in the history of
geographical exploration and discovery in the Far East, and how is
it different from other expeditions?

This work attempts to answer these and other questions, relying on many previously unknown archival documents.

From ancient times the boundless expanses of Siberia have cap-
tured the interest of the Russian people. As early as the four-
teenth century the people of Novgorod crossed the Ural Mountains. A stream of overland travelers flooded into the East in the
sixteenth century after the Russian central government elimin-
ated, one after another, the khanates of Kazan, Astrakhan, and
Sibir, the original barriers to such movement. Following private
individuals acting at their own risk and peril, a group of state servitors began to move out to the East. To consolidate the new
lands and impose tribute on the local native peoples, they built
ostrogs and *zimov'es*, and in this manner they founded Siberian
towns: Tiumen (1586), Narym (1596), Turinsk (1600), Iakutsk
(1632), and others.

These trekkers moved east not only by overland routes, but
also by sea, along the northern coast of Siberia. The voyage of the
seafarer Dezhnev, one of the most remarkable of these men, is recorded in historical literature of that time. It is true that the results of this voyage were not always recorded on maps with complete accuracy. For example, on the 1667 Godunov sketch map of
Siberia |1|, the northeastern extremity of Asia is washed by the
sea, but Chukotka is not located, nor are the Diomede Islands nor
even the Anadyr River, which the seafarer had discovered. The
Lena and Kolyma rivers are moved to the east coast of Asia. A
1673 sketch map of Siberia exhibits similar inaccuracies. The
map that best indicates Dezhnev's discovery is that of Peter
Müller, which includes information from the maps of Dezhnev
and Mikhail Stadukhin, neither one of which has survived to the
present |2|.

From the 1680s on, cartographers tended to deny or doubt the
possibility of sailing from the northern Arctic Ocean to the Pacific. A sketch map of Siberia from 1684–85 provides an example
of this. It shows the results of Dezhnev's voyage, but at the same
time depicts the Chukotsk Peninsula as extending beyond the
edge of the map. There are a number of such maps. Several have
inscriptions near capes that extend beyond the edge of the map:
"The Mountain has no end" (1673 map of Siberia) or "Impassable
cape" (Remezov's 1700–01 ethnographic map). Elchin's map of
1718 or 1719 depicts the southeastern part of Kamchatka as extending beyond the map, and near it is the notation, "According
to the account of the Kamchatka *cossack* Ivan Eniseisk and his

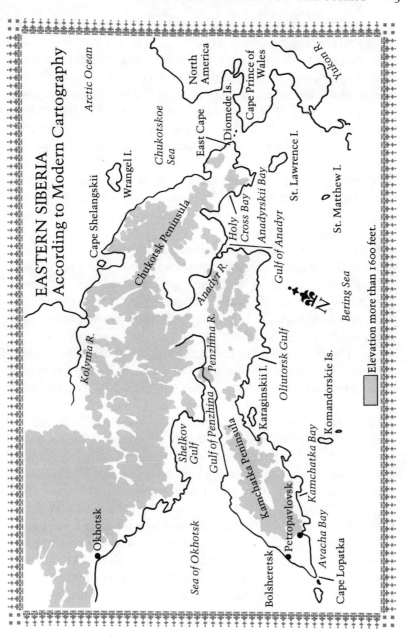

EASTERN SIBERIA
According to Modern Cartography

Arctic Ocean

North America

Cape Prince of Wales

Yukon R.

Diomede Is.

East Cape

Chukotskoe Sea

Wrangel I.

Cape Shelangskii

Chukotsk Peninsula

Holy Cross Bay

Anadyrskii Bay

St. Lawrence I.

St. Matthew I.

Anadyr R.

Gulf of Anadyr

Kolyma R.

Penzhina R.

Bering Sea

Oliutorsk Gulf

N

Shelkov Gulf

Gulf of Penzhina

Karaginskii I.

Kamchatka Peninsula

Komandorskie Is.

Kamchatka Bay

Okhotsk

Sea of Okhotsk

Petropavlovsk

Bolsheretsk

Avacha Bay

Cape Lopatka

Elevation more than 1600 feet.

comrades ... between the warm and the frozen seas many natives told them they did not know of any strait through this land
from one sea to the other." We also find this depiction of Kamchatka as a barrier to sailing from the Arctic Ocean to the Pacific
on a map discovered in the collection of the State Historical Mu-
seum |3|. The denial of a northeastern sea passage is also charac-
teristic of a group of foreign maps. On a 1687 map by N. Witsen of
Holland, in the place where Chukotka should be, we find the
notation, "Icy cape, the end of which is unknown." And on the
1706 map of Tartary by Guillaume Delisle, a mountain ridge in
the northeastern corner of Asia is shown with the notation, "It is
not known where this mountain chain ends, and whether it is
joined to some continent."

How can we explain the appearance of maps on which
Dezhnev's voyage either was not shown at all, or was distorted?
The question about a strait did not arise during Dezhnev's
lifetime, and his voyage was never properly evaluated in official
documents, so very likely it was not widely known by his contemporaries.

Such objective factors as the backwardness of feudal serfdom in
seventeenth-century Russia and the low level of geographical
knowledge contributed to this problem. We know that Dezhnev
himself was inadequately schooled in geography and that even he
did not realize that by rounding Chukotka he had discovered the
strait that separates Asia and America. Dezhnev's petitions are
evidence of the fact that his feat did not receive the recognition it
deserved during his lifetime. He applied repeatedly to the Tsar in
petitions to be compensated for his long years of service, and to be
promoted. In a 1660 petition he wrote, "I have served you, Great
Sovereign ... without your Sovereign's recompense in money
and provisions ... I have suffered every need and privation, I
have eaten the bark of pine and larch trees and every kind of foul
mess—for 21 years" |4, p.150|. In the end he received only thirty
eight rubles instead of the 128 that had been authorized, and a
certain amount of broadcloth; but he was promoted, as he had requested, to the rank of cossack *ataman*.

Because of the absence of a clear official evaluation of his discovery, cartographers, in placing coastlines on the maps, used not
only the charts of Dezhnev and Stadukhin, but also the oral ac-

counts of sailors; this simply added to errors in transmitting the results of the voyage.

Dezhnev faded from memory, and consequently the overland route via the Anadyr River, which Semen Motora and Stadukhin had discovered a year after Dezhnev's feat, was the only known route to the east. Further, unsuccessful attempts to repeat Dezhnev's voyage gave new reason for believing even more firmly that there was an "impassable" cape on the northeastern extremity of Asia. Once these capes were depicted on maps, the notion that there was no sea passage between the continents in the north was bolstered.

Until the seventeenth and early eighteenth centuries, even the names of the earliest explorers and the details of their voyages were buried in the depths of the archives. There was no mention of Dezhnev's discovery even in such important documents as *gramotas* of 1698 and 1700 from Tsar Peter I to Dorofei Traurnikht, the *voevoda* [administrator] of Iakutsk. These gramotas instruct Traurnikht to ascertain whether it is possible to sail along the coast of Siberia from the Lena River east to the Kolyma River. Bering's First Kamchatka Expedition is an even greater confirmation of the oblivion into which Dezhnev's voyage had fallen. The very conception of the Bering expedition and the numerous documents relating to it testify to the fact that Peter, members of the Admiralty College, Bering himself, his associates, and even most of the Siberians were not aware of Dezhnev's voyage—and Bering's associates included such old-time Siberians as Nikifor Treska and Kuzma Sokolov, who had found a route across the Sea of Okhotsk to Kamchatka in 1716, and Fedor Luzhin, a member of Bering's expedition who had already taken part in an expedition to Kamchatka and the Kuril Islands.

Thus in the 1720s Dezhnev's remarkable discovery was not acknowledged, and there were two opposing opinions about a strait between Asia and America. The purpose of the First Kamchatka Expedition was to end this uncertainty.

Peter's gramotas to Traurnikht outlined an extensive program of exploration, for Peter was interested in new lands, unknown peoples, the mineral wealth of Siberia, and the possibility of sailing along the northern shores of Siberia.

As this program was carried out, a major discrepancy developed between the broad scope of the project and the limited resources to carry it out. Such vast enterprises could not be undertaken by the small, poorly outfitted groups who had conducted earlier expeditions.

In 1716 an expedition far more important than any before was organized to go to the Far East—the Great Kamchatka Expedition. It was to explore Kamchatka and Chukotka and send out vessels from the mouths of the Anadyr and Kolyma rivers to search for islands and "mainland" opposite Chukotka. Some two hundred men were assembled and fitted out with a vast amount of provisions and supplies. There was little to distinguish this expedition from previous ones, however, for it was local in character; the Siberian governor drew up the instructions and the Iakutsk voevoda, Ia. A. Elchin, carried them out. The expedition did not include scientists and it had neither a clear plan of action nor adequate funding. The best indication of this is that Prokofei Nagibin, the navigator assigned to oversee the voyage to Bolshaia Zemlia (America), had to build a ship with his own money. Elchin had previously made a sketch map of northeastern Asia on the basis of information he obtained by asking questions, but it was very inaccurate and had no grid. The expedition failed, clearly a result of not only the scale but also the plan of the enterprise.

This was the last expedition organized in the spirit of old traditions.[1] The first scientific expedition was that of Ivan M. Evreinov and Fedor F. Luzhin, who were sent by Peter to search for precious metals on the Kuril Islands. Geodesists who had been trained at the Naval Academy were in charge of the expedition; the central government supplied them with necessary instruments, but they were poorly fitted out, and they sailed in such a flimsy little vessel it was a miracle they were not shipwrecked. The map of Siberia that the expedition compiled was more accurate than previous ones. This expedition had certain new elements, but basically it was transitional in nature.

The first major scientific naval expedition to the Far East was the Kamchatka Expedition of 1725–1730, also initiated by Peter the Great. The Admiralty College and the Senate provided overall leadership; the government appropriated significant funding. In its goals, the makeup of its participants, outfitting, methods of work, and eventual result, the expedition was scientific in the fullest sense. And in its very scale it was distinctly different from all previous Russian expeditions. Credit for the organization and execution of the First Kamchatka Expedition, which set off for the East almost before the newly founded (1724) Academy of Sciences had begun to function, belongs to the regular Navy, which had already earned an illustrious reputation through its brilliant victories. Subsequently it became a tradition for naval personnel to participate in peacetime exploration.

This first major Russian scientific naval expedition occupies an important place in the history of Russian science. No history of the discovery and development of the Russian Far East could be written without studying it.

ONE

*Reasons for
Organizing
the Expedition*

THE MATTER OF THE GOALS and objectives of the Kamchatka Expedition of 1725–1730 |6| is extremely complex. For some time this expedition was looked upon as a purely geographical undertaking. Peter I was the first to express this view. His written instructions read:

1. You are to build one or two boats, with decks, either in Kamchatka or in some other place.

2. You are to proceed in those boats along the land that lies to the north, and according to the expectations (since the end is not known), it appears that land [is] part of America.

3. You are to search for the place where it is joined to America, and proceed to some settlement that belongs to a Euro-

pean power; or if you sight some European ship, find out
from it what the coast is called, and write it down; go ashore
yourself and obtain accurate information; locate it on the
map and return here |7, p.59|.

Thus the aim of the expedition was to explore the Asiatic coast
north of Kamchatka and search for the place where Asia "is
joined" to America. Then, in order to be certain that the discovered place really was America, and to relate the newly discovered land on the map to those lands already known, the expedition was to continue on to any European possession, or to a
place where it would encounter some European ship. So the immediate objective of the expedition was to resolve the age-old
geographical riddle about the configuration of the continents in
the north.

This is how the purpose of the expedition was understood by
the participants, by the contemporary scholars Ivan K. Kirilov and
Gerhard F. Müller, by the members of the Senate and the Admiralty College, and by the majority of scholars for the next century.

A proponent of that point of view during the Soviet period has
been the academician L.S. Berg |8, p.601|, who exaggerated the in-
fluence of G.W. Leibnitz whom he considered the instigator of
the expedition.[2] But the question of the strait had come up long
before Leibnitz raised it. By the thirteenth century Arab scholars
were considering the possibility of sailing from the Pacific to the
Arctic Ocean. In 1492 the Bechheim globe showed Asia as separated from America. In 1525 the idea of the existence of a strait
was expressed by the Russian envoy to Rome, Dmitrii
Gerasimov. From the sixteenth century on, we find this same
strait on many maps under the name "Anian." But on some maps,
indeed some of those previously mentioned, the continents are
joined. Such lack of agreement proves there was no precise information on the strait, and that an exploratory voyage would be
necessary to resolve the mystery. Leibnitz was one of the first to
suggest, in 1697, that the Russians should be the ones to solve
this geographical puzzle, and with commendable persistence he
reiterated his suggestion |11, p.192|. Thus in 1716 when Leibnitz
and Peter spent several days in Braunschweig, this matter was
raised in their conversations. Leibnitz wrote, "... his [Peter's]

An exuberant London portrait of a young and imperious Peter, executed in the royal mode flaunted by Sir Godfrey Kneller. (Courtesy, the Royal Collections, Kensington Palace.)

primary interest is focused on everything that relates to navigation ... I hope that through him we will learn whether Asia is
joined to America" |12, p.187|.

There was another theory of why the expedition was organized
and what its aims were, and this one had to do with Peter. The
Tsar, a serious intellectual and outstanding statesman, would
hardly have undertaken an expensive expedition just out of
curiosity, especially since the country was at that time exhausted
by long, drawn out wars. An ultimate goal of exploration was the
discovery of a northern route. And that nothing is mentioned of
that in the instructions can most probably be explained by Peter's
intention to use the results of the expedition in the future.

John Perry speaks of Peter's practical attitude toward the expedition. In his book, published in 1716 upon his return to En-
gland from Russia (and translated in Moscow in 1867) |13, pp.40–
41|, he writes that the Tsar intended to send out the expedition in
order to determine whether it was possible to sail along the north
coast of Siberia to China and Japan.

Further confirmation of the utilitarian approach to the expedition is given by Fedor S. Saltykov's project of 1713–14, which is
evident from its title, "Concerning the search for an open sea
route from the Dvina River to the mouth of the Amur and to
China," and likewise A.A. Kurbatov's project of 1721 in which he
proposed searching for a sea route from the Ob and other rivers
and organizing voyages with the aim of trade with China and
Japan.

Certain obviously erroneous points of view have also been ex-
pressed. A.A. Pokrovskii |14, p.21| maintained that the purpose of
the expedition was "to proceed along the coastline of the American continent to some European town" and establish trade with
that town. Since the northernmost European possession in America was Mexico, which belonged to Spain, he concluded that Mexico was the ultimate goal of the voyage. He was not troubled by
the fact that the expedition carried neither trade goods nor money
with which to trade, and that at that time no foreign ship could
put into shore in that part of western America without special
permission from the King of Spain |15, part VII, p.524|.[3] Further-
more, the seafarers had taken on provisions for only one season
and thus could not have sailed to Mexico, for they could not have
had time in one summer to reach the strait, proceed to Mexico,

and return to their own shores. At that time a winter voyage on the stormy sea was out of the question.

Other scholars have also held to the "Mexican version," among them Aleksandr I. Andreev[4] and Dmitrii M. Lebedev.[5]

We find a very broad interpretation of the aims of the expedition in the work of Mikhail I. Belov. He felt that the expedition, apart from clearing up the question as to whether the continents are joined, "at the same time also resolved a related problem—whether it was possible to sail from Arkhangel to the Pacific Ocean and America" |19, p.53|. In reality, the duty of the seafarers was not to seek a route to America, but to determine whether a strait existed, and thus in the final analysis to contribute to the solution of the more important problem, the discovery of a northern sea route.

Vadim I. Grekov held a special position in considering that the expedition had no relation to the strait but was to reconnoiter a route to America and ascertain who lived there. However, this is clearly not in accord with Peter's instructions and with other documents.[6]

In 1964 Boris P. Polevoi advanced a completely new hypothesis, which the authors of a massive work on the history of Siberia accepted on faith |22, p.162|. He maintained that the purpose of the First Kamchatka Expedition was to resolve the question, not of a strait between the continents, but of the union of the mythical "Da Gama" land with America, with the aim of seizing the northern regions of the latter. For that reason, the expedition was to sail not north, but east, along the southern coast of Da Gama land |21, pp.88–92|.

If one is to rely on Pokrovskii, Grekov, or Polevoi, it is necessary to ascertain the failure of the expedition, since not only did the seafarers not discover a route to America, they did not even make the slightest effort to do so. A court would have imposed severe punishment for such a disregard for instructions—even a death sentence. In 1745, M.P. Spanberg was sentenced to death, although the Tsaritsa commuted this to a reduction in rank to second lieutenant, for willfully leaving Siberia. But Bering was promoted, given a raise in pay, and named commander of a new expedition.

In the 1870s, Karl E. von Baer was the first to approach a true understanding of the motives for sending out the expedition. It was not until one hundred years later that A.V. Efimov supported his view and enlarged upon it |5, pp.34–40,164–165|. However, he exaggerated the threat to Russia's eastern borders in relation to the colonization of North America. At the beginning of the eighteenth century the vast territory in Northwest America not only was not claimed by Europeans; they had not even discovered it. Between America and the Russian lands in Asia lay the still unexplored boundless expanse of the Great Ocean. None but the Russians knew a sea route to Kamchatka, and for a long time navigators had strict instructions to keep this route secret from foreigners.[7] History does not support Efimov's point of view.[8]

V.A. Divin overestimates the possible threat to the eastern borders of the realm in considering this one of the primary concerns in organizing the First Kamchatka Expedition. He writes, "Once they had discovered and conquered new lands in the northern part of the Pacific Ocean that were not claimed by Europeans, they had to strengthen the security of the borders of the realm" |25, p.43|.[9] However, subsequent events such as the sale of Alaska and the islands in the North Pacific for a mere pittance testify to the fact that the possession of these islands only complicated the defense of Russia's eastern borders.

What then were the real motives for organizing the First Kamchatka Expedition?

At the beginning of the eighteenth century in Russia there were new developments in various spheres of material and spiritual life. Shipbuilding was considerably improved, the regular navy and army were created, there were great cultural advances, the school of mathematical and navigational sciences was founded and had an astronomical laboratory, the naval academy was established to educate navigators and shipbuilders, and a significant number of schools of general education were established to train future seafarers and others in mathematics, naval architecture, artillery, and other subjects.

As a result, at the end of the first quarter of the eighteenth century the country had established through financial support and material means a cadre of shipbuilders and navigators and was in a position to organize a major scientific naval expedition. However, this was still only a possibility. The transformation into reality depended on the requirements of the economy and on political factors.

The seventeenth century began a new era in the history of the country characterized by gradual economic mergers of separate *oblasts* [provinces] and areas into a unified entity. There was an increase in the demand for foreign goods such as tea, spices, silk, and dyes; these came into Russia through second and third hands and were sold at exhorbitant prices. The attempts to establish river routes to India, dispatch ships with trade goods to Spain, and prepare an expedition to Madagascar all testify to Russia's desire to establish direct communication with foreign markets. Nearly always at that time the prospect of direct trade with China, Japan, and India was related to a northern sea route.

The entire accelerated process of the primary accumulation of capital likewise had great significance in that "soft gold"—furs— played the role of precious metals in forming an important source of private enrichment and a considerable item in the state budget. In order to increase the acquisition of furs, it was necessary to find new lands, especially since by the end of the seventeenth century the Russians had already exhausted the wealth of furs in previously conquered regions.

From the newly settled lands came furs, walrus ivory, and other precious goods; and into these lands were sent grain, salt, and iron. However, the transport of goods overland was attended by incredible difficulties. The cost of grain sent from Iakutsk to Okhotsk, even by the end of the eighteenth century, had increased more than tenfold,[10] and Kamchatka was much farther away. There was a saying that was all too true, "Overseas a heifer costs only a kopeck, but transport costs a ruble." It was necessary to find a new and better route. And contemporary thought again turned to a northern sea route.

Russia had become a vast power stretching from the shores of the Baltic Sea to the Pacific Ocean. Under the onslaught of the bold overland explorers and seafarers, the *terra incognita* had "retreated" to the northeastern corner of Asia. There, for a distance of a thousand kilometers, no one as yet knew the precise coastlines of the continent. It was necessary to define these clearly on the maps, to subdue the lands within these boundaries, and to secure them for Russia, so that in the event a strait did exist, that country might undertake a voyage via the northern sea route to the eastern shores of its own land and to other realms in the Pacific Basin.

This robust portrait purported to be the famous Dane, Vitus Bering, hangs in the main gallery of the Central Naval Museum, Leningrad. Artist presently unknown. (Published with permission of VAAP, Moscow.)

This is confirmed by a report of 18 August 1727[11] from the Senate to the Tsaritsa Catherine I in regard to preparations for Afanasii Shestakov's expedition, that had the goal of securing the lands beyond Russia, west of the maritime regions which were to be explored by Bering with the First Kamchatka Expedition. The two expeditions were to be complementary, and the Senate directed the leaders, "Wherever you serve ... you are to assist one another."

The importance of describing the conquered lands and discovering new ones was even mentioned in the charter of the Academy of Sciences. "The most useful seafarers in the realm will be those who not only make accurate descriptions of all known lands, but can also sometimes divine those unknown" |28, p.9|.

In the last analysis, the aspiration for knowledge was also a stimulus for organizing the expeditions. Peter and his associates wanted their country, already occupying a leading place in the political life of Europe, to be among the foremost in dissemination of culture and learning. They understood that the resolution of the question of a strait, in which scholars throughout the world were keenly interested, would confer great prestige upon Russian science.

The following fact attests to the interest displayed by foreign scholars in this geographical puzzle. At the time of Peter's visit to France in 1717, the Parisian Academy proposed to him that they would organize a French overland expedition to clarify whether a strait existed between Asia and America. It is doubtful whether this proposal actually indicated a genuine intention on the part of the French, for it would have been much easier for them to send such an expedition by sea. One may suppose that the French really wanted to emphasize the importance of the problem and to urge the Russians on to its solution. Knowing the difficulties the Russians had in penetrating the territory of Siberia, we may be quite positive in stating that if the French expedition had indeed been organized, it would certainly have ended in failure. The Tsar refused permission, declaring that he himself intended to send out such an expedition. Why then was it postponed?

The primary reason for the delay was the situation that had resulted from drawn out wars that had required enormous expenditures. It was no coincidence that Kirilov's 1734 project proposal

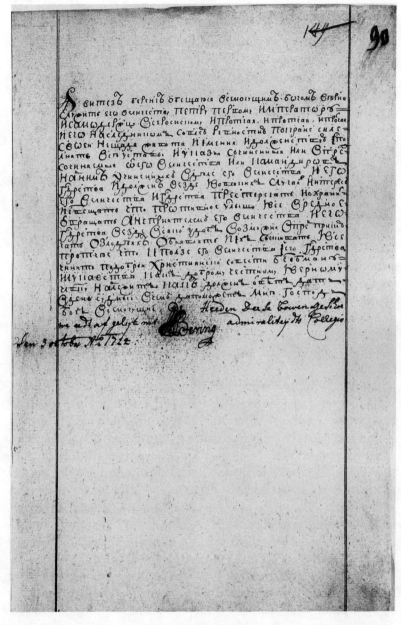

Oath sworn by Vitus Bering and signed by him on 3 October 1724. (Published with permission of VAAP, Moscow.)

commented in regard to the expedition that "although the desire was there on the part of His Highness, he could not instigate [the expedition] in wartime and during the campaign on the lower [Volga]" |29, p.289|.

But even during these years of intense struggle for an outlet onto the sea, the Tsar did not lose sight of the distant regions in the northeastern part of the land. In his instructions to Evreinov and Luzhin (1719), Peter ordered, "Determine whether America is joined to Asia; make a very thorough determination of what lies not only south and north, but also east and west, and locate everything accurately on a map" |17, p.5|. Peter's contemporary Fedor I. Soimonov also attested to this attitude during the war with Persia (1722–23).[12]

It is possible that frontier disputes served as the immediate stimuli for preparing the expedition. The Senate Oversecretary, I.K. Kirilov, recounted that when Peter appeared before the Senate in December, 1724, he wanted to see "maps of the Siberian lands." Kirilov directed Peter's attention to the discrepancies between the Evreinov-Luzhin map and a foreign map made in 1721, compiled from information gathered by French missionaries in 1708–1710. At that point, the Tsar ordered information from the two maps to be combined into a single map. Kirilov carried out this assignment and presented Peter with the new map. A copy of this map was apparently included with the instructions for the Bering Expedition |29, p.289|.[13] Kirilov's account refutes the versions of Homann's map, which Polevoi advances.

In any event, precisely a year after the Persian campaign, when the country had still not recovered from the wars which had been waged almost continuously for twenty-eight years, Peter again turned to the idea of the expedition. It is very significant that on one day, 23 December 1724, he signed two ukazes: one ordered work to be speeded up in compiling a map of all the *gubernias* and *uezds*; the other organized the First Kamchatka Expedition.

This is the earliest extant official document concerning the expedition. There were five points, each of which included Peter's orders and the response of the Admiralty College. Opposite certain points marks were made in the margins in the hand of the Tsar himself. The full text of the ukaz |33, ll. 110–111| reads:

1. *Find geodesists who have been in Siberia and have returned.* [Response from Admiralty College:] On orders from
the Senate the following geodesists were [previously] sent to
the Siberian gubernia: Ivan Zakharov, Petr Chichagov, Ivan
Evreinov (deceased), Fedor Luzhin, Petr Skobeltsyn, Ivan
Svistunov, Dmitrii Baskakov, Vasilii Shetilov, Grigorii
Putilov.

2. *Find a qualified naval lieutenant or sublieutenant to go
with them* [geodesists] *to Siberia and Kamchatka.* [Re-
sponse:] In the opinion of Vice Admiral Sievers and Rear Admiral Seniavin, any of the following are qualified for such an
expedition: lieutenants [M.P.] Spanberg, Sverev, or [A.N.]
Kosenkov, or sublieutenants [A.I.] Chirikov or [D.Ia.] Laptev.
Either Captain [Vitus] Bering or [K.P.] von Verd is recommended as commanding officer. Bering has been in East India
and knows conditions, and von Verd has been a navigator.

3. *Find a student or an apprentice who can build a decked
boat there, similar to the ones here that accompany large
ships. For that purpose send him four young shipwrights
with their tools, a quartermaster, and eight seamen.* [Re-
sponse:] The apprentice shipwright Fedor Kozlov is capable
of building boats either with or without decks, according to
designs.
[Note in the margin:] *It is very necessary to have a navigator
and assistant navigator who have been to North America.*

4. *For this expedition send from here half again as much*
[note in margin: *Twice as much*] *sailcloth, pulleys,* shif [a
boat or a vessel], *cordage, and the like and four falconets
with appropriate ammunition and one or two sailmakers.*
[Response:] The rigging is being sent.
[Note in margin:] *Everything else is fine.*

5. *If such navigators cannot be found in the* [Russian] *Navy,
then immediately write to Holland via the Admiralty Post
and request two men who are familiar with the sea north toward Japan.* [Noted by Vice Admiral Sievers:] If there are
any such navigators in the [Russian] Navy they will be sent
without delay.

Of those who took part in the expedition, six are mentioned in the ukaz: Bering, Spanberg, Chirikov, Luzhin, Putilov, and Kozlov. It is obvious from the ukaz that Peter did not intend to send senior officers on the expedition and that the proposal concerning this was suggested to the College on the basis of the opinions of Sievers and Seniavin. In historical literature it is frequently emphasized that Bering had spent time in the East Indies.

Peter's efforts to locate a navigator and assistant who had been to North America attracted a good deal of attention. But it was doubtful that such men were anywhere to be found. Two navigators took part in the expedition—the Englishmen Morrison and Enzel. It is difficult to say where they had previously sailed, but we know for certain that in the end neither of them went to the strait with Bering.

The rank and file members were taken from the Baltic fleet, following a principle that later became a tradition of taking volunteers from among the youngest and healthiest Russians. Literature pertaining to the expedition does not reveal the complete list of the leaders, not to mention the crew, or even the number of persons who were members of the expedition.[14]

On the basis of archival documents it has been established that thirty-four men including Bering set out from St. Petersburg, and that together with the soldiers and craftsmen who had gathered in Siberia there were more than 140 men. If we count the workmen, the number of participants is nearly four hundred.

Who made up the expedition's complement in St. Petersburg?

> Captain Vitus Bering
> Lieutenants Martyn Spanberg and Aleksei Chirikov
> Naval cadet Petr Chaplin (not a warrant officer as V.A. Divin suggests)
> Navigators George Morrison and Richard Enzel
> Geodesist Grigorii Putilov (sometimes erroneously called Potulov)
> Medical Officer Vilim [Philip Wilhelm] Butskovskii (for some reason called Nieman) |43, p. 123|
> Clerk Semen Turchaninov
> Apprentice mast-setter Ivan Endogurov
> Apprentice Fedor Kozlov

Vitus Johanssen (Ivan Ivanovich, or Vitiaz as he was sometimes called) Bering, a Dane by birth, was born in 1681, entered Russian naval service in 1703 in Amsterdam, and was assigned to the Baltic Fleet with the rank of Second Lieutenant. In 1710, at the time of the war with Turkey, he was transferred to the Azov Fleet where he was advanced in rank to Captain-Lieutenant. In 1712 he was sent back to the Baltic. He did not take a firsthand part in battles, but sailed on cruisers. In 1715 he was sent to Arkhangel, where he took command of the fifty-two gun ship *Selafail*, which had been built there, and sailed it to Copenhagen. In 1716, commanding the ship *Perle*, he sailed as part of an allied fleet to Bornholm. In 1715 he was advanced to the rank of Captain third class, and in 1720, Captain second class.

Following the conclusion of the Peace of Neistadt when, in 1722, the veterans of the Northern War were rewarded, Bering did not receive promotion. Offended, he submitted a request to the Admiralty College on 20 January 1724 to retire and take leave to "my own country." A month later he repeated his request. In making this request, as it appears from documents in the archives, he was motivated by the fact that he had served in the Russian Navy for more than twenty years, during nine of which he had been a captain, but as he wrote, "I have been denied the raise in pay given to several of my fellow officers who are much junior to me in service as captains, several of whom I have actually commanded. I much regret all of this . . . but I very much doubt that I can expect any further advancement" |34, l. 85,86|.

On 26 February 1724 Bering retired with the rank of Captain first class and two months' pay for the trip to his homeland, but he remained in Vyborg and did not go on to Denmark.

However, he did not have sufficient means to provide for his family, and five months later, apparently through the efforts of his fellow countrymen Vice Admiral Sievers and his son-in-law Rear Admiral T. Sanders, Bering returned to Peter with a request to accept him into service again in his rank of Captain first class. On 5 August Peter gave verbal orders to the President of the Admiralty College, Fedor M. Apraksin, concerning Bering's return to the Navy. On 18 August the mariner was summoned to the College and asked whether he actually wanted to return into service. Bering confirmed in writing his readiness to serve the Sovereign, offered his most humble thanks for permission to return to the Navy in his rank, and added at the end, "But I humbly request that my seniority not suffer." That same day the Admiralty College reached its decision, signed by General-Admiral Apraksin and the members of the College, to return Vitus Bering into service. On 3 October "in a meeting of the College" Bering took the oath and set out for Kronstadt under orders of the commander of the Baltic Fleet, where he was assigned to the ninety-gun vessel *Lesnoe*, which he had commanded prior to leaving the Navy.[15]

Thus, thanks to his brief retirement Bering was promoted to the rank of Captain First Rank, which had been denied him during his previous service.

However, it was not through his service in the Baltic and in the Sea of Azov, or in battle, that Vitus Bering achieved fame. It was his two vitally important scientific naval expeditions to the Arctic and Pacific oceans that brought him glory. Of the thirty-eight years that Bering served Russia, sixteen were spent on these expeditions.

Many capable officers were in the Russian Navy, but it was Bering who commanded the First Kamchatka Expedition, a choice unprecedented in those times, and in spite of every difficulty it was he who led the expedition to its conclusion. No matter how highly we value the service of Chirikov or others of his assistants, the main role, of course, belongs to the leader. Although in the interests of an objective interpretation of the history of the First Kamchatka Expedition in this study we shall note Bering's personal shortcomings, as well as his errors in judgment, this will by no means negate his merits.

In the archives one will not discover any information about why, of the two candidates for the position of leader, it was Bering who was chosen. Most likely he was given the assignment at the urging of Sievers. G.F. Müller, a member of the Second Kamchatka Expedition who was well versed in the details of the staffing of the 1725–30 expedition, maintained that Bering had proposed himself as a candidate |35, p. 7|.[16] It is possible that in doing this Bering was influenced by his hope of acquiring furs in Kamchatka. As we will see, he and Spanberg took with them a large amount of goods specifically to trade for furs. The seizure of Bering's personal baggage in Siberia confirms this. In any event, one of the prime motives for his continued service was his desire to serve until he had achieved the rank of rear admiral and could thus provide for his family in his old age. Not coincidentally Bering later wrote to Andrei I. Osterman, a powerful favorite of the Tsaritsa, "I have been thirty-seven years in service and have not advanced to a position where I am able to provide a permanent home for myself and my family. I live like a nomad." Bering even asked Osterman to release him from the expedition in a letter of 20 April 1741, written from the harbor of Petropavlovsk in Kamchatka.[17]

The recruiting of the complement began early in January 1725 and was finished by 8 January. A quartermaster and thirteen sailors were taken from the squadron of eight warships in the Baltic Fleet stationed at Kronstadt, and nine artisans were taken from the Admiralty in St. Petersburg. Thus twenty-three men in all were taken into the expedition at the capital, eight more than had been specified in the Tsar's ukaz.[18]

The president of the Admiralty College, General-Admiral Apraksin, to whom Peter had assigned the overall leadership for outfitting the expedition, naturally could not scrutinize every detail. The leader had to supervise the work of preparation personally. And since Bering had gone on leave to visit his family in Finland,[19] all the responsibility fell on Lieutenant Aleksei Ilich Chirikov. The decision was made to take on in the capital only those supplies that would be impossible to obtain in Siberia, and to take on the rest later when they were nearer Kamchatka. In the archives there are notes regarding every item that was obtained in the capital. Specifically, they had to carry across the entire country six anchors weighing from nine to eleven *puds* [equal to thirty-six pounds or approximately sixteen kilograms]; eight three-pound falconets; thirty cannon balls; ninety *dreifgagl* [double balls used to fire at mast and rigging], twenty-four guns, swords, and pistols, nine compasses, six sounding leads; four hour, half-hour, two-minute, and half-minute bells (sand glasses); rigging, sails, canvas, and many other items [39, ll. 2–5]. They did not forget to take a set of Naval regulations and a chest of "appropriate medications."

Evidently, as a foretaste of delays, by the early part of January, Chirikov had already begun to experience difficulties in regard to receiving clothing. From the documents it is apparent that the sailors in the Russian fleet at that time were very haphazardly supplied with apparel. According to Chirikov's report, at the beginning of 1725 some of them still had not been issued their clothing allotment for 1722 and 1723. Even with a special ukaz from the Admiralty College ordaining that they be issued uniforms, it was no simple matter. Almost half a month of correspondence dragged on until at last, five days before they were due to set out on their journey, the decision to issue uniforms was reached. But much was lacking in the warehouses, and the sailors were not given the required seajackets, "kaftans with canvas breeches, eighteen pairs of hosiery, and a pair of boots to last two years," and other items. For this reason Chirikov made urgent demands that the missing uniform components be sewn.

On 21 January the Admiralty College reached the decision that the personnel of the expeditions were to be issued their pay for 1725, as well as provisions enough to last until May, 1725,[20] and they ordered that 750 rubles be sent on ahead to hire horses to Tobolsk |37, ll. 40–43,94,96,111–116; 40, ll. 19,25,26|.

Then at last they could set out on their way.

T W O

From
St. Petersburg
to Tobolsk

A T ELEVEN O'CLOCK on a wintery Sunday morning, 24 January 1725, a long line of twenty-five sleds slowly pulled away from the Admiralty College courtyard and set out on the long and arduous journey. Ahead of them lay nearly ten thousand *versts* to surmount. They all knew the journey would be difficult, but none could even remotely imagine it would involve such incredible hardships and distances.

Chirikov commanded the main detachment of the expedition, twenty-seven men who traveled with all the expeditionary baggage. Bering, Spanberg, two navigators, and three seamen remained in the capital.[21]

Several days after the departure of the first detachment, Peter I died, but this did not threaten the expedition with failure, for Peter's dying wish was law for his successor to the throne and for his comrades-in-arms.

In order to inform the Siberian governor about the expedition and to order him to render aid, on 30 January 1725, the Empress Catherine I sent an ukaz to Siberia. It was too general in nature, however, and therefore, upon Bering's request, a second ukaz was sent two days later, which enumerated all the kinds of assistance the expedition needed. In particular, the ukaz instructed the governor to assign soldiers to do sentry duty, and carpenters, blacksmiths, and others to supply various materials to build ships. It also requested "wages in both cash and provisions" for 1726 |39, ll. 7–8|.

On 4 February, Bering received instructions from the Admiralty College |7; 39, ll. 14–15| that read:

1. In accordance with the ukaz of Her Imperial Sovereign Majesty, you are commanded to lead the assigned expedition and to proceed according to the instructions given you, written in the own hand of His Imperial Majesty of blessed and eternal memory.

2. In order to carry out this expedition, orders have been issued and carried out to send with you both naval and Admiralty servitors, senior officers and junior officers, and thirty-three men of rank. The Admiralty has also sent with them naval and artillery and other supplies and the required amounts of rigging.

3. Funds for your salary and for servitors under your command for the year 1725 have been sent with you in the full and correct amount, also the official record book in which you are to enter all income and expenditures, under your seal, for all the servitors in your command for the year 1725, according to the rate of pay for third rank as specified in the regulations.

4. For the year 1726 there will be both money and provisions for you and for the servitors under your command; there will also be all the timber and lumber needed to carry out such an expedition, and iron and tar and caulker's tools and the like. In addition, master blacksmiths and carpenters will be sent

out from St. Petersburg, as well as soldiers to serve as sentries, and all the provisions needed for the naval detachment. Regarding funds to carry out all your instructions, the Governing Senate is sending two ukazes with you to the local governor, which you are to deliver to him immediately upon your arrival. You are to ask him for everything you need, in accordance with these ukazes that are being sent with you.

5. The sum of 1,000 rubles is being sent with you for payment of your travel and all related necessary expenses and for the expenses of your stay. You are being given an official record book for such entries.

6. For transport from Vologda to Tobolsk you are being given two orders for post horses, per the ukaz. For *uezd* travel, a Senate order to the local official will provide you with the necessary transport, for which you will pay by the verst. You are to enter all these expenses in the same account book.

7. There is also being sent with you, to provide you with information on local places, a map drawn in 1721;[22] and if upon your arrival there you find yourself in need of help from geodesists, you are to select one or two of the men you find there.

8. There are also being sent with you thirty-four oaths to be sworn. When you join up with the rest of your command, order each man to sign one of these personally. If any of the men are illiterate, order them to make their marks instead. Send these to the Admiralty College immediately, with your report.

9. You are to keep a journal from the time you set out from St. Petersburg until you reach the assigned place, and during your stay there, enter all suggestions for improving such an expedition [in the future]; send monthly reports to the Admiralty College.

[signed] General Admiral Count Fedor Apraksin
3 February 1725

These instructions, as we see, were issued after Peter's death and do not pertain to the aim or sailing instructions of the expedition. Most of the points enumerated had already been carried out.

After giving the instructions to Bering, Apraksin sent a personal letter to the governor of Siberia on the same day that the Senate's ukaz was confirmed. He wrote, "With his command Navy Captain Bering has been sent from here to Siberia. Kindly receive him in good fashion and render him every assistance in obtaining everything he needs for this expedition, so that the enterprise will lack for nothing. Such an expedition is no small matter" |33, l. 113|.

On 5 February 1725 Bering was summoned to the tsarist court, and Catherine I presented him with the final and most important document, the instructions written by Peter.

The following day, having loaded his personal baggage on eight sleds, Bering set out with three foreigners in Russian service and three seamen, traveling light, to catch up with Chirikov's detachment.

On 7 February Chirikov's detachment reached Vologda, some 620 versts away. They traveled an average of forty-five versts per day. A week later Bering arrived, and two days after that they all set out together to continue their journey.

They passed through Velikii Ustiug, Solvychegodsk, and Solikamsk, then Verkhotur'e, Turinsk, and Tiumen. After covering 2,659 versts they reached what was then the principal town of Siberia—Tobolsk. Chaplin noted that the town is located at 58°05' of northern latitude on a steep hill above the Irtysh River, which at that point is three hundred sazhens wide.

Bering immediately gave the governor all the ukazes and a complete list of the members of the expedition, with notes as to their various rates of pay. Two days later he conferred with his officers, wrote his report, and delivered it to the Tobolsk gubernia chancellery with various requests. In particular he urgently requested twenty-four soldiers and two gunners "who have had sea experience, for I have too few naval servitors with me to man two vessels at sea" |39, ll. 27, 28|. To construct the ships and smallboats he asked for "sixty good carpenters," seven blacksmiths, two coopers, a turner, and a stove-setter, all with the requisite tools. He requested sea rations for sixty men for one year: 879 puds of sea biscuits, 195 vedros of beer, 78 puds of fish, 195 puds of oats, 94 puds of buckwheat, 195 puds of peas, 117 puds of cow's butter,

121 vedros of spirits, and other items. In all there were about two thousand puds of provisions |36, l. 211|. Then there were the provisions for all the men for the overland part of the journey which was to last two years; Bering expected that the expedition would last three years. He emphasized, "There will be no provisions except fish in these places, and no garden produce is grown there." He also requested various necessary items such as three hundred puds of iron and three puds of steel for blades. Here, as everywhere farther on, he tried to hold strictly to the rule not to carry with him anything that might be obtained closer to Kamchatka.

The governor of Siberia, M.B. Dolgorukov, having been notified by the Senate ukazes and by Apraksin's letter, promised every possible assistance. But he had warned Apraksin about the difficulties ahead, and even expressed skepticism about the success of the expedition. "I am afraid they may return without having accomplished their aims. . . " he wrote |36, l. 207|.

The seafarers at first intended to use the winter route. But they soon realized that it was unlikely that they would receive everything they needed in good time, and since it was already nearly April, they decided to travel by river. This would also require less money than was provided in their travel allowance, and Bering was thinking of ways he might effect economies. "While at sea," he wrote, "should a fierce storm or contrary winds, God forbid, force one to another land, one must not be without money" |39, l. 29|, indicating that the expedition might find itself in another land only by chance, not deliberately, as some scholars have suggested.

Bering found the details of business burdensome, and he therefore asked for someone familiar with local customs who would act as the representative of the governor for the expedition and "could render accounts of income and expenditure to the Siberian gubernia."

Having learned that there were two soldiers in Tobolsk, Boris Vyrodov and Semen Arapov, who had taken part in the Evreinov-Luzhin expedition to the Kuril Islands, Bering asked the governor to include them in his expedition. In general, all during the journey across Siberia, Bering diligently searched for persons who had been to Kamchatka. He was eager to meet with them, seeking to extract from their accounts as much information as possible.

Many of these accounts have been written down and, referred to as *skazkas*, are preserved in the archives.

In Tobolsk, the first of such persons was encountered, Lieutenant Safonov from a St. Petersburg regiment, who was returning from Kamchatka. He provided the information that the Kamchatka native people were not always peaceful toward the Russians and that lumber for shipbuilding at Nizhnekamchatsk would have to be hauled two hundred versts. This news disturbed Bering, who asked for thirty additional soldiers and more workmen; as there were no horses in Kamchatka, the lumber would have to be carried by the men.

By 29 April the Tobolsk district office advised that it had assigned laborers and pilots for the *doshchaniks* [river boats] plus sixty carpenters, two gunners, and seven blacksmiths "with bellows and anvils," and that the office was issuing wages of 1,723 rubles, 62 kopecks, for the year 1726. Half of the artisans would have to be taken on in Eniseisk and the rest, together with the two coopers, the turner, and the stove-setter, in Irkutsk province, along with the provisions. Everything not in the government warehouses would have to be purchased from private persons using "customs duties or liquor taxes." Bering was assured, "If you ... need anything ... from these provinces, the voevoda and the *kamerir* [provisioner] have been ordered to send it to you without delay ... so nothing will hinder the purpose of your journey" [39, ll. 17–21]. The question of the soldiers was also settled: instead of fifty-four, he was given only thirty-nine, since as the governor announced, "the garrison does not have a full complement" [39, l. 30].[23] The soldiers comprised an important part of the expedition. The hardest work fell to the sailors and soldiers, who often fulfilled important assignments without assistance.

As April drew to a close, the spring sun grew warm. On 23 April the ice in the Irtysh River broke up with a deafening roar, and three days later the river was completely free of ice. On 26 April the first spring storm broke with great thunder and lightning. It was time to be off on the journey, but nothing had arrived except for the four doshchaniks and seven *lodkas* [river boats].

On 5 May Bering became impatient and sent a document to the gubernia chancellery entitled "Concerning our dispatch from Tobolsk and the time of our departure on our journey." Five days later he wrote, "there is only one sailing vessel on the Lama River [in Okhotsk], which lies across the sea from Kamchatka, and it is impossible to use this because it is in such bad condition. Therefore I urge you, it is imperative that you issue ukazes to have two ships built there" |41, l. 8|. The reason for this entreaty was Lieutenant Safonov's warning that the vessel was in such bad condition he could barely make the crossing in it.

Not until 12 May did they receive the funds for the travel expenses, for hiring workers, and for purchasing materials. They were counting on four doshchaniks and seven lodkas with twenty-four to thirty workers, "but we were sent only eighteen men," Bering wrote, "so we added servitors to the usual number at work" |39, l. 29|.

THREE

From Tobolsk
to Ilimsk
via
the Irtysh, Ob,
and Ket Rivers

A T LAST on 14 May they sailed down the Irtysh. Bering was aboard one of the doshchaniks, Spanberg on another, and on the third were Chirikov, a geodesist, an apprentice boatwright and mast-setter, two sailors, and several soldiers. When the wind was favorable they moved along under sail, and the rest of the time they used oars. The current in the river aided them; Chirikov determined its speed at more than two and a half versts per hour. They usually made between forty and fifty versts per day and sometimes even more. To the left, then to the right, they encountered islands covered in green, sometimes reaching twelve versts in length. The picturesque shores of the Irtysh were covered with dense forests. They frequently came upon little settlements, and in some places they caught sight of Ostiak iurts [dwellings]. If the wind was favorable they even sailed at night.

They often had to halt because of bad weather. More than once "snow fell and there was a hard frost."

On 21 May they came to the Samarovsk post station not far from where the Irtysh empties into the Ob. All the next day they made rudders for the boats and on 23 May they once again set out on their journey. From there Bering sent Chaplin ahead by lodka with Corporal Anashkin and nine soldiers. Bering ordered him to proceed "with dispatch, day and night, as quickly as you can, as the season and wind permit, with all zeal" |39, l. 42|. At all the major population points Chaplin was to present ukazes and leave one soldier to hasten the preparation of everything they would need. When he had fulfilled the assignment, Chaplin was instructed to proceed to Iakutsk, deliver ukazes there, and do his best to see to it that the men were sent as quickly as possible to Okhotsk "to build ships, or if possible repair the old ship already there, so that ... we can proceed to Kamchatka without delay." Evidently Bering felt that as they already waited two months to receive the men and equipment they needed in Tobolsk, where the governor personally made all the decisions, the situation might well be much worse in the more remote parts of Siberia. The advance guard was hardly of sufficient strength to hasten preparations significantly, but it could be conducive to success.

On 25 May the flotilla entered the Ob and now had to sail against the current. They had to pull in close to shore and proceed with a tow line or barge poles. Often they had to turn into lateral channels where the current was not so strong. Sometimes they had to make detours in order to avoid headwinds. It was hard to use the tow line where the undergrowth along the banks of the river was flooded. Thus the entry in Chirikov's journal for 13 June reads, "I had to row harder, for the water was high in the river and it was impossible to proceed using the tow line." There was an interesting entry on 26 May. In the morning they proceeded by tow line. At 7 A.M. there was "a strong wind, and we stopped on the sand and waited until 40 bells—20:00." Sometimes they lost a great deal of time waiting for each other to catch up. On 29 May Chirikov was far ahead of the others; when he reached the village of Pinkin he waited thirteen hours for the rest.

On 30 May they reached Surgut. The journal entry reads, "Surgut is on the right bank of the river, not on the big hill, and there is forest near it." Here they had to spend more time, as Bering wrote to the governor, because "Iagodin [the administrator] was so obstinate he refused to give us guides. He took the letter I had written to him requesting guides and threw it down on the ground." This shows the resistance that the envoys from the capital encountered from time to time, despite tsarist and gubernatorial ukazes. They often had setbacks.[24] Sometimes they were prevented from going on by heavy rainfall. For example on 6 June Chirikov wrote, "Heavy rain fell all night. We put in to shore and waited sixteen and a half hours."

On 21 June they waited at the mouth of the Staritsa River, one verst from the town of Narym. "Near Narym we observed the breadth of the Ob River through the instruments and found the width to be 435 sazhens."

They continued on under sail along the Ket River. After 8 June they more frequently encountered shoals, marked by blazed trees on shore. The river became ever narrower and shallower. Therefore "we struck the mast and proceeded with barge poles." On 19 June they reached Makovsk. "The village stands on the right bank of the river, on a hill, and on the left bank of the river we came to a low place, and there was forest everywhere along both shores of the Ket River, from the mouth on." From Narym they proceeded along the Ket for 1094 versts. Bering noted, "from Tobolsk to Makovsk by rivers, where our route lay, live Ostiaks who were previously idol worshipers."

The second stage of the journey, along the rivers of the Ob system, was finished. Now in order to enter the Enisei they had to face the prospect of the Makovsk portage, leading to the town of Eniseisk.

Hopes that horses and carts could be ready at Makovsk ostrog proved unfounded, and they had to wait. Conditions here were even more shocking than in Surgut. Under-skipper Belyi turned to the local *prikashchik* [supervisor] with a request for men to unload provisions from the expedition's boat, but the prikashchik refused rudely "and began to swear and curse the captain." The next day he wanted to beat the soldiers who were standing guard, charging, "You are all swindlers and you should be hanged." Bering lodged a complaint, and the insolent prikashchik was punished.

Several days later they proceeded to Eniseisk. This town was founded in 1618 and was an important trade center. The width of the river here was 790 sazhens.

It rained day after day. July drew to a close and the expedition still had more than a thousand versts to go even to reach the Lena River. Bering lost patience and on 31 July wrote to the Eniseisk office, "I assume this delay has been deliberate. I am obliged to write to His Excellency the Governor in Tobolsk in regard to it" |41, l. 19|.

However, this complaint had an adverse effect on the Eniseisk administrator; he caused new delays. Recall that in Eniseisk in addition to boats and provisions they were to receive artisans. But herein lies a sorry tale.[25] Bering wrote to the Siberian governor that the commissar "repeatedly appointed ... men, of whom few were suitable, and many were blind, lame, and ridden with disease." The carpenters he was given did not have guaranties. This is a very interesting detail. In order to recruit trustworthy craftsmen for the expedition who would not desert halfway, Bering insisted that each post a guaranty. This was generally given by a relative or a neighbor who had already been hired.[26]

The Eniseisk administrator disbursed in advance "the salary in provisions and cash" to all the carpenters and blacksmiths for 1726. The seafarers were afraid that men who had been paid in advance would not have the necessary enthusiasm for the job, and as we will see presently, this fear was well-founded.

But perhaps the lowest trick the administrator played was in engaging all the men for the boat only as far as the mouth of the Ilim River, whereas he should have hired them to the town of Ilimsk.

An important addition to the expedition was the geodesist Fedor Luzhin, who "had been in Kamchatka and had made a map of it."

In Eniseisk the seamen met the famous Siberian explorer Daniel G. Messerschmidt, who had just returned from his travels. He showed them materials he had gathered, and his sketch maps of Kamchatka. It is possible copies were made of several of the maps, but this is not definitely known |43, p. 125|.

On 12 August the entire crew left the town that had given them such an inhospitable reception and sailed up the Enisei.

Again the days dragged by, filled with strenuous labor. More often than before they came upon hamlets and settlements. Forty versts from Eniseisk they reached the Tunguska River, as the Angara River was then called, below the mouth of the Ilim. Several times they had to cope with *shiveras* and *byks*. "A shivera is a swift current that pulses from rocks all across the river. A byk is a similar current, but only along one shore."

On 2 September Chirikov made the following entry in his journal. "Frost and rime in the morning." Two days later, "dismal weather with heavy snowfall."

Having traveled 804 versts along the Tunguska, on 11 September the flotilla entered the Ilim River. The river was nearly six hundred versts in length, but navigable only in the lower part. It was still 150 versts to Ilimsk. All the workers who had been hired only as far as the mouth of the Ilim River abandoned the expedition. The men who were left were not strong enough to portage the doshchaniks over the nearest rapids. They would transfer the small goods by lodka to the rapids. Spanberg was sent to supervise the ferrying of goods across the rapids. He was energetic, authoritative, and tough, a man who would not disdain any means to achieve a goal.

When the sixteen lodkas arrived from Ilimsk, "the men portaged the materials around the rapids and loaded them onto the lodkas, which were hauled by horses to the town of Ilimsk."

FOUR

Winter
in Ilimsk

O N 26 SEPTEMBER Bering reached Ilimsk. According to Chirikov's description, the town stood "between high hills. There is forest everywhere . . . and the town is on a slope that falls down to the bank of the river. There are some ninety dwellings in and around the town." Founded in 1631, Ilimsk was still a village and up to that time did not have any significant commercial importance because it was located on an unnavigable part of the river. But in the opinion of members of the expedition, the location of Ilimsk "was not altogether devoid of charm." They were fortunate here in that Petr Ivanovich Tatarinov was serving as the town administrator. For several years, from 1713 on, he had served as prikashchik at Anadyrsk ostrog and in Kamchatka, and was very familiar with local conditions. He treated the expedition with great understanding and concern |39, l. 45|.[27]

On 29 September the Ilim froze over. Chirikov and his men who had been left at the mouth of the river had to use sleds to reach town. Winter travel was difficult "because there was no road along the river bank, only a narrow trail where one could walk or go by horse."

Having learned from Tatarinov that it would be better to build vessels for future travel on the Lena River at Ust-Kut where the forest extended for a verst and a half, "and where there would be no portage of billets, and one could buy the necessary provisions," on 10 October Bering sent Spanberg in command of thirty-nine men onto the Lena, some 135 versts away. Among his men were the pilot Enzel, the apprentice Kozlov, a *desiatnik*, six soldiers, twenty-six builders, two caulkers, and a blacksmith. They hired peasants to bring wood to the construction site.

It was primarily Chirikov with his inquiring mind who handled scientific observations on the expedition. On 10 October 1725, he conducted a detailed observation of the eclipse of the moon. From his journal we learn that he determined the latitude of Ilimsk to be 56°37', and the angle of the center of the moon 43°10-1/3' "on the eastern side of the meridian." Because of the clouds, he wrote, "I could not readily observe the angle of any of the stars that were visible." The eclipse began at 11:31:01 P.M. and "at the St. Petersburg meridian the eclipse began, as the calendar indicates, at 7:03:31 P.M." The difference in longitude between St. Petersburg and Ilimsk is 66°57' (4 hours, 27 minutes, 48 seconds). Farther on Chirikov observed, "According to the mercator map, the rhumb from St. Petersburg to Ilimsk is east-by-south 5°52' to the east. The distance is 2,121 Italian miles, or 3,694 Russian versts ... and by the shortest geographical distance, 33°52' or ... 3,539 Russian versts. The angle of location from St. Petersburg to Ilimsk is 65°24', that is, east-north-east 2°6' to the north." At the end of his notations he observes, "the method of determining the hour for the beginning of the eclipse through the above mentioned observation does not seem to produce the proper results here, and therefore I have made a separate notation about this." Where he made this "separate notation" is not known.

The same entry made in Chirikov's hand in his journal on the day of the eclipse, and the words, "I have made a separate notation" rule out any doubt that Chirikov personally carried out the observation and reached the conclusion.

Bering repeated Chirikov's entry about the eclipse word for word in his report to the Admiralty College. However, he should not be criticized for that, although some of his remarks give the impression that he had personally made the observations and drawn the conclusions. For example, where Chirikov had written, "some variation in distance was found," Bering substitutes the words, "I find a variation in distance...." Later it was found that Chirikov was in error by more than 6°, and Bering repeated this mistake exactly, without any variation.[28]

From Spanberg's reports the seafarers learned that it would not be possible for the entire expedition to be billeted at Ust-Kut; by the beginning of October there were to be 107 men, of whom 98 were already present. For this reason, a large number of the men were settled in Ilimsk for the winter.

The first year of the journey ended, but a good half of the way still lay ahead. They not only had to build boats, but also plan the rest of the route from Iakutsk to Okhotsk, the most difficult parts of the trip. Wanting to profit from the experience of other expeditions, Bering obtained from Luzhin and his former companions a description of their route. It was thus that the accounts of the participants in the 1719–1722 expedition appeared |39, ll. 52–54|. On the basis of these descriptions and the information received from Tatarinov, a detailed document was compiled, "the location of the route by which means our journey from Ilimsk to Kamchatka will be carried out" |41, ll. 50–52|. This document was sent to the Admiralty College 30 November 1725. It describes the water route along the Lena to Iakutsk and on to Okhotsk, via low water rivers and overland by packhorse. The entire cargo weighed nearly ten thousand puds. If the vessels were ready in Okhotsk, as the ukaz sent out from Tobolsk had ordered, then "You are to take one of them and go to Bolsheretsk ostrog and from there proceed overland, carrying your provisions with you, or else leave some of the supplies in the ostrog and proceed along the Kamchatka River as you are able. When you have found timber and a place suitable for building boats, build them."

Upon the arrival of the expedition the Iakutsk officials were to purchase or hire four hundred horses with saddles, and prepare one thousand rawhide saddle bags.

If the vessels were not ready when the expedition reached Okhotsk, or if in Iakutsk they found that it would be impossible to transport the cargo overland across Kamchatka in the course of one winter, Bering had a plan. "Since the portage between the Bolsheretsk and Kamchatka ostrogs is long and mountainous, and it will take nine or ten days to traverse it with dogsleds, and since I believe it will be more difficult than any of the other portages ... I plan to spend the winter of 1726–27 on the Lama [Sea of Okhotsk] building boats, and then spend the summer of 1727 transferring provisions and material to Bolsheretsk ostrog; but I do not expect to transfer everything in one summer on these Lama boats.... We will use boats to round Cape Kamchatka, which extends to the south, and to reach the mouth of the Kamchatka River, and with them we will transport the heavy goods that would be impossible to carry by a direct overland route." Thus Bering intended to hasten his advance to the east coast of the Kamchatka peninsula, for otherwise, he wrote, "we will not be able to set out on our voyage by 1728." The captain expected that the cost of transporting each pud of cargo would be one ruble.

For the history of the First Kamchatka Expedition, the document "The location of the route ... " has exceptional significance. In the middle of the last century the historian A.S. Polonskii declared that apparently Bering learned in Eniseisk from local inhabitants about the existence of the strait, and he proposed to sail there not from Kamchatka, but from the other direction, from the mouth of the Kolyma River. In corroboration Polonskii quoted from Bering's report, which was supposedly sent to the Admiralty College from Eniseisk |46, pp.548–9|.

For more than one hundred years the Polonskii version was considered plausible and was accepted as fact by scholars, on the basis of the obscure document from which Polonskii had taken the citation. The search for this document turned out to be very difficult, for it was not related to Eniseisk. Neither in the single report of 4 August[29] nor in other documents drawn up in Eniseisk was there a word of any intention to sail from Kolyma around Chukotka.

Only a thorough study of archival materials revealed the source that proved to be "The location of the route...." However, a comparison of the extract quoted by Polonskii with the original source revealed a clear distortion of the text of the document, which Polonskii apparently made in order to substantiate his assertion that Bering knew of the existence of the strait by the time he was in Eniseisk.

Here is the full text of the paragraph that Polonskii took from the document (the words Polonskii excised are in italics):

> If, *when I was sent out from St. Petersburg*, I had been definitely ordered to go *by an overland route* from the mouth of the Kolyma *River* to *the mouth of* the Anadyr *River*, which I believe to be entirely [possible], which the [new] Asiatic maps indicate, and which many local people say they have been accustomed to using, then I am confident the desired goal could have been achieved at *much* less expense."

By omitting the word "overland," Polonskii misrepresents the sense of the original text. It appears as if Bering were speaking of sailing from the mouth of the Kolyma to the Anadyr by sea. But he actually had in mind the unexplored possibility of traveling overland from Iakutsk across the Indigirka, Kolyma, and Anadyr rivers to Kamchatka.

In actual fact people had traveled by that route every year until the discovery of a better route across the Sea of Okhotsk.

In another document Bering himself described the manner of using this route: "From Iakutsk overland to Zashiversk with horses, from Zashiversk along the Indigirka River, then across the mountains to the Kolyma River by reindeer, from the Kolyma to Anadyrsk by dogsled, from Andyrsk to Penzhina Bay and to Oliutorsk by reindeer, and from Oliutorsk to Kamchatka" |27, l. 115|.[30] But the route across the Indigirka, Kolyma, and Anadyr rivers lay through extremely barren and remote places. Although a small mobile party of *promyshlenniks* [hunters] traveling light might manage this route, it would be fatal for a huge expedition with a cargo of ten thousand puds. And where in this unpopulated region could they obtain dogs and reindeer? They would need more than a thousand of them. That this route was not usable for the expedition we will see further on, when we learn of the tragic winter trek made by Spanberg's detachment from the Gorbeia River to Okhotsk. And Spanberg had to cope with only part of the expedition's cargo and the prospect of traveling less than five hundred versts, whereas the journey by way of the Kolyma and Anadyr was several thousand versts.

Some scholars have mistakenly asserted that the Admiralty College did not respond to Bering's discourse concerning the route. But in fact, in a special session on 1 August 1726 the College decreed, "Instruct him to go to the assigned place in accordance with the ukazes and instructions that have been issued, bearing in mind optimum service and benefit for Her Highness and convenience for the servitors with him, according to his judgment, since the Admiralty College, because of a lack of firsthand information on local places and conditions, cannot issue precise ukazes concerning his actions en route" |15, part v, pp.345–6|. Bering did not receive this instruction until August 1727, before sailing to Kamchatka |39, l. 91|.

The Polonskii version is accepted as true by L.S. Berg, A.I. Andreev, V.I. Grekov, and V.A. Divin |25, p.40|. Given the Dutch maps of 1726 and 1727, which contain improbable legends, and given the map of the Swede Stalenberg, Berg even asserted that in 1725 "not only in Siberia, but even in western Europe it was already well known that Asia is not joined to America" |32, p.57|. But the point is that none of the foreign and Russian maps at that time, nor literary sources, offered irrefutable proof of the existence—or nonexistence—of the strait. Therefore Peter, to whom Stalenberg had presented his map, did not trust it. But even if he and all the statesmen and scholars had trusted this map, it would still have been just one of numerous contradictory maps, compiled on the basis of oral accounts.

We now are well aware that indeed there is a strait but we must not lose sight of the fact that this was not known then, that it had yet to be proved. And it can be firmly stated that none of the members of the expedition itself knew anything of Dezhnev's voyage. One is forced to this conclusion not only by the failure of the Polonskii version, but also by a number of indirect proofs. Literally every step of the expedition and every bit of information received was entered into the logbook, the books of entry and exit documents, in oral accounts, and the like. There are many hundreds of these documents, and in not a single one of them is there even a mention of previous voyages through a strait. On the contrary, Chirikov, who was better than the others at comprehending the problems and interests of science in his time, later wrote, when he was actually in the strait, ". . . we do not have information as to what degree of latitude from the Northern Sea along the eastern coast of Asia European inhabitants of known nations have gone . . . " |39, l. 227|. This statement of Chirikov's leaves no doubt. The seafarers did not know about Dezhnev.

Finally, one further documentary confirmation of this is a personal letter of Bering's, written seven years after the conclusion of the expedition. In it Bering writes that he had asked Müller "to make a firsthand inquiry as to whether people used to go by *koch* [small sailing vessel] from the mouth of the Lena by sea to the Kolyma." This indicates that even in 1737 he was still uncertain whether it was possible to sail between the Lena and the Kolyma. And Müller's report on Dezhnev's voyage around Chukotka was greeted by Bering with the words, "This information is not altogether reliable" |29, pp.256–7|.

Having sent off to St. Petersburg his report and a statement about his onward route, Bering again turned his attention to current affairs. It was necessary to prepare provisions and deliver them to the mouth of the Kuta River, prior to the opening of navigation on the Lena River. To ensure that authorities in Iakutsk would carry out all their assignments in the allotted time, the captain wrote, "So that during this coming summer of 1726 [*sic*, 1727] we can proceed to Kamchatka with the artisans . . . " it was necessary to build boats that could be used to sail on the Lena to Iakutsk, and then on smaller rivers to Iudoma Cross.

In December (not spring, as Andreev states) of 1726, Bering set off for Irkutsk "to consult with the voevoda of Irkutsk, Izmailov, since he had previously been the voevoda in Iakutsk" |41, l. 57|. But it is doubtful whether it was necessary to spend the entire winter in Irkutsk for this reason. Apparently one of the motivating factors was the convenience of spending the winter in a town that was large by Siberian standards. He took with him the only physician on the expedition.

In Irkutsk Bering received two reports from Chaplin, informing him that long before his arrival in Iakutsk on 5 September carpenters had been sent on to the Sea of Okhotsk with supplies to build ships |39, l. 60|. In order to hasten matters, Chaplin had also sent Corporal Ivan Anashkin and the soldier Aleksei Shchepetkin to Okhotsk, and with them a servitor to act as interpreter. Chaplin's news about the interrogation of the Iakut people who lived along the Sea of Okhotsk was very important. They gave information about the low-water rivers Aldan, Maia, and Iudoma. On the basis of this, Bering ordered Spanberg to reduce the dimensions of the doshchaniks "to a length of five sazhens and a depth, fully loaded, of twelve *vershoks* [unit of measure equal to 1.75 inches]."

FIVE

From Ilimsk to Iakutsk

IN MARCH of 1726 they transferred the cargo and most of the men, using the winter route from Ilimsk to Ust-Kut. They transferred all the heaviest things, such as the anchors, cannon, and three hundred puds of iron, to the Muka River in order to transport them to Ust-Kut by water when the river opened. Soon after Bering's departure for Ust-Kut, the Russian Ambassador Plenipotentiary to China, Savva Vladislavich Raguzinskii, passed through Ilimsk in state.[31]

When he was in Irkutsk Bering had been promised that everything necessary would be delivered to Iakutsk in February, but it was not until 29 March that seventeen carpenters and two blacksmiths arrived there, bringing tar and other materials with them.

Around the middle of April the ice broke up in the Kuta and the Lena. The seafarers began to build lodkas, and soon launched all but one of the doshchaniks into the water, and braided rope for rigging. At the end of the month they fitted the ship with cannon, anchors, and other heavy goods from the Muka River.

On 8 May Bering and Spanberg took eight doshchaniks and sailed down the Lena to Iakutsk. Chirikov and sixty-four men remained at Ust-Kut. They were to await word from Sergeant Liubimskii from Ilga about sending flour from there to Ust-Kut. Soon they were notified that the flour was ready but that it was impossible to send it because the river was too low. The soldiers who had been sent to Ilga advised that "This spring there has been almost no snow or rain here since the 28th of March, and it has been very warm . . . which has caused the water to be very low in the local rivers" |41, l. 73|.

On 1 June, without waiting for the flour, Chirikov's detachment sailed down the Lena on seven nearly empty doshchaniks. In his journal Chirikov observed, "The Lena River . . . in most places is no more than sixty sazhens wide. The depth in various places holds at more than three sazhens." On 6 June Chirikov noted, "People in various places along the Lena River said that on the evening of 14 May there was a great earthquake that lasted about an hour." The width of the Lena was already one verst, and the speed of the current was three and one-quarter miles per hour. The air was often blue-gray and smelled strongly of smoke; somewhere there was a forest fire. "The lack of rain is responsible for a huge fire," observed Chirikov. The next day he noted in his journal an observation about the weathering of the hills along the shore. "On the right bank of the river, stretching for fifteen versts into the distance, there are rocky cliffs like worn pillars, at a height of five to seven sazhens or more. In ancient times these must have been entire mountains, which have been worn down by rain and wind over the ages, for even now rocks break off. . . . "

On 16 June Chirikov's detachment reached Iakutsk, Bering having arrived there fifteen days earlier. This town was previously called Lensk ostrog and had been founded in 1632 by the cossack *sotnik* Petr Beketov.

The most difficult part of the journey remained, without a hint along the way. There are no words adequate to describe the transport of cargo by *telega* or even by *volokush* (heavy dragged webbing). Only a man on horseback or a man on foot with a packhorse could manage the mountains, the impenetrable forests, and boggy quagmires—and even then such a person would have great difficulty.

Having gathered information on the route, the members of the expedition began to prepare for the trip. They needed men, horses, and transport equipment for the packs; provisions; and materials. Nothing had been prepared in Iakutsk, although the governor's ukaz had long since arrived, and Chaplin had been there for nine months. Chaplin had done his best but had been able to accomplish almost nothing.[32]

In May, from the Irkutsk office, which was under the jurisdiction of Poluektov, the voevoda of Iakutsk, there came orders to issue to Bering, on credit, 4,200 puds of flour, and to hire three hundred horses for him, prepare hide saddle bags, and the like. The orders concluded with a stern warning: "If these orders are not carried out promptly, in order to make up for having delayed your important journey, then both the voevoda and his commissar will be harshly punished."

Bering flooded the Iakutsk voevoda with a torrent of papers containing requests, demands, and threats. Having determined that he needed six hundred horses rather than three hundred, he asked that he be supplied with them in three lots, and that there be one handler for every five horses. He wanted to have the first lot of horses by 20 June, in order to send the artisans to Okhotsk more quickly; and he wanted the next lot by 4 August.

These dates both seemed unrealistic. "Horses for hire were not to be found in Iakutsk," Bering reported to the Admiralty College, "and it would have been too costly to buy them ... so they are being taken from the Iakuts" |39, ll. 87,88|.

To assemble the men and the horses special officials were sent with orders "to carry this out immediately," then for "the compulsory requisition of horses" yet another soldier was sent. Upon Bering's request, Ivan Shestakov was attached to the expedition, a man "who is familiar with native customs." Then they decided against using the Polish exile, I.P. Kozyrevskii, the first explorer of the Kuril Islands, for "there is no way in which he could be of assistance," and furthermore, he was ill |39, ll. 54,55,58; 41, ll. 90,94|.[33]

Here in the last large eastern town it proved to be more difficult to hire laborers for the expedition than anywhere previously.

Many of the Russian inhabitants of Iakutsk, as well as Iakuts from nearby areas, had been to Okhotsk more than once and knew the route there very well, but could not be enticed to go there for love or money. "A notice was published regarding hiring

140 workers for the boats," Bering wrote to the Iakutsk office, "but not a single Russian or native came to be hired. . . . And it was impossible to send the materials and provisions by river and overland without help. Because of this we are asking that servitors be assigned to us."

Correspondence with the voevoda about assigning men brought no results. When Bering became tired of writing, he could send Chaplin to the office to negotiate, because he was tactful enough to be able to establish good rapport with the local administrator. After one such encounter, the first fifty of the necessary 140 workers were sent. Time to dispatch the boats so they could reach Iudoma Cross before winter was running short. They conceived of one more way to coerce the voevoda: all the officers, under the leadership of Bering, went to the voevoda's office and "demanded that he send the men and horses."

Of course it would be a mistake to suppose that all the difficulties resulted from the stubbornness of the voevoda. At that time these regions were thinly populated, and the requirements of the expedition were on an extraordinary scale.

In order to break down the voevoda's stubbornness they resolved to try one more ploy: they threatened to set out on their journey traveling light and leave all their cargo with him. He then would be solely answerable for the failure of the expedition.

This threat produced an effect. The voevoda sent them a few more men. Now there were 119 men. It was pointless and impossible to wait any longer.

In order to review what further needed to be done, Bering, in accordance with the demands of Naval Regulations, gathered his officers for consultation. They unanimously decided, "In order not to lose the time during which they could travel by water, to send off the thirteen boats that could carry the men, and leave two boats behind" |39, l. 108|. They unloaded eight hundred puds of flour from these two doshchaniks and sent it to the voevoda so that he personally would take charge of sending it on to Okhotsk before the onset of winter.

Before setting out on their journey they made wooden rudders and masts and loaded the flour, cannon, and anchors onto the doshchaniks. On 25 June they began to ferry the packs of flour onto the right bank (looking upstream) of the Lena, and early in

July, the cattle, horses, and various supplies. Bering ordered local
authorities to pay for the hire of horses and drivers, but they were
unfair to the Iakuts and paid them much less than previously, two
rubles instead of three rubles for a horse, and one ruble instead of
three rubles, fifty kopecks, for a driver.

By River
and Overland
to Okhotsk

O N 7 JULY the first detachment of 205 men set out for
Okhotsk aboard the thirteen doshchaniks with Lieutenant Spanberg in command. In the detachment there
were eighty-three members of the expedition, one hundred eighteen Iakut workers and three guides. The heaviest and most un-
wieldy articles were loaded on the boats—the cannon, anchors,
iron, cables, and more than 2,700 puds of flour—in all, a cargo of
4,200 puds.

Spanberg's instructions ordered him to sail into rivers,
"upstream, whenever possible" |41, ll. 96–101|. One of the points
reads, "At the Iakutsk office three hundred horses have been requested for use in unloading the boats in places where it will be
impossible to proceed because of low water or ice." Orders were
given to "both the navigator and geodesist ... to keep journals,
with the usual notations about travel on rivers and corrections for

the maps that have been given to us. Note the latitude where these occur and the compass variations."

They were forbidden to distribute provisions in advance. Foreseeing that along the way they would not be able to avoid losing men, Bering wrote, "If it happens ... that any of the naval or admiralty servitors ... or soldiers or carpenters die, take back any pay he did not earn."[34]

On 27 July the first overland party left for Okhotsk under the command of the shipbuilding apprentice Fedor Kozlov. In the instructions that were issued to him he was told to cut hay in Okhotsk, prepare *iukola* [dried fish], and "if the [old] ship has come from Kamchatka, look it over and help make it ready for our arrival."

Before sending the rest of the detachment on its way, and before setting out himself, Bering insisted that the voevoda issue ukazes to the Lamsk, Bolsheretsk, Upper and Lower Kamchatka ostrogs, and even to the Anadyrsk ostrog, which read as follows: "Upon receipt of this, Her Imperial Highness' ukaz, you, the local administrators, upon the request of Navy Captain Bering en route, are to supply him with all available goods and provisions for his departure, with all assistance in building ships, and with everything relating to unwritten amendments to his instructions, so that he may set out more conveniently and quickly.... Harsh punishment and fines may be anticipated for anyone not carrying out the provisions of this ukaz" |41, l. 102; 39, ll. 121, 159|. The sailor Andrei Bush, who had come from Okhotsk, was assigned to the expedition, "because he knows another sea route to the Bolshaia River."

By the beginning of August it became clear that it would not be possible to make rawhide packs for all six hundred horses. Bering decided not to wait any longer. Upon his request the *syn boiarskii* [member of the minor nobility holding military rank] Timofei Antipin, "who knows the settlements along the water route from here to the Lama," was ordered to bring 120 horses to a place that Spanberg's detachment could reach by water so that the cargo could be transferred from there to Okhotsk on these horses.

From 6 to 13 August one detachment after another set out under the direction of the doctor, Butskovskii, Sergeant Liubimskii, and the carpenter desiatnik, Vavilov. There were three carpenters and one servitor in the first detachment; with 103 horses they transported 120 packs of flour and groats. In the second group there were three soldiers and two servitors who transported 174 packs with 124 horses; in the third group two soldiers and a carpenter took 64 packs of flour with 133 horses.

On 15 August Antipin and two soldiers gathered together, driving 120 horses. This group was to await Bering on the Mga River.

On 16 August Bering left Iakutsk and took with him Chaplin, the clerk Turchaninov, six sailors and soldiers, three artisans, two servitors, and two Tungus. This detachment set out with light loads on seventy-seven horses. Bering already had his hands full with his own personal baggage. Chaplin wrote in his journal that in Vavilov's detachment "it took thirty-five horses to carry the captain's baggage." An entire string of horses!

The best time of year, June and July, had passed, and considerable difficulties lay ahead for the travelers. Furthermore, before they set out on their way, they discovered that the orders for the expedition had not been conscientiously carried out by the contractors. Thus 380 packs turned out to be shortweight, packs "made and sold at a much dearer price than we had ever paid at Iakutsk" |39, l. 119|. The flasks for vinegar were not well made, and the vinegar had to be left behind. They were often supplied with bad horses; on one occasion they could accept only fifteen of sixty-eight horses presented to them.

Because of the shortage of horses and packs, they could not manage to send 1,500 puds more of flour to Okhotsk. For this reason they had to leave seven members of the expedition in Iakutsk under Chirikov to be responsible for transporting the flour the following year. Chirikov was ordered to set out for Okhotsk in March of 1727 |41, ll. 108–109|. This was unrealistic, for there is deep snow in Siberia in March, and hard frosts and raging blizzards, and there is no forage for horses along the way. The lieutenant was also ordered to help Spanberg if requested; he was to see that eight hundred puds of flour were sent on to Spanberg with the two remaining boats, and in the event of problems, he was to write to Irkutsk and to the Admiralty College.

The overland detachments made slow progress. They would start out in the morning, make a midday stop for dinner, rest their horses, and then in the evening, having covered between twenty and forty versts in all, they would stop for the night. On the second day out, the first of the horses in Bering's detachment dropped dead. The farther east they proceeded, the more horses died. "From the Lena River to the Tata," Chaplin wrote in his journal, "there are stretches of dry land, lakes, great deciduous forests, and broad meadows in some places." After two days the detachment headed by the sergeant and the carpenter desiatnik caught up with them at the Mga River. They stopped at the settlement of the Iakut princeling Nirgai. Concerning the Iakuts Chaplin wrote, "They live in iurts ... covered with birchbark. They have about seven thousand head of horned livestock and horses." On 22 August the following notation appears: "There was a light frost during the night." Farther on the mention of frost becomes ever more frequent, sometimes alternating with mention of rain. Then we encounter reports of snowfall, and on 29 September the entry reads "hard frost."

The desiatnik was the first to set out on the way from the Mga. He was given twenty horses from Antipin's party for reinforcement. On 26 August Bering's detachment set out, and after him the sergeant's group, to which twenty horses had also been added. After they had travelled several versts, they crossed the Kinekhta River and came upon a marsh where for the first time they built a corduroy road. In the days ahead they had to corduroy quite often, and in order to cross the Bolshoi Kholym River, they even had to build a bridge.

On 1 September they came to the Aldan River. It was nearly 150 sazhens wide, and "down the right bank of the river there are high rocky hills, and low hills along the left bank." The next day they began to ferry the horses and cargo across the river on boats that Spanberg had left there. On the third day they finished ferrying and resumed their journey. For the first time they spent the night in the forest, right in a boggy marsh.

For five days in succession, beginning on 5 September, they went "like pebbles" along the Iunakan River, "which has very swift high water." The hills came right down to the river, now on the left and then on the right, forcing the travelers to cross from one bank to the other as often as six times a day. "There was a small amount of grass and marestail for the horses to graze on." Several times they settled into their camp for the night by four or five in the afternoon so they could graze the horses and let them rest, since the mountains that lay ahead were devoid of vegetation. Before they reached the Ukachan River they came upon "a place where the ice was seven feet thick." On 19 September Chaplin observed, "The road was dry. In some places the road was dusty and in other places it was frozen over. Poor forage for the horses." After two days Bering ordered Antipin to let the rest of the horses graze for two days and then to set out for Iudoma Cross. (It was so named because a cross had been erected on the bank of the Iudoma River; later a zimov'e was built there. The place is presently call Iudoma-Krestovskaia.)

On 22 September Bering reached the Iudoma River, opposite Iudoma Cross, where he left two soldiers and two Iakuts with twenty-seven horses. In their instructions the soldiers were told to report to Okhotsk "when the Iudoma freezes over, or when you hear from Lieutenant Spanberg.... In regard to the horses that are being left with you, if someone is going back and needs them, give them horses, but tell them that unless they are in desperate circumstances they are not to take any provisions. If you run out of provisions and have not yet heard from the lieutenant, then you are to proceed to Okhotsk ostrog" |41, l. 111|.

Several days later Bering's detachment set out for Okhotsk. On 27 September they managed to cross the Urak River "with great difficulty, for it was very swift and there was ice on it." After they had crossed a hill they came to the Okhota River. Chaplin observed, "We did not see a single inhabited iurt all the way from the Aldan to this place.... Along the right bank of the river there are fine meadows and tall grass." In his report Bering wrote, "Truly, I cannot put into words how difficult this route is. If we had not had a frost and light snow, not a single horse would have made it" |41, l. 111|. On 1 October Kozlov arrived, Butskovkskii on the 11th, Liubimskii on the 19th, and Vavilov on the 22nd. The last group arrived on 25 October.

The trail was difficult and many of the servitors—forty-six out of 122—deserted; influenced by them, a number of the Iakuts deserted as well. Three men died. In Kozlov's detachment even the guide deserted, and the group "remained on the Iunakan River for seven days for lack of a guide and because of high water." Sometimes the deserters stole horses. An embittered Bering wrote stern letters to Iakuts |41, ll. 111,121–122|. The text on one of these reads, "We are requesting that if ... any servitors appear without leave from us or from the lieutenant, such scoundrels are to be punished in accordance with the ukaz of Her Imperial

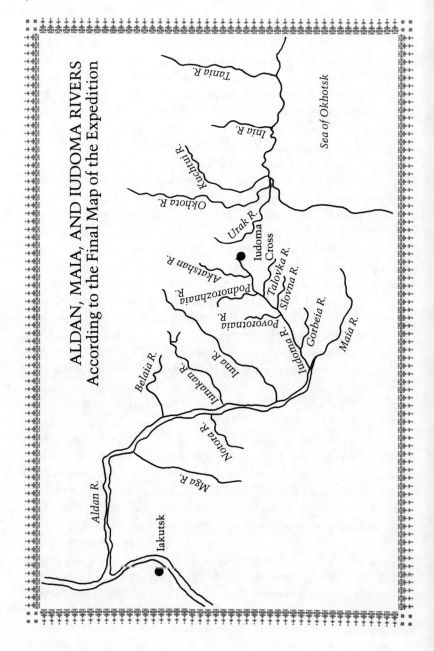

ALDAN, MAIA, AND IUDOMA RIVERS
According to the Final Map of the Expedition

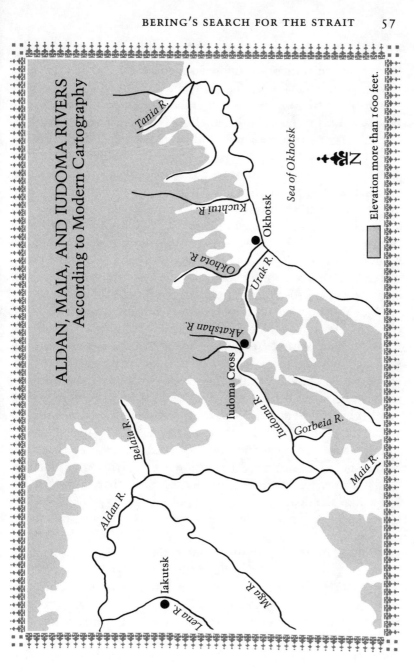

ALDAN, MAIA, AND IUDOMA RIVERS
According to Modern Cartography

Tania R.

Kuchtui R.

Okhotsk

Okhota R.

Sea of Okhotsk

N

Urak R.

Akatshan R.

Iudoma Cross

Iudoma R.

Gorbeia R.

Belaia R.

Maia R.

Aldan R.

Iakutsk

Msa R.

Lena R.

Elevation more than 1600 feet.

Majesty, so that in the future this will be an example to others. Whatever punishment is imposed, send us word of it so that I will have no need to make further complaints about this."

A great disaster on the Iakutsk-Okhotsk transfer was the loss of horses. Only 393 out of the original 660 horses reached Okhotsk.[35] On the way to Iudoma Cross and from there to Okhotsk more than once they had to remove the packs from the horses who were straining to the utmost, and they had to leave 1,500 puds of provisions at Iudoma Cross.[36] But the Iakuts suffered an even greater loss than the expedition from the death of the horses, for all the horses had belonged to them. The Iakuts were dismissed from Okhotsk with a large part of the surviving horses. There is no information as to how many horses were returned to the Lena, but considering the winter conditions, deep snow, and lack of forage, one can suppose that scarcely any of them made it back.[37]

There was no word of Spanberg's detachment, which as we will recall had been dispatched from Iakutsk to Okhotsk by the river route. Bering sent a Tungus to meet Spanberg, but even he vanished without a trace. Nor was there any news from the soldiers who remained at Iudoma Cross. Since there was nothing more to be done, Bering decided to wait. It was not until 1 November that he sent a servitor to the lieutenant with a letter in which he wrote that if the detachment had only a short distance left to reach the Cross, they were to "send such things as cannot be transported in summer." Bering did not ask what condition the men were in, or whether they needed assistance, although he knew that the doshchaniks would not be able to go as far as the Cross and that Spanberg's men would have to carry the cargo overland on their backs. At the conclusion of the letter he authorized the servitors "to be issued a pud of flour for the month of November ... so they will not die of starvation" |41, l. 117|.

On 17 December Bering received his first news from Chirikov that Spanberg's men had carried the cargo on their backs over the ice of the Iudoma River. He ordered a band of fifty men under the command of Corporal Anashkin to prepare to set out for Iudoma Cross to meet Spanberg. However, before dispatching them, he decided to await word from Spanberg himself. At last on 21 December a messenger from the lieutenant reached Okhotsk. Spanberg sent word that on 4 November, using ninety sleds, he had "taken all the materials without leaving any behind," and that at the zimov'e near where the Gorbeia empties into the Iudoma, sixty-four versts above the mouth of the Iudoma, he had left the navigator Enzel with some men and flour. Only in one instance in the report was there a mention of the severe hardships the detachment had undergone: "Today I left forty sleds along the way because the servitors were ill, and there were so few mountains left." The report was written on 27 November.

On 22 December Bering sent ten men under Anashkin to Iudoma Cross, carrying sixteen puds of dried meat and fish, and the next day he sent thirty-nine more men and another thirty puds of meat and other provisions on thirty-six sleds.

On 6 January Spanberg and two soldiers reached Okhotsk, and between 10 and 16 January the rest of the men in his detachment arrived, sixty in all. Many were ill. The geodesist Luzhin and the navigator Morrison were in such bad condition that it was impossible to carry them to Okhotsk, and they had had to remain at Iudoma Cross. Forty-seven men had either deserted or been dismissed. Seven had died. Along the way they had to leave cargo and sleds and ten men with these supplies. They carried only the geodesic instruments, the carpentry tools, the government funds, and the apothecary supplies to Okhotsk. (Many authors have mistakenly stated that most of the cargo actually reached its destination.)

What had happened to Spanberg's detachment?

The experience of this detachment is the most tragic page in the history of the expedition, and it is a saga that remained unknown until Spanberg's report was found in the Archive of the Navy [VMF] |41, ll. 123–125; 38, 131–134|.

Recall that the detachment set out from Iakutsk on 7 July. At the mouth of the Aldan River they prepared barge poles, rudders, and other equipment. They towed the doshchaniks along the Aldan with ropes. On 21 August they reached the mouth of the Maia. On this river, Spanberg wrote, "there are rapids, extremely difficult to ascend, and fast water." On 2 September they were at the mouth of the Iudoma River "which is very shallow, swift, and full of rapids . . . it is not possible for the men to haul a boat over the rapids in some places. For that reason . . . at times I used the crews from four boats to haul a single boat on the worst rapids and ascents, and in such places we made only one verst a day." In this manner they pushed on until 13 September. Up to this time forty-seven men had either deserted or been dismissed because of illness. It was impossible to haul the doshchaniks any farther, so they built two more lodkas and loaded onto them all the cable, anchors, cannon, sails, and other materials "that could not be carried overland in packs," and continued to travel along the river. Some of the men stayed with the doshchaniks with the navigator Morrison. Spanberg instructed them to build a zimov'e for the men and storehouse for the rest of the provisions and materials that were left on the doshchaniks.

On 21 September they reached the mouth of the Gorbeia River "and there was no way we could proceed farther upriver." They unloaded the materials from the boats and built a storehouse and two zimov'es. They sent two lodkas on to Morrison for "the treasury" and the crew's belongings, and then began to prepare birch to make sleds. At the end of the month Morrison arrived and reported that his boat could not go as far as the Gorbeia because an early freeze had choked the river with ice. Spanberg ordered his men to transfer the cargo on their backs from the ice-bound boats onto the sleds. The Iakut servitors refused. Spanberg ordered them to be sent to work under guard, "and any instigators of this evil are to be put into stocks and beaten for this. . . . Punishment will be imposed by five men flogging with the cat-o'-ninetails. . . ."

By 11 October the cargo was transferred to an island in the Gorbeia River and put in storehouses. They prepared one hundred sleds and loaded onto ninety of them everything that could not be carried by packhorses in summer: anchors, cannon, rigging, and the like. They also took the medications, the government cash, ammunition, and flour for November and December, nearly a thousand puds in all. More than three thousand puds of cargo were left, which the navigator Enzel and seven others were to guard.

The workers, who in Iakutsk had been issued only enough flour for October, found themselves in a desperate situation. Spanberg wrote, "I realized their need, and so they would not starve to death I ordered that they be issued three and a half puds per man for the two-month trip in November and December."

On 4 November they set out on their way with foreboding. They took only ninety sleds because there were not enough men to pull the rest. They still had nearly five hundred versts to cover and, as usual, not enough provisions, and their clothing was not adequate for such an undertaking. The weather was unfavorable. "From 4 November on there were hard frosts and blizzards," wrote Spanberg. The men made slow progress. They became exhausted from having to wade through snow up to their waists, and soon many became so weak they could not move their legs. The weaker had to be carried on the sleds, and because of this the rest were all the more quickly put out of action. On 15 November one of the Iakut servitors died.

At the end of the third week they had to stop near the Povorotnaia River. By this time six more men had deserted, and "many of the others appeared ill." Here they left forty sleds and four men "who were so sick they could not go on." They pulled the sleds up on the high bank and "built a *balagan* over them for protection." Soon afterward they had to abandon one hundred cannon balls, a falconet, and several kegs of gunpowder right on the trail.

On 1 December they reached the Talovka River. Six more men deserted. Provisions were at an end and "every day twenty or more men fell sick." They had to leave another twenty sleds with six anchors, seven falconets, two thousand rounds of ammunition, and most of the cable.

After twelve days of unbelievable hardship they reached Krivaia Luka. "We were in great need of provisions; none of us had any left." They began to starve. The situation was desperate. Spanberg wrote, "I distributed all my own provisions to the men—flour, groats, meat, and peas—and shared their need equally with them."

It was only after this that Spanberg resolved to go on ahead of his detachment. He rapidly covered the sixty versts to Iudoma Cross and sent his men flour from there. The several days of waiting were terrible for the men. "Until the provisions reached them they were eating the leather straps on the sleds, the leather packs, their leather breeches, boots, hide bedding, and dogs." Many were severely bloated and lay without moving; some suffered frostbite. During these days another four men died. The flour furnished to the soldiers saved the rest from death. Somewhat recovered, they abandoned the heavy loads and again set out on their way. Exerting themselves to the limit, the men slowly dragged the sleds, from which the groans of their sick comrades reached their ears.

On 17 December the first sleds reached Iudoma Cross. Three days later everyone who could move set out for Okhotsk on forty sleds with the cash, apothecary supplies, and the instruments;

they left behind the sick men, including Luzhin and Morrison, and also the grenades, powder, and sheet iron.

Again everything happened the same way. Help from Bering was delayed and the standard of provisions continued to be inadequate—and this at a time when they had to exert colossal strength in Siberian winter conditions. The flour ran out after several days. "Until the 29th we proceeded with great privation, in a fierce freeze," wrote Spanberg. "There was no food left at all, so on the way we ate whatever we had—dead horses and every bit of leather." Men dropped from weakness and fatigue, struggled to their feet and fell again, as if they had been scythed down. Progress was slower. At last their final dregs of strength were exhausted and the detachment halted.

Again Spanberg set out ahead in order to save his men from certain death. We learn their condition from the following passage of his report. "I went on ahead to Okhotsk ostrog because the men were all too weak to go on. I walked day and night." On 31 December Spanberg met Anashkin's detachment, which had been sent out from Okhotsk. Spanberg returned with them and distributed meat and fish to his men. Soon another thirty-six sleds arrived from Okhotsk with provisions. The men were saved.

In his report Spanberg states that "the guide Kolmakov was totally unfamiliar with the route from the zimov'e to the Cross, and from the Cross to Okhotsk ostrog, and everything he told me was a lie. When there was no trail or road we strayed a good deal and went much out of our way unnecessarily." Naturally a poor guide aggravated the difficulties. However, Bering was not altogether accurate when he wrote in a letter to Chirikov that Spanberg's men "suffered much privation on the way because of the guide's deceit," and that "there was more expense for the Iakut servitors than help from them" |41, l. 120|.

Thus the outcome of the Spanberg detachment march was completely deplorable. A major part of the cargo was left halfway to the Gorbeia and the rest was abandoned in four places along the banks of the Iudoma.

During their stay in Okhotsk they had to build a ship so that during the summer of the following year they could cross to Kamchatka. They also had to recover the cargo that had been left along the Gorbeia and in other places, and then finally they had to bring in provisions from Iakutsk.

Twenty-six men were engaged in building the ship under the leadership of the syn boiarskii Iakutskii. By July of 1726 there was "a new seagoing ship under construction, but at present we cannot finish it because it is impossible to caulk it and make it watertight ... for there is no hemp or tar to be had in Okhotsk."

The builders experienced great difficulties with provisions. No grain was grown there and merchants almost never came. When they did come it was not to trade in grain, but in pursuit of precious furs. Therefore it was practically impossible to buy flour.

When Bering arrived in Okhotsk he was given the reports from Corporal Anashkin, the soldiers, and the Iakuts who had been hired for construction work. The soldiers wrote that they had received only enough provisions to last until the first of January 1726, and they had already been without bread for nine months. In fact, they had had to take twelve puds on credit from local people.

Bering made an unexpected decision: to issue them flour and groats for only four months and for the rest of the time to pay them a cash equivalent—but at the Iakutsk price, which was less than one-tenth the Okhotsk price. With the arrival of the remainder of the expedition they faced the prospect of going hungry several months more, for the flour received was not even enough to repay the local people.

The Iakut servitors complained that they were not receiving their wages and asked that each be paid his due of five rubles, twenty-five kopecks. Bering ordered that they be paid two rubles, fifty kopecks.

SEVEN

Winter in Okhotsk

M ANY PERSONS ARRIVED in Okhotsk with Bering. Now the ship could be built more quickly. But building a ship would not resolve the situation; it was already too late to sail to Kamchatka, for winter was coming on.[38] It was necessary to prepare to spend the winter there.

From the trees that were cut along the shores of the Okhota River they built barracks for the men, *izbas* for the leader and officers, and a bathhouse, which was a necessity for a Russian settlement. The cattle that had been driven from Iakutsk were butchered for meat. The reindeer purchased from the Tungus went into the common pot.

It was more complicated to assemble and bring to Okhotsk the cargo that had been left on the way from Iakutsk. To accomplish that would certainly take all winter.

In his report to the Admiralty College, Bering wrote, "At the present time I cannot order anything more to be done because of the increased number of those who are ill, until the materials and provisions that were left along the way are collected and brought to Okhotsk ostrog. . . . This winter there have been heavy snows here and terrible freezes and blizzards, and the local people who have lived here more than twenty years say that it is the worst winter in memory" |41, l. 122|.

At the end of January Bering and Spanberg carefully examined all their men and even the Iakut servitors not subject to them who were being sent to Kamchatka with commissar Tarabukin. They separated out the healthy persons, and soon the order was given that on 13 February they were to set out after the cargo that had been left on the Iudoma. Each servitor who went to the Iudoma was to be given two puds of flour and one pud of meat for three months. Even the thirty-one Tungus were given provisions —one and a half puds of flour and meat, and a ruble and a few dengas for each.

Spanberg's detachment went first. He was ordered to gather up everything and proceed to Okhotsk. If he did not have enough strength to transport the entire load during the winter, he was not to take items that could be carried by packhorses in summer. "Leave such things in a high place where they will not be damaged by high water; build *balagans* and cover them so animals will not ruin them" |49, l. 1|. Ninety-five men set out from Okhotsk, including Chaplin and Anashkin. They also took seventy-six sleds. There were several dogs harnessed to sleds, but most were pulled by men.

It was especially difficult for the servitors and carpenters. The servitors had been short of clothing for more than six months as had the carpenters for the year they had been with the expedition. They were not eligible to be given uniforms, their wages from Iakutsk had been delayed, and they had only a miserly ration of provisions. The order to set out on the trail made them grumble. "The captain sends us out naked, barefoot, without wages, to certain death, and he does this deliberately," they said. "We will go, and if we can do it we will pick up the government goods, but if we cannot, then we will not touch them" |50, pp.542–543|.

On 14 February the detachment set out. Soon they came upon the body of a dead carpenter. Then they had to leave fourteen of the weakest men who, Spanberg wrote, "could not go on with us. I ordered them to make their way however they could." For several days "there was a great blizzard, with snow and a headwind, and the snow became very deep." Finally after two weeks the first sleds reached Iudoma Cross. The sick geodesist Luzhin and seven other men were living there. Luzhin informed Spanberg that on 2 February the navigator Morrison had died. The men were so weak they could not bury him.[39]

Two groups traveled along the Iudoma River. Chaplin was at the head of the first, with thirty men, and the corporal and a sailor led the second with forty-two men. The "severe frosts" continued. After a day they crossed the mountain to Krivaia Luka and found the first part of the abandoned cargo. Here they met the carpenter who had walked from the Povorotnaia River and was barely alive. It is difficult to imagine the self control one had to have to be alone in such godforsaken places, without food, in the terrible frosts and blizzards, day after day, stubbornly pushing on. After three days, two carpenters became ill and had to be left on the trail.

On 8 March they reached the Bolshaia Elovka River. Here they found the body of another dead comrade. The next day the corporal's group went on, while Chaplin's group loaded the cable, six anchors, and seven cannons onto sleds and returned to Iudoma Cross.

On 15 March Chaplin observed, "we were unable to go any farther because of the bitter frost," and they had to stop for several hours.

At Iudoma Cross on 18 March they learned that Fedor Luzhin had died the previous week. They had to continue on to Okhotsk, but the servitors and the Tungus had no provisions left. They turned to Spanberg with a plea for help, and he ordered that rations be distributed to them, and so Chaplin's group continued on their way. They made slow progress because "the trail is bad everywhere," as Chaplin wrote in his journal. "There are snowdrifts everywhere ... little food for the men. Many have eaten all their rations."

March was already drawing to a close, and the help that Bering had promised had not materialized. Spanberg sent a report from Iudoma Cross to Okhotsk in which he advised of the problems with provisions and made the sensible observation, "On this journey I have more than once seen the men run out of provisions because they have such appetites on the trail that they eat twice as

much as they would at home" |39, l. 116|. Then Spanberg himself
set out for Okhotsk in order to obtain help for his detachment
more quickly. Leaving Chaplin behind, on 29 March he met the
envoys from Okhotsk who were bringing meat and fish.

Meanwhile, straining to the utmost, Chaplin's half-starved
men were hauling the loaded sleds. When they met the envoys
from Okhotsk they kept eight men with them and sent the rest to
Corporal Anashkin at Iudoma.

On 6 April, after almost two months on the trail, Chaplin's
group reached Okhotsk and delivered the cargo from the Iudoma
River, with the exception of one anchor.

But the most trying ordeals befell Anashkin's men. If the Iakut
servitors feared Spanberg's rage and respected Chaplin's gentle-
ness, they apparently neither feared nor respected Corporal
Anashkin. There was a rebellion in his detachment. This is how
the corporal himself described it. "We reached the Povorotnaia
River where the goods were, and made a halt. I went on ahead
with eight men ... the twelve Iakutsk servitors ... came up in a
strange throng. I told them to get the sleds loaded with the materials, but they silently went right by the things. . . . Seeing that
they were up to no good I yelled at them to stop. . . . I said 'What
are you doing?' They replied, 'We do not want to die like the
others did, so we are going straight to town and you cannot stop
us.' They snatched knives and axes from the shafts of the sleds
and came tramping across the snow and said, 'If you try to make
us go against our will, we will run you through.' I kept on talking
to them and said, 'I am doing the same work you are. . . . You
have been given wages and rations from the largesse of Her
Majesty, and meat as well, and up until now we have not been
short of food.' Then they said to me, 'We worked for this largesse
before this shipment came. All fall we worked building quarters
for the captain, and we hauled lumber and firewood and moss.
The captain and the other officers insulted us ... they said, "You
are heathens and miserable folk." And you, Mister Corporal, you
are coming back alive, and you do not do anything but bow to the
captain for the largesse.' I did not have enough strength to argue
with them and curse them. There were too few of us [Russians]"
|39, ll. 167–168|. (There is no mention of this rebellion in previous
historical literature.)

The soldiers and the carpenter who were with Anashkin confirmed his report. This rebellion clearly showed the resentment over the inequalities and back-breaking work.[40] The rage erupted in open rebellion. In other expeditions when men died of malnutrition and scurvy it was because of a lack of food, but here there was plenty, for at the end of the expedition, as we shall see, the amount of flour alone that was left over exceeded two thousand puds.

When Corporal Anashkin's group had special difficulty with provisions, he sent a Tungus to Iudoma Cross, from whom Spanberg learned, as he wrote in a report to Bering, that "the men have little food left, especially the Iakut servitors and the Tungus, and they have started to eat the dogs." On the return journey Anashkin's group buried two of their comrades and reached Okhotsk on 8 April.

They transported the rest of the cargo to the sea and deposited it into warehouses. However, there was quite a bit of material, mostly light in weight, still at the Cross. On 12 April a detachment of twenty-four men under the command of the apprentice Kozlov was sent out after these things on a last sled journey.

On 21 April an unusual thing happened. The scribe Semen Turchaninov announced to Spanberg that he had "important evidence" against Bering.[41] The law provided that in such cases the informer was to be taken into custody and immediately sent to the capital. The scribe was shackled and sent to Iakutsk under the guard of two soldiers.

There is still no information on the content of the denunciation. But it evidently pertained to some abuse on Bering's part. In this regard there is a very significant note in the journal of the Admiralty College. "An ukaz is to be sent to the Tobolsk governor, ordering that any available person in Iakutsk in the Siberian expedition take Captain Bering's baggage, his trunks and portmanteaus, to Tobolsk. Have the luggage brought to your office under seal, inventory it, and make a list of the contents. Do not return the baggage to the captain until you receive instructions from the Privy Council or an ukaz from the Senate" |15, l. 680|.

With every passing day the sun became warmer. The third spring for the Siberian expedition was commencing. By 10 May Chaplin commented in his journal, "High water in the river. The ice is going out." Two days later the water began to subside, and soon the last of the ice was gone.

Now all attention was focused on building the ship. On 13 May Bering sent the carpenters, caulkers, blacksmiths, and navigators, with Spanberg in charge, to the building site where they transported the coal and necessary supplies.

Fishing commenced at the end of May. Chaplin wrote in his journal, "All the servitors have been sent out from the ostrog to sea to catch fish for themselves." Bering, however, observed that there were fewer fish in 1727 than previously, "and if the provisions had not arrived overland from Iakutsk, we certainly would have died of starvation" |49, l. 24|. The fresh and nutritious food quickly restored the men's strength and had a beneficial effect on the sick who were evidently suffering largely from scurvy. After a month the number of the sick was reduced to one-fourth.

At the beginning of May, Kozlov's detachment arrived from Iudoma Cross. On fifteen sleds they delivered the cable, sails, more than one thousand rounds of ammunition, powder, iron, and other things. In his report Kozlov advised that it had been especially difficult for the Tungus along the way who by 27 April had already consumed all their provisions. "Our trip was extremely difficult," he wrote. "There was tremendous snowfall, very wet, and there was so little freezing weather that we could not walk either on the trail or alongside it. When it was cold enough to freeze in the morning we could press on until midday, but then we would have to make a halt because the trail would become too difficult" |39, ll. 178–179|.

It was not possible to move everything because the condition of the trail deteriorated. Part of the cargo was put on rafts to be sent via the Urak River to the sea. But because of a long period of stormy weather it could not be transported to Okhotsk by sea.

There was great anxiety over sending for the cargo that had been left at the Gorbeia zimov'e. On 7 June five men went there under the command of commissar Durasov. They took the rawhide packs and an order to the navigator Enzel, who was spending the winter there, to take the iron, tar, groats, and other provisions to Iudoma Cross. For the construction of the boats they had to send men out from Iakutsk to replace those who had deserted from Spanberg's detachment. Not waiting for the Iakutsk office to act, Bering himself sent Enzel thirty-two men. It was later learned that the men who had been sent from Iakutsk had gone as far as the Aldan and then deserted in various directions. Enzel did not have many men with him, so Bering ordered him to take the cargo, not to Iudoma Cross, but to Iakutsk, so that from there he could send 150 puds (out of the total of 2,050 puds) of flour and groats to Okhotsk by packhorse.

At last, on 8 June 1727 they ceremoniously launched the new ship. They named it *Fortuna*, perhaps in hope of good fortune in the future. It was a single-masted sailing vessel. A week after the launching they set the mast in place and rigged the ship.

Now they needed a plan for their further activity. At Bering's request Spanberg expressed his opinion. He gave wise advice: send men to Kamchatka with everything they would need to build a new ship there. The *Fortuna* was already fully loaded with nearly 250 puds of flour and groats, 32 puds of iron, 18 puds of dried meat, and other things, and it did not make sense to wait until new cargoes arrived. After her run to Kamchatka the *Fortuna* was to return immediately to Okhotsk.

Why did Bering and Spanberg propose building a new ship, rather than deciding to sail north on the *Fortuna*? Unfortunately a description of the ship is not to be found in the documents, but likely it was not capacious enough and above all did not have the necessary strength and seaworthiness. After all it was a *shitik* or "sewed" vessel, made of birch planks fastened, or sewed, together with withes.

On 1 July 1727 the *Fortuna*, under Spanberg's command, set out into the Sea of Okhotsk under oars. There were forty-eight men on board, including Putilov, Kozlov, six sailors, seven soldiers, the carpenter-desiatnik, three Admiralty carpenters, a caulker, a blacksmith, twelve Eniseisk and Irkutsk carpenters and blacksmiths, and a Kamchatka commissar and thirteen servitors who were en route to their assignments.[42]

Chirikov was expected to arrive in Okhotsk any day. What had happened to his detachment, which had spent the winter in Iakutsk, and most importantly, how had they fared on their journey to Okhotsk?

At the end of August 1726, Chirikov's men had unloaded into the warehouses flour from the two warehouse vessels that Spanberg had left in Iakutsk in July of that year. More than 2,500 puds of the flour that had been delivered from Verkholensk was put into a storehouse, and then eight hundred puds of flour were sent on by packhorse to Okhotsk with the Iakut servitors. The servitors, however, had to winter on the Aldan River because they had been given bad horses and all the forage on the trail was trampled by the time they passed along.

The first snow fell in Iakutsk on 2 October. In December there was a hard freeze. On 31 December Chirikov noted, "Dark days. Bitter cold. Air heavy with frost. . . ." The terse notes in his journal are filled with observations on the weather.

From February on, Chirikov began to prepare for the trip to Okhotsk. He bought reindeer hides from the local people for sweat cloths, and thirty-one head of cattle, and he sent a soldier out into the *ulus* [Iakut settlement] to assemble the horses more quickly.

On 1 May he and his men left Iakutsk. They crossed the Lena on the ice and then moved along the Tata River. On 9 May they reached the Mga River. The ice had broken up three days earlier and the river was running swiftly. They made rafts to transport the flour to the birchbark lodkas and used two rafts, three-by-four sazhens, to ferry all the horses and sixteen of the cattle across the river. The other twenty cattle managed to swim across.

In order not to be delayed on the Aldan, Chirikov sent the quartermaster Borisov and the Iakut servitors on ahead and instructed them to build rafts there. They again built rafts and even bridges on the Nakha, Elgeia, and Chepontsa rivers.

On 23 May Chirikov's detachment reached the Aldan at the point which even now is called the Okhotskii Perevoz (Okhotsk Ferry). Here six rafts were almost ready. Beyond the Aldan they found 312 horses to transport provisions to Okhotsk. On 1 June they ferried the livestock and provisions to the other bank of the river. Using good judgment, Chirikov sent a soldier to inspect the trail ahead, and then sent his men to clear the way.

Finally, between 3 June and 8 June 1727 the five groups, ninety-seven men in all, reached Okhotsk. They brought in 1,500 puds of flour on 140 horses |39, l. 188|. Only a small part of the livestock, thirty-nine head of cattle, ten cows, and two pigs, were kept back in order to fatten them up for the rest of their trip.

The farther they went the more difficult it was to travel. In the swampy marshes the horses became blanketed with clots of mud, and the men often had to stop "to wipe off the mud and lighten the horses."

On 24 June Chirikov's detachment reached the zimov'e at Iudoma Cross. Chirikov's journal reads, "The Iudoma River is forty sazhens wide and moderately swift in this place. At low water there is a place to ford it. We made the horses swim across and ferried the provisions on a raft."

From the Iudoma they moved along the shores of the Ozernaia River, and on 29 June they reached the Urak River. Three times in four days they crossed from one bank to the other. On 2 July they reached the Okhota River and the next day were in Okhotsk.

Thus Chirikov made a quick and successful trip from Iakutsk to Okhotsk. Whereas the overland groups were only beginning to set out from Iakutsk in July, Chirikov's detachment was already in Okhotsk by the early part of that month. The three main groups in his detachment lost seventeen horses in all. Not a single man deserted. This is obviously an indication of the fine relationship Chirikov had established with his men.

At the end of July the Iakut servitors delivered eight hundred puds of flour to Okhotsk, and the last to arrive was the soldier who was herding the livestock. Now everyone had assembled there except for the men on the Gorbeia River.

Since they had lost the two thousand puds of provisions that had been left at the Gorbeia zimov'e, they decided to use local food resources, primarily fish. They also thought of the possibility of preserving various kinds of duck meat.[43]

On 10 July the old ship that had gone to Kamchatka in 1725 with the two commissars returned.[44] Bering demanded an explanation for their prolonged absence. The commissars defended themselves by saying that the ship was not fit for a return voyage in 1726. In confirmation of this they exhibited a copy of the "statement" of one of the navigators. The two navigators on the ship were Nikifor Treska, who had discovered the route to Kamchatka across the Sea of Okhotsk in 1716, and Ivan Butin. Bering also took written testimony from them.

Nikifor Treska wrote, "On 7 October 1725 we set out from Okhotsk for the Kamchadal ostrogs. . . . When we were still two hundred versts away from Bolsheretsk ostrog a strong wind came up and the ship was beached by the waves, and several of its seams opened. . . . We spent the winter in that place. In the spring of 1726 . . . I went to the ship and repaired it, the one on which I had sailed to Bolsheretsk in the early part of June, and I told the commissars it was time to set out to sea. But they did not go last year. . . . Many times they sat me down in their cabin and told me to swear that the ship was not seaworthy. But I would not do it" |39, l. 194|.

Butin added the following remarks to Treska's statement. "When I sat in their cabin I refused to sign a statement that the ship was not seaworthy. The commissars urged me, Ivan, to do this, and got me drunk and wrote out a false statement and gave orders for someone to sign my name for me. But I did not give this account and I did not authorize anyone to sign it for me."

In Kamchatka the native population suffered greatly at the hands of the local authorities. The commissars there gave full freedom to their "appetites." It seemed to them that even an entire year was not enough to "warm their hands" collecting the iasak.

In order to transfer the rest of the cargo, they decided to use the old ship as well as the *Fortuna*. But first it was necessary to make capital repairs. They careened the ship on shore, replaced part of the wooden planking, and caulked and tarred it. On 5 August they put it back into the water and finished their work afloat. After five days the *Fortuna* returned from Kamchatka for new cargo.

On 14 August Bering asked his lieutenants to give him their opinions on the following questions:

1. Should they take both ships to Bolsheretsk or leave one in Okhotsk to wait for the men from the Gorbeia River?
2. If they did not wait for the men, how long would their money and provisions last and from what account would provisions be issued?
3. Should they take with them to Kamchatka all the servitors and carpenters who had been sent to the Gorbeia or dismiss some of them?
4. Should they leave some of the livestock at Okhotsk until their return?

Bering and his two officers were unanimous in their answers to these questions and consequently the following decisions were made:

1. As long as there were enough provisions and materials to load both ships, "have them load both ships and dispatch them from here immediately. When they reach the Bolshaia River have one ship return with the first favorable wind."

2. In case head winds prevented the ship from being dispatched, or in case the servitors were so late in arriving from the Gorbeia that it would be impossible to sail to Kamchatka, six months' pay should be left for them, enough flour for ten months at the rate of one pud per man per month, and also one bull and all the entrails from the cattle that had been slaughtered.

3. All the artisans should be sent home and issued passports.

4. Six or seven live cattle should be entrusted to the local inhabitants so they would be there when [Bering's men] returned. "If there are no cattle, then give them two good reindeer instead of each head of cattle."

Signed by Bering, Spanberg, and Chirikov |39, ll. 199–200|

In Okhotsk they gave the sick Endogurov the instructions and two hundred rubles in cash for wages. A sailor and five soldiers remained there with him. They were to slaughter sixty head of cattle and put the meat up in storehouses, cover it with snow, and then salt it, having obtained the salt through evaporation.

On 18 August they finished loading both ships. In its hold the old ship had room for 1,095 puds of cargo while the new ship could carry 987 puds. In addition they loaded onto each ship some thirty-five puds of iron and sixteen 10-vedro (one vedro equals one pail) barrels of water.

Everything was ready to put out to sea. Bering and Spanberg chose the more reliable *Fortuna* and Chirikov was ordered to sail on the old ships, along with Chaplin, the hieromonk, fifteen sailors and soldiers, and the four navigators.

Everyone was in good humor. At last, after nearly three years of ordeals on land, they could raise the sails to be filled with the fresh sea wind. Everyone received rations for September, rye bread and dry biscuits for the journey. The pilots were particularly pleased because they had been given their wages for the past year as well as for 1727.

Before they put out to sea Bering sent back with one of his traveling companions his last report from Okhotsk with a map of the expedition's route from Tobolsk to Okhotsk. In the report he listed the participants in the expedition and indicated their whereabouts. There were eighty-five men in all, thirty-five on the two ships, twenty-one in Kamchatka, seven in Okhotsk, seventeen on the Gorbeia, one ill in Iakutsk, and four en route to St. Petersburg |49, l. 39|. In this report there is one puzzling entry. Bering wrote, "I intend to have both ships go around the cape to the mouth of the Kamchatka River." These words are contrary to Chirikov's, who wrote in his journal, "I was ordered to take the old ship on our voyage . . . to Bolsheretsk." On a ship that had already served many years it would have been dangerous to sail even in the Sea of Okhotsk, let alone out in the Pacific. At Bolsheretsk both ships, the old and the new, immediately unloaded, and almost the entire cargo was transferred to the east coast of Kamchatka along the rivers and by sleds. Why did Bering permit such an inaccuracy in his reports? Possibly he wanted to absolve himself of guilt in advance for the overland transfer across Kamchatka, which was attended by such colossal difficulties as those they had encountered in Ilimsk in 1725.

EIGHT

Across
the Sea of Okhotsk
to Kamchatka

O N 22 AUGUST at about noon the ships set out for the shores of Kamchatka. From that day on the dates are calculated from one noon to the next, as was customary with sailors at that time.

The weather changed often. It would be dead calm, then the wind would come up, and it rained often. Several times they were blown off course. On the morning of 28 August they were becalmed. They measured the depth and found it had decreased to thirty-two sazhens, which indicated their proximity to shore. And in fact three hours later they sighted Kamchatka. A steady headwind forced them to drop anchor three versts from shore. On the morning of 29 August they sent a lodka ashore, which brought back three barrels of water. The sailors identified the stream as the Krutogorova. They stood at anchor for three days.

On 3 September at about noon, when they came to the mouth of the Bolshaia River in southwestern Kamchatka, the wind began to carry the ship out from shore, and they had to stand at anchor. At this time Chirikov wrote in his journal, "Quite a sizable leak opened up in the prow of our vessel." When the tide turned they towed both ships into the river with ropes and tied up on shore. The next day Bering and Spanberg took twenty-one lodkas, the surplus baggage, and the government cash and set out for Bolsheretsk, which was located some thirty-four versts from the mouth of the river. Several days later Chirikov and Chaplin also arranged to reach Bolsheretsk. The Russian settlement there at that time consisted of seventeen dwellings.

Now they faced the problem of transferring the entire cargo across the peninsula to the mouth of the Kamchatka River. Bering asked the *zakazchik* [administrator] of Bolsheretsk ostrog, Aleksei Eremeev, what would be the most convenient, quickest, and cheapest way to transport the cargo across the peninsula, and whether there were any persons available who had gone around Kamchatka by sea in baidaras, "who could go by boats around the cape to the mouth of the Kamchatka River, and who would be engaged to transport the goods between this ostrog and the Okhotsk ostrog" |49, l. 39|. It is a curious fact that Bering inquired about the possibility of rounding Kamchatka on the old ship, which was not even safe for crossing the Sea of Okhotsk, when he had a new ship available, the *Fortuna*.

Eremeev gave him the names of servitors who had sailed in baidaras along the east coast of Kamchatka from the southernmost tip to the mouth of the Kamchatka River, and explained how many days this trip required and how much time was necessary in order to transfer the goods by river.

Bering was not venturing to sail around the Kamchatka peninsula; he asked for this information when the ships had already been unloaded in Bolsheretsk. Later he wrote, "We were hindered by strong headwinds and rain . . . by the fact that it was already late in the season by local reckoning, and that the area was unfamiliar since no such vessels had ever been there before" |49, l. 51|. However, it was only 3 September then, and judging by the entries in the journals, the weather did not hinder the continuation of the voyage.

The main problem was that Bering, overestimating the danger, did not want to sail around Cape Lopatka and along the east coast of the peninsula. On the decrepit, leaking old vessel, to embark on such a voyage certainly would have been dangerous. But if he had decided to round Kamchatka by sea on the *Fortuna*, it would have been a much shorter journey than the overland transfer. And by September 1727 a significant part of all the personnel and cargo would have been at Nizhnekamchatsk, which would have allowed them to build the ship more quickly and embark earlier on the voyage to the north.[45]

In order to unload the ships and transfer the cargo ashore, Bering asked the officials of nearby settlements to send men and lodkas. Until 9 October most of the members of the expedition and some eighty Kamchadals as well were busy with this work. Forty local lodkas, called *batas*, were used.

On 19 September twelve men under the leadership of Lieutenant Spanberg set out on thirty lodkas to go up the Bystraia River. They carried everything necessary for building and outfitting a ship, and also 107 rawhide packs of flour. The cargo was to be taken as far up the river as possible, then portaged overland to the Kamchatka River. At Verkhnekamchatsk they were to request men with boats, then sail down to Nizhnekamchatsk and build the ship there. At Nizhnekamchatsk they were to buy twenty to thirty reindeer from the local people and begin to prepare tar and coal, then ask for men, including eight or ten who were experienced carpenters.

After seventeen days part of Spanberg's men returned, led by Moshkov. They reported that it was very difficult to take lodkas along the Bystraia River. One Kamchadal had drowned, and two anchors, the cable, and eight packs of flour had been lost.[46]

Everything that had been transported to that point with such difficulty over many thousands of kilometers was of exceptional value. Therefore, Bering equipped the entire party for salvaging the equipment that had sunk.

As soon as Spanberg's men arrived, Bering sent another fourteen lodkas up the river with flour, iron, grenades, and the like. Misfortune also befell this group: at the final rapids a lodka capsized and four bags of flour, the accoutrements, guns, and powder went to the bottom.

At the end of October Bering promoted the naval cadet Chaplin to midshipman ahead of schedule for "diligent service beyond the call of duty."

The weather at Bolsheretsk remained unusually good. Although the first snow fell on 7 October it was not cold. The river did not freeze over for some time. In November snow fell often, but sometimes it rained as well. And strange as it may seem, there was still thunder on 30 October. On clear days they trained the men in the manual of the rifle and in target shooting.

In December freezing weather began. They went to the sea with sleds to get whale blubber, for a dead whale had washed up on shore. They brought back some two hundred puds of blubber, which they later gave to the Kamchadals as food.

To transport the cargo to Nizhnekamchatsk, Bering requested from various settlements in Kamchatka upward of six hundred Kamchadals and more than five hundred draft dogs; three hundred men would be needed in February and two hundred in March. For this region, this was an absolutely astronomical number.[47] Several officials replied that to send out men and draft dogs "is impossible during the present winter season ... the iasak natives have gone out hunting sable and fox and there are very few servitors in either the lower or upper ostrogs" |49, l. 143; 59, l. 209|. Some of the officials did not even reply to Bering's letters.

The captain instructed Spanberg to hasten to assemble the men and draft animals at Nizhnekamchatsk, and he ordered the soldier Kapotilov to the western part of the peninsula. He would have liked to take all the iasak people away from their winter hunt and appropriate them for transporting the cargo of the expedition as payment of their iasak. But he understood that to gather up the hunters who were spread out all over "hill and dale" was practically impossible. Furthermore he was afraid of being held responsible for the failure of the winter hunt on the entire peninsula, which would have had an adverse effect on the income of the state.

Bering changed his mind and requested that the men be sent out only after they had paid their iasak. He also ordered that he be supplied with local fish and even with mutton fat. But the population of Kamchatka was greatly impoverished since there had been a poor catch of fish the previous year and in some places, such as Verkhnekamchatsk, famine was widespread. It was very difficult to obtain dogs. The iasak collector from Verkhnekamchatsk sent only nineteen dogs and wrote, "I could not round up any more, nor will I be able to in the future, because the natives in the ostrogs do not have any dogs. There were some *kaiurs* [slaves] ...

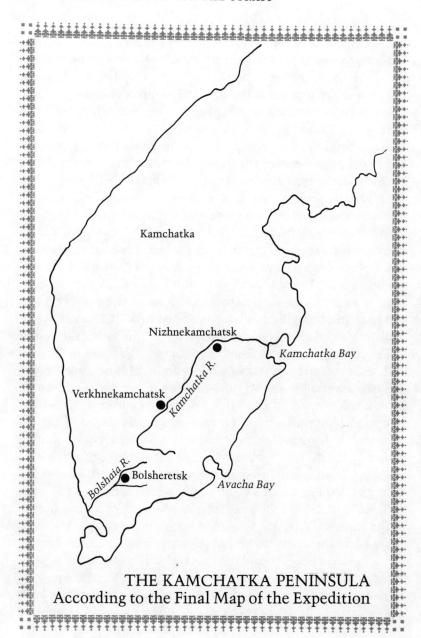

THE KAMCHATKA PENINSULA
According to the Final Map of the Expedition

who were bringing iukola to the hostages, but all their dogs died on the trail and the natives went back to their settlements on foot" |49, l. 210|.

At the beginning of January they managed to send sixty-three loaded sleds from Bolsheretsk to Verkhnekamchatsk. Since there were so few dogs only three or four were harnessed to each sled and six men walked ahead as *"peredovshchiks* [guides], to lay out the trail." Soon another twenty-two sleds were sent. Of the eighty-five sleds, thirty were being used to carry Bering's personal baggage.

Finally on 14 January Bering himself set out for Verkhnekamchatsk with the doctor and Chaplin.[48] They arrived eleven days later. At that time there were seventeen dwellings in all in Verkhnekamchatsk. As Chaplin observed, the river had not frozen in some places, and along the shore "there was quite a large birch forest."

In Bolsheretsk, Chirikov was the senior officer. In March he was to carry out the 340 packs that had been left with him, and for that purpose he was to receive 180 pack animals from various places.

In January Chirikov's men sewed up cowhide-covered wooden barrels to hold the gunpowder. They distilled spirits from sweet grass (probably *solodka*) for distribution as sea rations. Around the middle of February the soldier Kapotilov returned to Bolsheretsk. He brought only nineteen of the draft animals that Chirikov had sent to Verkhnekamchatsk, and he had loaded each sled with seven puds of cargo to be pulled by four dogs.

Always carefully observing natural phenomena, on 15 February Chirikov noted in his journal that at sunset there was an eclipse of the moon. "But because the moon was rising through clouds, we did not see how far it was into the eclipse at the time of its ascent. At five o'clock in the afternoon the moon appeared, breaking through the clouds, with no eclipse on two or two and a half inches of its eastern edge where it had already emerged. At the end of the eclipse the height of the star Sirius was observed on the eastern side of meridian 19°18', and direct height without refraction 19°13'; there is a southern declination this year of 16°16', and a right ascension of 97°26', while the sun then had a declination of 9° and moved to near 18°. After that it was found in a real ascent of 33°7'51", and therefore it is known that Sirius reached the meridian at 7:58:20 in the evening and across the latitude of that place with variation and observation of the star it was found one hour, twelve minutes, forty seconds from the meridian, and from the time of its appearance at the meridian it was six hours, forty-five minutes, and forty seconds ... until the end of the eclipse when it was above the horizon passing across the center of the earth parallel to the horizon, appearing above the earth's surface at that place."

In February Bering managed to send sixty-seven sleds from Verkhnekamchatsk ostrog to Nizhnekamchatsk with flour, iron, hemp, instruments, apothecary supplies, and treasury cash. Bering himself reached there on 2 March. In his "Brief Account..." he wrote, "We transported everything to the upper and lower ostrogs in the local manner by using dogs. Every evening en route we made camp for the night in the snow, and took cover because there are great snowstorms here, which in local parlance are called *purgas*. When one of these storms hits in an open area, if one cannot take cover and becomes buried with snow, one will die" |53, p.92|.

After three days of travel, in the distance "we saw a flaming mountain." Five days later they reached the Ushka settlement where the artisans were preparing lumber for the ship, and they spent the night there. The next day they reached Nizhnekamchatsk ostrog. They settled along the right bank of the river and counted forty households, which stretched out along the shore for a verst.[49]

Later Bering wrote, "During our stay in Kamchatka in all three ostrogs [Bolsheretsk, Verkhnekamchatsk, and Nizhnekamchatsk] there were no more than 150 servitors to collect iasak ... the Kuril people live in the south of Kamchatka and the Kamchadals in the north. They have a number of words in common in their languages. Some of these people are idol worshipers, and almost none of them are believers. They are alien to all good customs. Russians who live in Kamchatka, as well as the local inhabitants, have no grain nor do they have livestock except for dogs, which are necessary to them for travel and transport, and whose pelts they make into garments. They eat fish and roots and wild berries and in summer wild birds and all kinds of sea animals. At the present time they grow barley, hemp, and white radishes; turnips ... grow at all three ostrogs to a size seldom found even in Russia, so that four turnips may weigh one pud. I brought ... rye and oats which were sown near us, but I do not know whether they will ripen because the frost comes early and there is no manure on the soil since there is no livestock here and the soil is tilled by hand. All these people from whom iasak is collected in the form of furs are under the authority of the Russian state" |53, p. 92|.

Farther on Bering describes some of the customs of the Kamchadals, especially the custom of killing the second-born infant when twins are born, but also moving critically ill persons away from the settlement, burning corpses, and others.

The expedition's stay on Kamchatka was detrimental to the Kamchadals. In addition to the constant requisitions, there were transport obligations. Although Bering requested a great number of people and sled dogs only after the iasak had been paid, many Kamchadals nonetheless worked on the expedition all winter long. True, Bering relieved some of them from the payment of iasak, but they were no better off because of this, for the winter hunt usually produced furs for the native hunters themselves, which they exchanged for provisions and supplies of the utmost importance. Furthermore many collectors secretly took additional iasak for their own use even from those who had been excused from paying it; some managed to collect two or even three iasak payments from each native man. In addition to furs they took iukola, ducks, geese, and hare from the defenseless people, food which was used for the expedition's needs. Any persons who protested paying iasak were beaten or else saw their wives and children taken away into servitude |54; 73, p.117|. The Kamchadals personally had to deliver all the items that were taken from them to the ostrogs, where officials often detained them for several months to work for them personally. Such a relationship between the officials and the Kamchadals resulted in a decline in the local population from one year to the next.[50]

The Kamchadals also suffered other calamities stemming from the expedition, including the almost total annihilation of their sled dogs, a large number of which died of starvation. There were often fewer dogs harnessed to each sled than were needed, and the sleds were loaded more heavily than usual. The weakened animals died by the hundreds. The uninformed, oppressed natives of Kamchatka, not understanding the significance of the expedition, saw little difference between the iasak collectors and the expedition members. Yet the Kamchadals' aid to the expedition was invaluable.

At Nizhnekamchatsk, Bering learned that Kozlov's detachment, which had come to Kamchatka on the first run of the *Fortuna*, had already prepared a large part of the lumber needed. However, the men had consumed all the provisions literally the day after they reached Nizhnekamchatsk, and it was with great difficulty that Kozlov managed to distribute his "master workmen among the servitors and have them provisioned, rather than having to forage for themselves..." |39, l. 205|. Later the natives at Nizhnekamchatsk, as Bering wrote, "refused to give provisions for the servitors in our command because they had none for themselves." Spanberg was instructed to request fish from the provisions of the local warehouse and also to request some at the monastery |49, l. 45|.

Having received three lodkas with nine Kamchadals and several servitors "who knew of good forested places along the Kamchatka River and other rivers that empty into it," Kozlov set out in search of trees suitable for construction lumber. It appeared that "there are a great many trees, but ... they are peeled and hollow." They cut trees until 18 October and prepared more than three hundred *kokoras* [the lower part of the trunk and major perpendicular roots] and two large pits of larch pitch. Sometimes they took the wood to the river on dog sleds, but more often the men carried it on their backs.

It was especially difficult to carry the keel, which formed the foundation of the ship. Kozlov's weekly reports give an idea of the speed of the work. For example, from 11 to 24 March they prepared the keel, stem post, stern post, and twenty-three frames, cut more than ninety boards, cleared a place for the ship foundation, and fixed blocks. From ten to fourteen servitors and twenty-four native men—in addition to members of the expedition—were occupied with this work. They were half starved. "The servitors who are spending their time preparing lumber repeatedly ask for food," wrote Kozlov in his last report.

Bering divided up the small amount of provisions, but these too were rapidly consumed, and Kozlov again advised in his report that "the servitors are persistently asking for food." One carpenter could not endure the privation and deserted. Five men fell ill and the caulker Matveev died. It was only after this that the medical officer was sent to the builders at the Ushka settlement.

The morning of 4 April was clear and frosty when they solemnly laid down the boat and "the captain gave out spirits to everyone." Immediately some of the Kamchadals and their dogs were allowed to return to their homes. At the end of April Spanberg recovered and went to the construction project, taking five master builders with him. The work was in full swing.

Bering sent the pilots Moshkov and Butin to take the *Fortuna* around "Cape Kamchatka" to the mouth of the Kamchatka River. They were to put out to sea with the first favorable wind and during their voyage were instructed to "make note of the wind and the lie of the land and the islands, the depth of the water in various places, and everything eventful" |49, l. 51|. Bering ordered the administrator of Bolsheretsk to provide ten men for the *Fortuna*, and to give every assistance to the pilots. The navigators Treska and Bush were ordered to take the old ship to Okhotsk and turn it over to the pilot Enzel or to Endogurov so that all the rest of the cargo left in Bolsheretsk could be delivered by 10 July.

During April Chirikov used 170 sleds to transport almost all the rest of the cargo and most of the men along the winter route to Verkhnekamchatsk ostrog. At Bolsheretsk, at his own risk and on his own responsibility, he left the sailor Selivanov and the soldier Kapotilov with the provisions and materials in order to send them from that point to Nizhnekamchatsk ostrog by sea on the *Fortuna*. Chirikov made this decision despite having been strictly ordered to transport the cargo overland.

Apparently Bering still did not believe in sailing around Cape Lopatka. But if he actually wanted to use the sea route, as he had written in 1727, why did he not send the men and cargo on the new ship now, when the voyage could have been undertaken in the best weather in June, and on a new ship rather than an old hulk?

On 30 May Chirikov arrived at Nizhnekamchatsk with the ailing geodesist Putilov. He brought more than two hundred packs of provisions. Meanwhile the shipbuilding was proceeding at full speed at Ushka. By 19 April the lower framework was finished and forty-three of the upper kokoras had been set. They built a special steamer to bend the lumber and also constructed a forge and living quarters. At first the builders had a problem with provisions, but in spring fish were available and the soldier Sodilov was sent to prepare them. To encourage local inhabitants to lay in a supply of fish, the expedition promised to buy iukola from them. They also tried to buy reindeer meat from the Koriaks.

At the beginning of May they began the exterior planking of the ship. Early in June they started the interior work and caulked and tarred the seams. Then they brought the ship down onto her port side and prepared to launch her. It was only on the evening of 9 June 1728 that the boat was finally launched, damaging two tackle blocks. On the occasion of the launching the builders were given two and a half vedros of spirits.

The ship was named *Sv. Arkhangel Gavriil*. It carried two masts and was 18.3 meters long, 6 meters wide, and 2.3 meters deep |49, l. 42|.[51] Fedor Kozlov, the apprentice shipwright, was the principal builder of the *Sv. Gavriil*. The vessel was built from plans for the best warships of the time. It was fastened with iron and nails and would be notable for its longevity, since it was not dismantled until 1755. The windows were of mica, which was usual for that time; anchors were ten and a half and nine puds in weight; cables were ten and fifteen centimeters. Armaments consisted of four harquebuses and several three-pound falconets |57, ll. 190–193|.[52]

The sailors loaded into the hold all the rigging, sails, anchors, cannon, various light objects, and two hundred packs of flour. Then, taking advantage of the high water that even flooded the ostrog, they launched the ship into the sea. All but eight men went out to complete the ship.

The day drew near when they would put out to sea. In the middle of June Chirikov presented Bering with his recommendations for the number of servitors and the amount of provisions to be taken along. As Chirikov wrote, Bering "listened, but did not take kindly to my suggestion to consult all the persons involved about taking provisions."

From the middle of June on, the water in the river slowly began to subside and the weather continued to warm. Everything that was not to be used on the voyage was put away in a storehouse they had built. On 21 June Bering, Chirikov, Chaplin, and other expedition members put out into the coastal water. There, fifty-five miles from the settlement of Kliucha, they continued to work laying the deck and building the cabins. At the end of June they set the rudder and with the help of high trestles set the mast. On 30 June they began rigging the ship, starting with the shrouds.

Toward the end of June the restless Chirikov "went to the captain in his quarters and proposed . . . taking an interpreter on the expedition with us, someone who could converse in Chukotsk or Koriak *with the Chukchi and other natives who inhabit the land beyond the Anadyr River*" [italics added]. He also proposed that they "take seines and nets so the men could fish wherever they went" |58, 26 VI|.[53]

On 5 July 1728 Bering held a council of officers who reached the following decisions |39, l. 225|:

> I, Captain of the Navy Vitus Bering, have summoned the present senior officers to me and have on the following points requested their opinions.
>
> 1. *Shall we take fifteen barrels of salted fish from the servitors and promyshlenniks of this ostrog for the sea voyage, for which they would be given the promised payment?*
>
>   Give back seven and a half of the inhabitants' reindeer to the servitors and promyshlenniks.
>
> 2. *The ship from Bolsheretsk, which was ordered around the Kuril Cape, has not arrived. If it does arrive, should it go with us or not?*
>
>   Even if the ship arrives it should not be taken to sea with us.
>
> 3. *The intention is to send the hieromonk back to Tobolsk because of the cramped conditions on board. Shall he now be given money and provisions for travel, and if so, for how long? Likewise the carpenters, when their work is finished—shall they be sent back to their previous command or not? What shall they be given in the way of money and provisions for the journey?*

Send the hieromonk back and for his journey issue him cash for his salary from 12 May to 1 January 1729.... In Bolsheretsk issue two packs of flour and send written instructions that on the Lena they are to help him reach Iakutsk. When the carpenters finish their work send them back to their command. Give them provisions and assistance for their journey home.

4. *The servitors who will be at sea with us are asking to be paid in advance.*

The servitors who will be at sea should be paid through 1 January 1729, so they can purchase winter clothing and boots and settle their debts.

5. *It may happen that we will not return here in 1729, but we are leaving the government cash here. Shall we order that it be taken to Iakutsk, or given up here with a receipt to the commissar along with the rest of the provisions and materials?*

If we have not returned in 1729 and there is no word of us, then the servitors whom we have here in Kamchatka should leave here in January 1730, and go to Bolsheretsk, taking the government cash with them, as well as the provisions and materials, and give a receipt to the Bolsheretsk commissar or administrator, and then they should go on to Okhotsk and take the cash to Iakutsk and give it to the Iakutsk office and obtain a receipt for it.

6. *Since the geodesist is ill, should he be left here or sent elsewhere?*

... He should remain here ... with our soldiers who are being left as guards; orders should be given that there always be one man with him.

7. *How many men shall we leave to guard the cash and*

provisions we are leaving here, and what provisions
shall we issue them?

Leave two of the servitors and give them enough provisions for one-half pud per month.

8. *How much flour and gunpowder shall be put aboard*
   ship?

   Load as much flour as there is room for and take ten barrels of powder.

9. *What monthly ration of provisions shall we give the ser-*
   vitors who will be with the pilot and Endogurov?

   Order each servitor to be issued one-half pud of provisions per month and write to the Bolsheretsk administrator to help them with supplies of fish.

It was signed by Vitus Bering, Martyn Spanberg, and Aleksei
Chirikov.

The next day the *Fortuna* appeared at the mouth of the Kamchatka River, having left Bolsheretsk 20 June. The sailor Selivanov, the pilots Moshkov and Butin, and twelve men from Bolsheretsk ostrog were aboard.

The *Fortuna* remained at Nizhnekamchatsk, as Bering explained, "because of the poor condition of its rigging and because
there was not enough time to make repairs and still have it set
out during the summer season; thus we had to go in one ship" |49,
l. 58|.

Even if there had been time to repair *Fortuna*'s rigging, the ship
would still not have been able to go north because of structural
problems and because of the lack of men. It was only from the
basic staffs in Iakutsk, Okhotsk, and other places that the more
than thirty men were to be found, including a pilot, geodesist, apprentice, corporal, sergeant, and the twelve servitors who had
come on the *Fortuna*, and these were persons who had come by
chance, not necessarily persons suited for the voyage to the north.

They finished construction and rigging by 6 July. They then dismissed the hieromonk, carpenters, blacksmiths, and servitors. They issued everyone passports, provisions, and salaries |49, ll. 55–58|. A written document was sent to the Okhotsk administrator in which he was ordered to give "every assistance" to those who had been sent.

To safeguard the materials and provisions and care for the ailing geodesist and soldiers on Kamchatka, three soldiers were left behind. On 9 July they finished loading 810 puds of flour, 175 puds of sea biscuits, 66 puds of fish oil, 21 puds of meat, 20 barrels of water, 6 sazhens of firewood, and other items. They left 268 puds of flour in the Kliucha settlement and 167 puds at Bolsheretsk. The command was transferred aboard the ship. In all there were forty-four men: Bering, Spanberg, Chirikov, Chaplin, the physician Butskovskii, the pilot Moshkov, apprentice Kozlov, quartermaster Borisov, eight sailors, a desiatnik, sailmaker, caulker, five carpenters, two blacksmiths, a drummer, nine soldiers, two interpreters (the servitor I. Pankarin and the local inhabitant Ia. Povirka), and six officers' servants. Each received his salary for half a year in advance, and all were dressed up and smartly turned out. Everyone was in good spirits. They waited four days for a favorable wind. Bering sent a report to the Admiralty College informing them that the ship would put out to sea on the first favorable wind.

Three and a half years had passed since the expedition had left St. Petersburg.

NINE

To the High Northern Latitudes

O N 13 JULY 1728 the *Sv. Gavriil*, with a sloop in tow, slowly made its way down the Kamchatka River. The day was foggy and a light wind was blowing. At 8:00 P.M., at the height of the tide, they cautiously made their way past the long sandy spit and then out the mouth of the river, where they stood at anchor.

At 3:00 A.M. on 14 July they raised anchor, set all sails, and, with a light wind and clear weather, set course for south by east.

The measured days of shipboard life stretched on. We learn of this from the watch journal, where there are entries for every hour telling the direction of the wind, the course, the speed in knots, and the drift of the ship. At the end of each day the latitude and longitude are given, along with the compass variation and the distance traveled, the number of sails that the ship carried at any given time, all the shore reference points observed, the current, weather, various incidents, and the like. It has generally been considered that we are indebted to Petr Chaplin for all this invaluable data, but this is a mistake. One man could not have made all the entries around the clock. Chirikov and Chaplin took turns making the entries, when they stood watch. Furthermore, Chirikov transferred the entries from the original journal into his own |58|,[54] in case the original journal was lost. The leader of the expedition did not keep a journal. Spanberg did not know Russian well and there were no pilots on the ship.

Initially the latitude and longitude were taken at the mouth of the Kamchatka River, the latitude being reckoned at ten minutes from the southernmost point. The days were reckoned, as previously noted, not from midnight, but from noon. The first half of a nautical day was the second half of the previous day on a civilian calendar.

There were only eight sailors aboard the ship, an obvious shortage, which meant that the soldiers had to take on some of the sailors' duties.

In the course of the voyage they of course experienced all the inconveniences and vicissitudes of proceeding under sail. Often when the wind fell the sails would droop helplessly and the *Sv. Gavriil* would drift; sometimes the ship's movement was slowed by head winds or by the current. The average distance per day in the first fortnight was fifty miles. Sometimes they made only six or eight miles, but at other times more than one hundred.

On 15 July they rounded Cape Kamchatka, and with a light southeast wind they set their basic course to the northeast. At night there was an offshore fog that obscured the coast, but it dispersed when the sun came up. The next morning was calm until the wind came up from the southeast and gradually increased in strength. The speed of the ship increased, and by noon they were making six knots. In all they made more than thirty-five miles.

All day 16 July and all the following night there was a brisk south wind, so they reefed sails several times. Their speed varied from four to six and a half knots. At 9:00 A.M. the wind changed to the north and their speed decreased to two knots. Fog set in and "mist dripped from the fog." At sunset they determined the compass variation as 16°59' easterly. For the first time they made more than ninety-five miles. They moved only along the coast.

The compass variation for all three days was uniformly one and one-quarter rhumbs easterly.

The next day was foggy with a light wind; the night was cloudy. At 4:00 A.M. to the northeast they observed "a hill where the coast vanished from sight." This was the southern extremity of Karaginsk Island.

On 18 July clouds covered the entire sky but eventually cleared up. At midnight there was "heavy wind and rain." They sailed under mainsail and foresail, the lower sails on the second and first masts. At 2:00 A.M. they broke a sideboard on the starboard side. The general direction was northwest. They made less than nine miles, since they repeatedly changed course from northwest to east-southeast.

The next day it began to rain, and the wind was moderate to strong at times. They sailed under mainsail and foresail. When the wind shifted from southeast by east to north-northeast, the mainsail halyard ripped. For an hour they drifted under the foresail. After midnight there was a light wind "with rough seas from land NNE." The constant north wind caused two days of high waves. They made about twenty-three miles per day.

On 21 July, with a fresh wind and under full sail, for the first time they made more than one hundred miles in a twenty-four-hour period. They sailed the entire time about thirteen to fifteen miles off the coast of Oliutorsk Bay. They sighted many prominent reference points on shore to which they gave descriptive names: "mountain, white with snow," "prominent mountain," "mountain with unusual aspect," "point which juts into the sea," "three- peaked mountain," and others.

The next day was cloudy with wind varying in strength from west and southwest. At 8:00 P.M. the speed reached 6.6 knots. They made 104 knots, as they had the previous day. That day they rounded the southern extremity of Oliutorskii peninsula. They held at twelve to fifteen miles offshore. From 4:00 A.M. on, "the radiance of the sun pierced the gloom." That day they went more than 3° to the east and reached a northern latitude of 60°16'. The compass variation from 17 to 22 July was one and one-half rhumbs easterly, and the next day it was one and three-quarters rhumbs easterly. The wind was moderate and the sun shone through the clouds. They sailed parallel to shore for twenty miles or so.

July 24 was warm and sunny. That night a "strong wind with gusts" brought "fog and mist." At 8:00 A.M. they turned on the other tack and proceeded first southeast by south, then east, and even northwest. From 9:00 P.M. until midnight the sky was overcast with an occasional drizzle. Although the wind was moderate the waves grew stronger. The compass variation was two rhumbs easterly.

On 26 and 27 July the weather was clear and the wind gentle, and the ship approached within twelve to thirteen miles of shore. "The land lies parallel to our course in a curve," wrote Chirikov. Soon land appeared ahead on their course; this was Cape Navarin. They held to a course of six and even three miles offshore and rounded the cape. At 6:00 A.M., Chirikov wrote, "On shore we sighted a waterfall and river that flows into the sea." Here the color of the water was different from the usual hue. In two days they sailed 160 miles and reached a northern latitude of 62°55'.

The sky was overcast and there was a drizzle of rain on 28 July. For the first time they observed a current southeast by south, with a speed of not more than one mile per hour. Here the sailors sighted whales with "varicolored hides," sea lions, walrus, and porpoise. Because of the fog it was difficult to see the shore, but they held a course fifteen miles offshore.

The next day was again overcast. They sailed parallel to shore at a distance of fourteen miles and then moved in closer, to a distance of three miles. It began to rain at midnight. The depth was twenty meters. They drifted for three hours, then again sailed near shore at a distance of one and a half miles. The sheer hills on the shore that fell sharply into the sea came to an end, and a low monotonous shoreline stretched ahead. The variation of the compass from 26 to 29 July was one and three-quarters rhumbs easterly.

At 2:00 P.M. on 30 July they dropped anchor a mile and a half offshore and sent the sloop ashore with Chaplin and four sailors. They did not find any potable water, nor did they discover a suitable moorage. The sloop returned after three hours, and the *Sv. Gavriil* continued on, holding at three miles or less offshore. At 7:00 A.M. "we were sailing north, and off to the port, between west by south and northwest by west an inlet appeared." This was the estuary of the Anadyr River, but in the watch journal it was not named, and the expedition's map is notably inaccurate in this area. There is no estuary shown on it, and the Anadyr River is located much farther to the south, at Cape Navarin (Thaddeus).

On 31 July it poured rain. They sailed along shore, but because of fog they saw it only intermittently. The land was low and there was snow everywhere. The depth of the sea was not more than twenty-two meters. "There was a high wind and land was not visible from 8:00 on." It was just at this time that they passed a bay. Following an old custom they named it for the feast day on which it had been discovered, thus Krest (Cross) Bay. This was the first opportunity for the expedition members to confer a name on-to a geographical feature. At 11:00 A.M. the color of the water changed—a sign that they were near land. They took a sounding and found the depth to be twenty meters. Soon the weather cleared, and the seafarers sighted, in the northern and eastern parts of the horizon at a distance of three miles, a low shore covered with snow. That day they made eighty-five miles and reached 65°40' northern latitude and 19°06' longitude.

Again on 2 August it was overcast, with a drizzle of rain. Because of a dead calm they stood off from noon until 8:00 P.M. at a depth of ten meters. That day Chirikov made an entry saying that from all sides the land "looks just like a certain sketch of it." It may be presumed that the omission of the name of the person who made the sketch suggests that it was Chirikov himself.[55] At 8:00 P.M. a wind came up from the northeast and they sailed out from the inlet. Holding five miles offshore they rounded the western tip of Meechken Spit. The compass variation from 30 July to 2 August was one and a half degrees easterly.

There was no change in the weather the next day. They made about eight miles and once again found themselves in a bay.[56]

On the evening of 4 August they noted a weak current from shore, flowing south by west. It was "cloudy and very quiet." After midnight it rained. In the morning they sighted land at a distance of two miles. Concerning the spit Chirikov observed, "There are rocky mountains, apparently, four miles from the coast and lying parallel to shore." In the morning they sailed along the shore at a distance of two miles (Berkh mistakenly gives this distance as ten miles) and in a depth of twenty meters. That day they advanced forty-five miles.

It rained incessantly on 5 August. At 6:00 P.M. the weather cleared and the seafarers sighted high ground on the coast five

miles ahead on their course. Proceeding along shore, they passed a
bay (Rudder Bay). The coordinates here were incorrectly stated; in
the journal the place is located on dry land in 65°34'78" northern
latitude and 21°40'34" east of the mouth of the Kamchatka River.

The next day when they lowered the jib a gust of wind snapped
the topsail halyard. At midnight "there was strong wind and we
lay to under one mainsail" seventeen miles out from shore, holding a course of south-southeast. At 2:00 A.M. the wind picked up,
and their speed increased to 6.5 knots. By 5:00 A.M. it reached 7.8
knots. At this time they were holding a course of east by south.
Only one barrel of potable water was left on the ship, so they decided to take on a new supply of water. At 6:00 A.M. they drew
near "a point of rocky mountains.... The mountains stretched to
the east, very high and rugged ... like walls, and from the ravines
lying between the mountains, the wind is changeable.... We
were about two hundred sazhens off the coast of the rocky mountains. We went between the hills into an inlet, the location of
which is shown in the drawing, and lay at anchor." (Chaplin does
not have this entry in his journal.)

The depth was twenty meters, with a stony bottom. At the beginning of the eleventh hour they sent the sloop into shore with
midshipman Chaplin. They managed to find "... a lake of
melted snow and two brooks on the western side of the inlet
which flow from the steep hills into the same area where we took
the boat. We took on some of this water. The inlet is quite deep
and we saw a dwelling, a human habitation...." In honor of the
feast day they named the bay Preobrazheniia (Transfiguration).
That day they made about seventy-two miles.

August 7 was cloudy "with sunny periods." At noon they sent
eight men with Chaplin ashore in the sloop to bring back fresh
water and to make a description of the bay. When they had gone
about three versts from the vessel, the sailors found a place where
Chukchi were living that year. Many paths were worn all around.
Toward evening the sky was completely overcast, it poured rain,
and a strong wind came up. By midnight they had filled fifteen of
the barrels with water, and by morning, the other five.

At noon on 8 August they raised anchor and proceeded parallel
to shore, which lay east by south. At 7:00 P.M. they came to an inlet nine miles across, which indented the shore in a north-
northeasterly direction. They held to a distance of three miles off

the steep and often precipitous bank. "From 7:00 P.M. until midnight," wrote Chirikov, "we observed a small craft paddling out from land toward us, in which eight persons were seated. When they had paddled up near our vessel they inquired where we had come from and why. They said they were Chukchi. But when we invited them to come to the ship for a little visit they would not come alongside. They put one man on a bladder made of seal hide and sent him to converse with us. This man made his way over to us on the bladder and told us that the Chukchi live along the coast and that there are many of them. He did not know how far the land extends to the east. They had long ago heard about Russians. The Anadyr River lies far to the west of them. At first he did not mention an island, but later he said that there is an island which on a clear day can be seen from the mainland and that it is not far off and lies to the east. Then he returned on the bladder to his boat and told his companions to paddle over to our ship. They pulled alongside for a very brief time but would not come aboard. Their little boat was made of the hide of sea lion and of other sea creatures. Our interpreters spoke with them in the Koriak tongue. They said that they had few words in common with that language, and for that reason we could not inquire of them in detail as to what they wanted."

A fuller and more detailed account of the questions that were asked of the Chukchi, and their replies, are recorded in an official document signed by Bering, Chirikov, and Spanberg. The text of that document |39, l. 227| reads as follows:

> August 8, 1728. Eight men came out to us from shore in a hide boat. Our interpreters, the servitor Ivan Pankarin, and the newly baptized man Iakov Povirka spoke with them in the Koriak tongue. By our command they questioned them on the following points:
>
> 1. *What are your people called?*
>
> Chukchi.
>
> 2. *Where is the Anadyr River? Is it far from here?*
>
> You have passed the Anadyr River. It is far behind. As

you came here, far away. No ships have ever come here before.

3. *Do you know the Kolyma River?*

We do not know the Kolyma River, but we have heard from the reindeer Chukchi that they go by land to a river and they say that Russian people live on that river, but we do not know whether that is the Kolyma River or some other.

4. *Do you have any forest land? Is there a big river that flows from the land into the sea? Where does your land extend? Is it far away?*

We have no forest anywhere in our land. There are no large rivers which empty into the sea. Any rivers that do are small. From here our land turns to the left and extends far, and all of our Chukchi live on it.

5. *Is there any promontory that extends from your land into the sea?*

There is no promontory which extends from our land into the sea. All our land is level.

6. *Are there not any islands or land in the sea?*

There is an island not far from land and when it is not cloudy you can see it. There are people on that island, but we do not know about any more lands, only all of our Chukchi land.

As Grekov observed (he published the document with two omissions and some slight inaccuracies |42|), when the Chukchi spoke of their land turning to the left, they meant that it turned not to the northwest from the present Cape Dezhnev toward the Kolyma, but to the northeast from Cape Chukotsk or Chaplin. In general the Chukchi were speaking only about the nearest area.

They had not gone to the Kolyma and were not familiar with it. Apparently they did not know about the Diomede Islands either, or about the northern littoral of Chukotka; at least they did not give any information about it. In short, the information received from the Chukchi was so scanty that it was not possible to gather from it any conception about northeastern Asia, much less about a division between the two continents.

However, we can scarcely agree with Grekov's opinion that "Ittygran and Arakamchechen islands ... were unknown to them." Indeed these islands are so close to the mainland that they are easily visible from shore.

Berkh maintained that the described meeting with the Chukchi took place in a latitude of 64°41'. This is incorrect. Even at the end of that day, five hours after the meeting with the Chukchi, the ship had reached a latitude of only 64°30'. Because there was no wind for nine hours during and after the meeting, the ship went no more than a mile to the southeast. F.P. Lütke's suggestion |59, l. 235| is much closer to the truth. One hundred years after Bering's voyage, Lütke sailed there in the sloop *Seniavin*. Lütke felt that the place where the meeting took place was between capes Iakun and Ching-An. To all appearances the meeting occurred in the approximate latitude of 64°32'.

The question of longitude is more difficult. According to Chirikov, at the end of the day of 8 August they had reached a longitude of 26°04'. But this is one whole degree east of Ittygran Island. We note that the location of the *Sv. Gavriil*, as indicated in the journal at the end of 5 and 6 August, is on dry land. This serves to emphasize the fact that one of the primary errors of the 1729 map of the expedition is that the Chukotsk peninsula is located farther north than is actually the case.

It is difficult to explain such errors. Might they have been results of the inaccuracy of the instruments, or of overcast weather and heavy clouds? The compass variation from 3 to 8 August was one and three-quarters rhumbs easterly.

The morning of 9 August was still and cloudy. At 3:00 P.M. "heavy clouds rolled in" and soon it began to rain. They were three miles offshore. "There was a great undulation to the sea." That day they made twenty-one miles (20.45 to the south and 6.69 to the east), not thirty-five miles as Berkh wrote, adding their speed to the distances of the two tacks. The latitude at the end of the day was 64°10' and the longitude 26°20'. The compass variation right up to 16 August averaged two and one-quarter rhumbs easterly.

The next day was clear with a light wind. From noon until 9:00 P.M. "we maneuvered along the shore, which concluded its eastward extension." They then sailed northwest, five and a half miles from shore. That day they made slightly more than eleven miles.[57] On 10 August (the eleventh, by naval reckoning), it was cloudy with a light wind. At 2:00 P.M. to the south-southeast they sighted the island that the Chukchi had mentioned to them. They named the island St. Lawrence in honor of the feast that day. They approached within four and a half miles of the island. In the report to the Admiralty College of 10 March 1730 |49, l. 98| Bering wrote, "When I approached the island the Chukchi had mentioned, I saw dwellings similar to those of the Chukchi." Other documents, however, do not corroborate that they sighted Chukchi dwellings on the island. The depth decreased from thirty to twenty-two meters. From 9:00 A.M. until noon there was "dense cloud cover." They made only eight miles that day.

In the watch journal the southeastern corner of Chukotka was more than once referred to by its proper name. We find the first mention of "Chukotskii Nos" in Chirikov's reply to Bering's question on 13 August 1728. Thus Grekov's statement that the name "Chukotskii Mys" did not come into existence during the voyage is unfounded. The term "Chukotskii Ugol" was also used by the seafarers on the final map in the "Catalog of towns..." in the "Brief Relation...." In this our navigators joined the presently designated Chukotskii Mys and Mys Chaplina, perceiving them as one entity, which is readily seen on the final map.

On these dates the expedition was in the strait between the continents. However, the seafarers, of course, did not realize that it was a strait.

On 12 August: "Strong wind, cloudy ... we lay to under one mainsail because of the heavy wind." At 4:00 A.M. they came about onto the other tack and proceeded at a speed of three knots. That day they changed tack three times. At 8:00 P.M. they sighted "a group on shore" to the northwest by west, and two and a half hours later, to the southwest by south-one-half rhumb westerly they noted "land behind us" at a distance of fifteen miles. This most likely was Cape Chaplin. Rounding Capes Chukotsk and Chaplin at some distance, the sailors did not notice the bay separating them and did not make out the islands of Ittygran and Arakamchechen. That day they made more than thirty-three miles. At noon they reached latitude 64°59' and longitude 27°04'.

From Cape Chaplin the ship did not proceed west to the shores of Chukotka as the instructions ordered, but held to a course of north-northeast, a considerable distance from land. As a result the men did not see land for forty-one hours starting from 10:30 P.M. 12 August.

The next day was cloudy, with a fresh wind. They proceeded under mainsail, foresail, and topsail. At 4:00 P.M. "a strong wind came up and we reefed the mainsail," and their speed increased to five knots. Then fog and mist closed in. At 4:00 A.M. the wind grew even stronger, and the sea was very rough; their speed was 5.5 knots. They made some ninety-three miles and reached 66°17' latitude and 29°06' longitude.

On 13 August a very important episode occurred, which influenced future events. At 8:00 P.M. when the ship had reached latitude 65°30' but was still quite some distance from Cape Dezhnev, Bering summoned Spanberg and Chirikov to his cabin and read through Peter's instructions. Then, referring to the statement from the Chukchi and to the fact that the Asiatic shore was turning westward and was lost from sight, he explained his opinion to them: the land of Chukotsk Nos, which they had previously believed to be joined to America, was actually separated from it by the sea. Thus would it not be possible to conclude that Chukotka was separated from America without actually proceeding as far as the latitude of Cape Dezhnev in the northeastern extremity of Chukotka? It is obvious that Bering mistook the southeastern corner of the peninsula for its easternmost extremity. Convinced of this, the captain did not ask the officers whether they believed in the existence of a strait. "Bering requested . . . a written opinion from Spanberg and Chirikov as to whether they could consider the 'indicated [Chukotsk] promontory as separated from America by the sea'"|17, p.10|.[58] Spanberg, giving concrete expression to his leader's order, wrote that it would be necessary to answer the question, "Which is more important, to proceed farther north, and if so how far, or search for a harbor, and if this, when, and where?" |39, 1. 228|.

Chirikov was the first to reply, that same day. He wrote:

> This day Your Excellency has summoned us and explained your opinion concerning the land of the Chukotsk promontory, that because of the accounts of the Chukotsk inhabitants, and by reason of the extent of the land from this promontory between north and northwest, and also the fact that we are presently in 65° northern latitude,[59] this indicates that although it had been supposed that this promontory might be joined to America, it is in fact separated from it by the sea. You have also asked that we state in writing our opinions as to what course of action this expedition should follow henceforth. Complying with this order, I humbly submit my opinion.
>
> Since we do not have information as to how far north along the east coast of Asia people known to Europeans have been, we cannot know for certain whether the sea separates Asia from America unless we proceed as far as the mouth of the Kolyma River, or as far as the ice, for we know there is always ice in the Northern Sea. For this reason it is certainly up to us, on the basis of the ukaz given to Your Excellency from His Imperial Majesty of Worthy and Blessed Memory, to proceed along land (if ice does not prevent us, or if the coast does not turn to the west, to the mouth of the Kolyma River) to the places indicated in His Imperial Majesty's ukaz. If the land still turns to the north, then it is incumbent upon us to continue until the 25th of this month to search in these places for an area where we could spend the winter, especially opposite Chukotsk Nos, where, according to the accounts Petr Tatarinov had from the Chukchi, there is forested land. If on the 25th there is a contrary wind, then at that time we should search for a winter harbor |39, 1. 227|.

On the basis of an analysis of his reply, Chirikov has often been called a born explorer in scholarly literature, in the present case making the only possible interpretation of the strict scientific determination about the age-old question of a strait. It only remains for us to agree with this conclusion and to emphasize the fact that

Chirikov's proposal was simple, wise, and logical. His conviction
that it was necessary to continue sailing was not founded on, for
example, "a profound knowledge of navigational conditions in
the Northern Arctic Ocean," as V.A. Divin believes |25, p.65; 61,
p.57|. Chirikov himself, in his reply to Bering, states that they did
not know what latitude men had reached previously by sailing
from the Northern Sea along the east coast of Asia; and even more
important, this is yet another piece of evidence that the seafarers
did not know about Dezhnev's voyage. Elementary logic requires
that for proof as to whether a strait exists between the continents,
one must go by sea to the Kolyma and by that means relate the
map of Chukotka with the map of the already known coast of
northern Siberia, extending a common shoreline, as Peter's instructions read; or go as far as the ice "which is always present in
the Northern Sea." If the ship encountered ice floes there in summer, it would indicate, as Chirikov suggested, that it was sailing
in the northern Arctic Ocean and that there was no isthmus between the continents in the north.

It was all the more necessary to continue the voyage because
the notorious Shelagsk Cape was depicted as extending beyond
the edges of the map, and this left doubt regarding a strait.

It is now completely clear to us how right Chirikov was. However, although his opinion has been known for more than one
hundred years, published in 1850 by A. Polonskii, even in our
own time one may find an inaccurate assessment or even an incorrect interpretation of it.

Most often it is only remembered that Chirikov advised con-
tinuing on to the mouth of the Kolyma. For example, Grekov
writes that Chirikov "said that Bering's supposition about the
separation between Asia and America could only be verified by
following the northern coast of Asia to the west ... that is, as far
as the Kolyma River" |42, p.34|.

Berg, Vize, Belov |62, p.402|, and other scholars have said ap-
proximately the same thing. Divin considered it was even possible to arbitrarily determine the date when they would have
reached the mouth of the Kolyma River. He wrote, "Bering
refused to go on to the mouth of the Kolyma ... although the
condition of the ice would obviously have permitted him to do so,
and by 25 August he could have reached the mouth of the river"
|61, p.51|. Divin repeated this opinion eighteen years later |25,

p.57|. Lebedev and Esakov |52, p.195| also acknowledge the possibility of reaching the Kolyma by 25 August. However, it is impossible to understand how the vessel could cover nearly three thousand miles in twelve days, when the greatest distance they ever made in one day was 104 miles.

In actuality Chirikov was thinking of something considerably more astute: he was advised that they proceed "as far as the mouth of the Kolyma River *or to the ice*" [italics added]. Clearly he realized that while the ice might prevent them from reaching the mouth of the Kolyma, it might also conclusively prove the separation between the continents. And if the continents were indeed joined by an isthmus, then he believed that in August any ice south of such an isthmus would not be very thick.

We must emphasize two points. First, in his reply Chirikov tactfully pointed out to Bering that his suggested course of action would be a breach of the instructions given him by Peter, which were to proceed without fail along the coast heading north. Bering was now ordering them to move away from the coast. Since they had not seen the coast for twenty-two hours, he concluded that the land "had ended," that the strait had been discovered, and that the goal of the expedition had been fulfilled. But the ship continued to proceed, as if automatically helping to cast doubts. And evidently Spanberg also had doubts, if even one day later, on 14 August, he proposed that they spend another two days sailing north.

Second, Chirikov, following the orders in the instructions to proceed to some place known to Europeans, considered the mouth of the Kolyma to be one of these places. It was considered the farthest eastern point of the northern seacoast of Siberia, which was then known to Europeans—in this case, to Russians. Therefore, Chirikov proposed that they sail not just along the coast, but "along the land . . . to places indicated in the ukaz of His Imperial Highness." In the orders of the instructions, "proceed to some town belonging to a European power . . . place it on the map, and return here." The town did not have to be a place of potential trade or of architectural interest; it only had to exist as some identifiable geographical point on the map. Therefore, the instructions would be fulfilled by placing on the map some coastal point instead of a town. It was important that the place be known to Europeans and be so designated on the map. In this case it is not of importance that Peter had in mind a point on the American continent, since he was inclined to believe that Asia was joined to America.

In regard to spending the winter in the high latitudes, Chirikov felt that would be necessary only if, when the voyage was prolonged, "the land still inclines to the north," or if there were constant headwinds. It is important to note that Chirikov was fully aware of how dangerous autumn sailing is in these latitudes. It was for this reason that he allowed a maximum of twelve days, until 25 August, for the voyage along the coast of Chukotka to the northwest and to search for a harbor.

We may suppose that the *Sv. Gavriil* would have reached ice before 25 August, and then, in Chirikov's opinion, it would no longer be necessary either to sail to the mouth of the Kolyma or to search for a harbor for a winter stay. And only in this way would the instructions have been fulfilled.

For us a very important point in Chirikov's reply is that he proposed if necessary to search for a base for wintering first of all "opposite the Chukotsk Nos, on land ... where there is forest." He was certainly suggesting "Bolshaia Zemlia," that is, America. Having learned of this from Petr Tatarinov in Ilimsk, Chirikov believed in the existence of this land, and in its proximity to Chukotka.[60] Bering and Spanberg evidently had either forgotten about Tatarinov's information or did not believe him. In any case, objecting to Chirikov, both were in agreement in repeating that there was no harbor on Chukotka suitable for spending the winter, since there was no forest and the Chukchi natives were hostile. If Bering had taken Chirikov's advice, Northwest America would have been discovered in 1728.

What did Spanberg think about their future actions? He gave his reply on 14 August, writing in German since his command of Russian was weak; Bering translated his reply.[61] It read as follows:

> Your Excellency has been pleased to ask, since we have reached a latitude of 65°30′ in the northern regions, and in your opinion and according to the account of the Chukchi we have reached the point opposite the easternmost extension of that land ... which is the better course of action: to proceed farther north, and if so, how much farther; or to search for a harbor, and [if so], where would it be best for the state's inter-

est to protect the ship and the men over the long winter? My
reply is that since we have reached the above-mentioned latitude, and on the Chukotsk land there is no harbor, firewood,
or river course where we can take cover under winter conditions such as prevail in this latitude, and since the natives are
hostile, and we were not informed as to how much we were
to observe in these places, nor do we know what our return
route is to be, I believe that if we continue sailing north on
our voyage until the 16th of the present month, and it is not
possible to reach 66°, then we should turn back, invoking the
name of God, in time to search for a harbor and safe place on
the Kamchatka River, from whence we set out, so that we
can keep the ship and the men safe[62] |39, ll. 227–228|.

It is often suggested that Spanberg was harsh with his subordinates and that he was noted for his resoluteness and was in-
clined to take risks |42, p.34|. He has also generally been consid-
ered a fine seaman. Andreev especially spoke glowingly of him
|17, p.7|. However, the materials of the First Kamchatka Expedi-
tion do not provide a basis for excessive praise. In all likelihood he
was not disposed to taking risks if, once they were positioned
near the Chukotsk peninsula in 65°30′ latitude, he was proposing
to proceed only another half degree to reach 66°. As we have seen,
Bering believed it was impossible to adopt this suggestion and
proceed farther to the north. Why did Spanberg propose sailing
past 66°? It is difficult to give a rational answer to that question.
The fact is that he was not very optimistic about reaching even
66°, although the ship so far had not encountered any serious ob-
stacle, such as severe storms or ice, and they had plenty of provisions and fresh water.

Spanberg's remarks about the fact that "we were not informed
as to how much we were to observe in these places nor do we
know what our return route is to be," do not provide a basis for
considering him a fine seaman, since Chirikov and Chaplin syste-
matically made observations, noting latitude and longitude at the
end of each day, and of course were well informed on the position
of the ship and the route that they followed to the north, and by
which it was possible to return to Kamchatka. Evidence of this is
Spanberg's doubt about the possibility of reaching 66°. But even
more obvious is the fact that at the end of the day on 13 August,

the very day when he expressed his doubt in writing, the ship did cross this parallel and reach 66°17′.

In scholarly literature one may find the statement that Chaplin also expressed his opinion as to whether to turn the ship onto a return course. Supposedly he spoke on behalf of the officers against Bering, having made a note in the watch journal that he had arrived at his decision without taking counsel with them |64, p.38; 65, p.256|. But a careful look at the watch journal reveals that there is no such note, nor could there have been. It is difficult to imagine such a note appearing in the watch journal of a naval ship. Furthermore, Chaplin, a midshipman, was not entitled to take part in the meetings of the officers, so he could not have expressed an opinion on behalf of all the officers, or even on his own behalf, either orally or in writing. Finally, in addition to Bering, there were two senior officers on the ship, and it was these men whom the commander was asking.

What did the leader of the expedition do after he had received responses from the senior officers? He himself said, "Having considered the given opinions, I have made my decision. If we remain here any longer, in these northern regions, there will be the danger that on some dark night in the fog we will become beached on some shore, from which we will not be able to extricate ourselves because of contrary winds. Considering the condition of the ship, the fact that leeboards and the keelboard are broken, it is difficult for us to search in these regions for suitable places to spend the winter. These lands, except for Chukotka [are unknown], the natives are hostile, and there is no forest. In my judgment it is better to return and search for a harbor on Kamchatka where we will stay through the winter" |39, l. 228|.[63]

There is hardly a person who will dispute the fact that sailing in unknown waters, even on clear nights with no fog and with favorable winds, is attended with definite danger. The *Sv. Gavriil* could have encountered danger. Nonetheless, Chirikov proposed that they sail farther, regardless of the risk.

Would Columbus, Cook, or Bellingshausen and Lazarev have made their discoveries if they had not taken reasonable risks? We recall the Antarctic expedition of the Russian seafarers of 1819–21. Granted they were sailing ninety years later, but they were also in wooden sailing vessels, and in more difficult conditions of ice, several times reaching beyond 69° southern latitude, and they had not only the fogs, dark nights, and contrary winds to fear, but also the far more dangerous enemies, ice and icebergs.

Quite apart from these dangers, Bering pleaded broken leeboards and keelboard. But in spite of these they could easily have continued the voyage. Neither Chirikov nor even Spanberg considered it necessary to mention these in their replies. The leader's concern over the dangers of wintering on Chukotka were completely justified; the possibility of wintering there was out of the question. But no one suggested that they spend the winter there. Bering's last sentence—"In my judgment, it is better to turn back..."—sounds quite lacking in confidence.

As we see, Bering basically did not reply to Chirikov's proposal concerning the main consideration in that situation—the necessity of proving that the continents were not connected.

Now let us return to the voyage of the *Sv. Gavriil*, which we have left in the strait.

On 14 August the weather was overcast. At noon it began to rain. Chirikov wrote, "In this place the ocean current is northwest by west.... Although there is also a counter-current, the flow is more on the indicated rhumb." From 2:00 P.M. until 2:00 A.M. there was a light wind. "We lay to without sail through all the watches," stated Chirikov, "because of the lack of wind but primarily because of the darkness."

In scholarly literature one may find mention of amazement at the fact that having passed through the strait, the sailors did not immediately see both shores, the Asiatic and the American. But from the deck of a ship both shores are readily seen only in very good visibility. Our seafarers, having passed through the narrowest part of the strait, thirty-five kilometers, because of "fog and mist" did not see either shore, although they were sailing fewer than ten miles off the Asiatic coast.

That day they made more than twenty-six miles and reached 66°11' northern latitude and 29°36' longitude, east of the mouth of the Kamchatka River. The compass variation was two and one-quarter rhumbs easterly.

At 3:00 P.M. on 14 August they encountered light northeast wind. Their speed decreased to 0.9 knots, and the ship began to drift to the northwest on the current. Just then in a brief moment of clearing they sighted "high land behind us" twenty miles to the south. This could only be Ratmanov Island, unknown to the sailors. After three and a half hours, when the ship continued to drift to the northwest because of the calm, "between west by south and west-northwest, at a distance of fifteen miles, high mountains appeared, which we believe to be on Bolshaia Zemlia," Chirikov wrote in his journal. This land was, of course, Cape Dezhnev.

The members of the expedition did not put the track of their voyage on the map. Later, cartographers tried many times to fill in this gap. The noted hydrographer and cartographer A. Nagaev |66, No. 58| undertook the first such attempt in 1767. In 1787 A. Vilbrekht |67, No. 111| filled in the course of the *Sv. Gavriil*, as V. Berkh also did in 1823. In all three instances, however, the track of the ship, particularly in the strait, is indicated by a straight line, without accounting for the change in current each day, and the return track is too far from the eastern shores of Chukotka. Vilbrekht, for example, in placing Ratmanov Island north of 66°, located the track of the ship east of it.

Even less exact are the manuscript maps of V. Krasilnikov of 1768 |67, No. 93|, which are preserved in the archives, and of an unknown writer also of the second half of the eighteenth century |67, No. 94|.

All the compilers apparently located the track of the voyage of the expedition on geographical maps of their time, which are notable for their significant inaccuracies, so that in their turn they are not conducive to the correct representation of the route of the ship.

We have reconstructed the track, on a contemporary geographical map, on the basis of the hourly entries in the log. In order to avoid errors made by the primitive instruments of that time, we have corrected the track, relying on the indications in the journal for the distances to points on shore and between various points of the voyage.

In accordance with the intention of the instruction, Bering should have gone to the shore he sighted, and sailed along it to the northwest. But he failed to do so, inasmuch as on 12 August he did not proceed along the eastern shore of Chukotka. The *Sv. Gavriil* sailed away from shore, north-northeast.[64]

The appearance of dry land on 14 August was a surprise to Bering. Now Bering related to this newly sighted land his thought about the "end" of land, stated on an earlier date, and everything

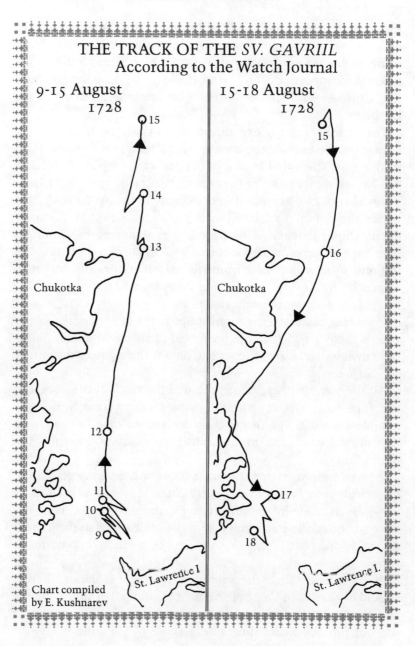

THE TRACK OF THE *SV. GAVRIIL*
According to the Watch Journal

9-15 August
1728

15-18 August
1728

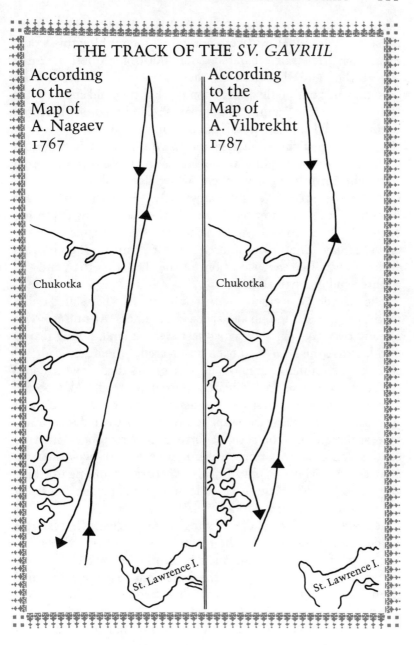

THE TRACK OF THE *SV. GAVRIIL*

According
to the
Map of
A. Nagaev
1767

According
to the
Map of
A. Vilbrekht
1787

Chukotka

Chukotka

St. Lawrence I.

St. Lawrence I.

he had thought about Cape Chaplin (that this was the eastern-most point, and that if it were not joined to anything this would mean that the strait separated Chukotka from America). But it was all the more ill-advised to consider that the land "ended" for certain, since one could easily suppose that it would appear again farther on, as it had appeared that day. Probably that is the reason Bering ordered continued sailing north-northeast.

On 15 August the wind died and there was periodic fog. From 9:00 P.M. until midnight it was overcast and there was rain. From midnight until 5:00 A.M. there were "fog and heavy mist." Chirikov observed, "We saw many whales. From the 12th of this month on, the seawater has been white in color. The depth has been 20, 25, and 30 sazhens." The current was the same as on the previous day. They made more than forty miles. The compass variation was like the "variation" of the ship from the wind—up to three and one-half rhumbs.

The next day was cloudy, with a dying wind. They sailed under mainsail, foresail, and jib at a speed of 2.3 knots. At sunset it was already two days since they had last sighted land. Bering finally decided that the strait had been discovered. When they had proceeded seven miles after noon, he gave orders that they turn onto their return course. In the watch journal we read, "At 3:00 the Captain announced that in accordance with the ukaz he must turn back, and turning the ship, he gave orders to hold to a south-by-east direction." The actual course, according to a calculation of the compass variation, was different, south-by-west, one-quarter west. The *Sv. Gavriil* made this turn, according to Chirikov, at 67°18'48" northern latitude and 30°14' longitude east of the mouth of the Kamchatka River.[65]

Leaving the coast on the evening of 14 August, the seafarers sailed for forty-four and a half hours in a north-northeasterly direction and made sixty-six and a half miles as the crow flies, although in literature one finds the statement that the ship sailed twenty-four hours and made as much as two hundred miles. This means that the expedition reached 67°06' northern latitude and 168°10' west of Greenwich, which is to say that the location of the site where they turned onto the return course, as marked in the journal, is inaccurate.

For the twelve hours following the turn, the *Sv. Gavriil* held to a course of south-by-west, one-quarter west, at a speed of 2.6 to 5.8 knots, and from 4:00 A.M. on they held to a course one rhumb closer west. After the turn they sailed for eighteen hours without sighting land, and were completely out of sight of land for more than sixty-two hours. It was only on 16 August at 9:00 A.M. at a distance of twenty miles on a course south-by-west, one-half west that there appeared "land with mountains, where Chukchi live." For another three hours, to the starboard of the ship at a distance of thirteen miles, they sighted high mountains "from whence the land extends south-southwest and northwest," and to the port side of the vessel at a distance of sixteen miles, wrote Chirikov, "there is land, which we believe to be an island." In the first of these two cases the mention is of the shores of Chukotka and in the second, of the island named by the seafarers Diomede Island, now Ratmanov Island.[66] On the map the sailors placed the island more to the north and somewhat more to the west than it should have been. That day they made about ninety miles and reached 66°02' northern latitude and 28°31' longitude east of the mouth of the Kamchatka River.

Holding course, the *Sv. Gavriil* on 17 August sailed along the east coast of Chukotka, not entering bays but sailing close to the cape, at a distance of one-half and even one-quarter of a mile. South of Cape Dezhnev "we sighted quite a few people and their dwellings in two places on shore. When they saw us they ran up onto a high rocky hill," wrote Chirikov. At 2:00 A.M. they noted land at a distance of a mile and a half in the direction south-by-west, and they sailed parallel to shore. They passed Seniavin Strait and Arakamchechen Island, not realizing that it was an island, and in the morning rounded Cape Chaplin. They did not name the cape. On the cape the sailors sighted Chukchi dwellings and temporarily referred to it as "a point of land with dwellings." Afterward, as Chirikov wrote, "we went to another point that we had previously sighted, which had a bay in the sea on the right." Thus the expedition discovered one more Chukchi camping site. In all on that day they made 115.8 miles.

On 18 August they rounded the southern tip of Chukotka— Chukotsk Cape. At first they proceeded along the coast at a distance of four and a half miles; then they continued south, and in the morning again sighted St. Lawrence Island twenty miles to the east. They again followed the southern shore of Chukotka.

Cloudy weather prevailed. On 20 August from midnight until 5:00 A.M. it was calm and "we lay to without sails." The depth was fifteen sazhens with a rocky bottom. Until 9:00 A.M. "we did not sight land because of the clouds." At 10:00 A.M. "there was no wind at all." They sighted land astern, and behind the ship appeared four lodkas. They approached the ship and engaged in conversation with the sailors. The following is the text of the actual notes of the conversation with the Chukchi.

Chukchi in four hide baidara paddled out from land to us. There were about 40 persons, both men and women, and one of them was a toion [leader] who could speak the Koriak tongue quite well. By our orders our interpreters questioned the toion and obtained the following answers.

1. *Where is the Anadyr River? Is it far from here?*

The Anadyr River is half a day [to the south] from here, not near. I have been to the Anadyrsk ostrog to sell walrus tusks, and I have known of the Russian people for a long time.

2. *Are you familiar with the Kolyma River? Is there a passage from here to the Kolyma?*

I know the Kolyma River. I have gone there overland with reindeer. The sea is shallow off the mouth of the Kolyma and there is always ice there in the sea. We have never gone by sea from here to the mouth of the Kolyma, but the people who live along the coast from here to the distant Kolyma all belong to our tribe.

3. *Are there islands or is there land in the sea opposite your land?*

Across from here people speak the same language as Chukchi used to speak.

The undersigned attest to the accuracy of the questions and answers: Vitus Bering, Martyn Spanberg, Aleksei Chirikov |39, 1. 228|.

From these notes it appears that again on this occasion the Chukchi did not give a definite answer to the question whether there was a sea route to the Kolyma, since they had never personally voyaged there by sea. Let us turn our attention to one detail pertaining to the geographical concepts of the natives, which indicates that it is impossible to place any reliance on their information. The Chukchi said the Anadyr River lay to the south of the place where they met Bering. This no doubt explains the fact that on their map the sailors placed this river, the mouth of which they had not personally observed, at Cape Navarin. In actuality the Anadyr does not lie south of the meeting place, but west and even somewhat north.

In the watch journal Chirikov, relating the meeting with the Chukchi, adds several details. "We go to the Kolyma River by reindeer, but we have not gone there by sea," he relates. He also gives the information that the Chukchi brought meat to the ship along with fish, water, and fox and polar fox pelts, "fifteen in all, plus four walrus tusks," to trade for needles and fire steels.

Bering points out in his report of 10 March 1730 that they met the Chukchi in 64°25' northern latitude, at Cape Iakun, somewhere south of the place where they had met the Chukchi the first time. (V.I. Grekov maintains that both meetings took place near Preobrazheniia Bay.) Straightening their course the sailors continued on to the southwest at some distance from shore.

On 22 August at 4:00 P.M. to the right of their course at a distance of twenty-five miles there came into sight "a point of land located near the Anader [sic] River, which we named Sv. Faddeia [Navarin]." Then the coast once more vanished from sight. That night "there were colored columns of light [aurora borealis] across the northern sky."

On 24 August at 1:30 P.M. they again sighted land twenty miles to the west-northwest.

The following day when the ship moved off from shore a strong wind came up "with heavy seas," and the halyard on the foremast broke. They lowered the sail and proceeded under reefed mainsail. Several times it began to rain. The land disappeared beyond the stern.

V. Berkh, speaking of the Sv. Gavriil's idiosyncracies, remarked on the fact that when it sailed close to the wind it made a speed of only one and a half to two knots, and its "variation" exceeded three to five rhumbs. On other tacks, however, its speed reached seven and even nine knots, and there were times when it even made eleven knots. The compass variation beginning 19 August was one and three-quarters rhumbs.

From 24 to 30 August they sailed some distance from shore. For the most part the course lay almost directly southwest. On 23, 28, and 29 August the current was correspondingly marked northeast by east, southeast-three-quarters-east, and south by east. There was not a single storm all this time. But from the evening of 30 August there was a strong wind on the approach to the peninsula beyond which lay the mouth of the Kamchatka River. It continued all night, and the next morning was particularly strong at noon, at which time "the mainsail ripped and because of the danger we reefed the main." When their speed reached 7.5 knots "we sailed with one straight foresail."

At 4:00 P.M. out of the gloom they sighted land ahead and to the right at a distance of three miles or less. A strong wind drove the ship toward the rocky shore, rising up in a sheer face. They had to put off to sea, especially since the shore here curved in an arc as if it were surrounding the ship on three sides. "Then we lowered the straight foresail and set the main and other foresails against the heavy wind and waves, but we could not accomplish this quickly, nor without great difficulty." The battle with the elements continued until late in the evening. Finally at 10:00 P.M. the halyards of two sails, the main and fore, ripped at the same time. The sails crashed down, and the rigging was so tangled it was impossible to straighten it out in such high seas. They hurriedly anchored a mile offshore. In total darkness and constant rain, with increasing waves and barely slackening wind, the crew worked through the entire night and the early part of the following day to put the rigging in order.

By noon the wind and waves had calmed and the voyage could continue. But then as they were raising the anchor the cable broke. Apparently it had been damaged by rocks right at the stock. They raised sail and proceeded along the coast southeast by south. At 8:00 P.M. they tried to take a sounding, but the lead would not reach bottom.

At last on 1 September they rounded Cape Kamchatka and entered Kamchatka Bay. On 2 September they entered the mouth of the Kamchatka River, went up river a bit, and anchored where they had stood prior to setting out on their voyage to the north.

The fifty-one-day expedition at sea had ended.

TEN

Mapping Bering's 1728 Voyage

WHAT FAR NORTHERN POINT did the *Sv. Gavriil* reach, and how far was it from the northeastern extremity of Asia?

The first historian of the expedition, G.F. Müller |68, pp.392–394|, was mistaken when he wrote, "On 15 August they reached 67°18′ northern latitude at the cape, beyond which the coast . . . extends to the west." It turned out that the northernmost point the expedition attained and the northeastern point of Asia are located in almost the same latitude. The final map of the expedition served as a basis for such a conclusion, where the northern extremity of Chukotka is shown to be in 67°18′, which is one entire degree north of its true location.

Müller's second mistake was an addition to erroneous geographical notions of the time. It was the assertion that from the northeastern point of Asia "the coast turns to the west, but this curve consists only of a large bay ... and from there the coast straightens out to the north and northeast up to 78° of latitude and beyond, to where the actual Chukotka cape is located...." On the maps of 1754 and 1758 Müller, not knowing the precise configuration of this cape, provisionally indicated it with a dotted line as a huge, mushroom-shaped "peninsula" that extended from east to west more than ten degrees and stretched north almost to the 75th parallel. The eastern point of this "peninsula" was shown 2°30′ farther to the east than Cape Dezhnev. On the "peninsula" described by the dotted line, an inscription read "land of the Chukchi, which extends to some unknown point."

In this mythical peninsula we readily recognize the reputed Shelagsk Cape, although it is not called that here. As we know, this cape was depicted on most pre-Bering maps, and likewise on the final map of the First Kamchatka Expedition (1729), and DuHalde's 1735 map, and even on the more accurate map of the Naval Academy (1746). The size, outline, and location of the cape changed, but its presence on the maps remained.

However, Müller was correct in stating that only by going to the northern part of the peninsula that was depicted, "would there have been grounds for stating that the two parts of the world were not joined." Thus Müller felt that Bering's conclusion about the separation of the two continents was unfounded. Müller's opinion did not coincide with Chirikov's proposal, expressed on 13 August, but it approached it: if Bering had gone along the northern coast of Chukotka he might have encountered ice south of Wrangell Island.

In Western European literature of the eighteenth and nineteenth centuries, still another mistaken notion was firmly held, which the Danish geographer Lauridsen called "an interesting misconception." He discovered on maps that were compiled during the first decade after the end of the expedition that from the present-day Cape Dezhnev the *Sv. Gavriil* supposedly went not north-northeast, sailing away from Chukotka, but along its coastline, to the northwest. Lauridsen was the first to call attention to the fact that Hazius in 1738, using information from the First Kamchatka Expedition, showed a mountain chain along the northern shore of Chukotka, somewhat above the 70th parallel, and on the coast he made the notation, "the limit to which the seafarer Bering followed the coast." In the same way this mountain chain was also shown on other maps from this period, the primary one being the final map of the expedition itself. DuHalde (1735), knowing the latitude that the expedition had reached but without a conception of longitude, ended the mountain chain at a latitude of 67°20' on the map of the expedition that he published |69|. Thus, the very character of the northern shores of Chukotka, as depicted, furthered the original error, which stated that the ship had sailed along the northern coast of Chukotka.

At the end of the nineteenth century the American scholar William H. Dall felt that the mistake on DuHalde's map was not a typographical error but rather a deliberate "clarification" of the original map to bring it into accord with the publisher's erroneous notions. "Bering, of course, was never on this northern coast of Chukotka," wrote the scholar, "but DuHalde's map was juggled so as to indicate that he had been there" |70, p.65|. However, this observation by the American does not answer the question as to why DuHalde engaged in such juggling. In complete bewilderment Dall |70, p.164| exclaimed, "How was it possible that men of such exceptional intelligence as DuHalde and D'Anville and Müller and Hazius, Euler and Campbell were all so deceived?" The scholar believed this was a result of the fact that the original source materials had remained unknown for a long time and that these fragments, which had become the property of the world, were notable for their difficult language and frequent distortions. He expressed the idea that a definitive explanation of this could be found in Russian archives.[67]

In Soviet literature a thorough analysis of the error has been made by V.I. Grekov |42, p.36|. He first points out that even James Cook was influenced by the representation of Bering's sailing in a westerly direction when he sailed through the Bering strait and north of it fifty years later. Cook maintained that the *Sv. Gavriil* went to Cape Serdtse-Kamen, almost eighty miles northwest of Cape Dezhnev |71, p.197|. Grekov believed that there was another major error connected with the name Serdtse-Kamen, committed by Georg W. Steller when he said that evidently the expedition had reached this cape located in Krest Bay (presently Cape Linlinnei). Grekov also pointed out two errors made by N.N. Ogloblin, that counter to all assertions, Bering was not in the strait between Cape Dezhnev and Ratmanov Island, since he had not sighted Kruzenstern Island, the second of the Diomede Islands; and likewise that the *Sv. Gavriil* had supposedly reached King Island, seventy kilometers south of the Cape of the Prince of Wales. But Grekov did not answer the question either, as to why this misunderstanding had occurred in the first place.

Probably DuHalde made his mistake because in the first document that was made known to the world, Bering's "Brief Relation..." to the Tsaritsa, which DuHalde recounts in his work, there was no information regarding the longitude that the expedition reached. The appearance of the misinformation was indirectly furthered, also, in the second point of Peter's instructions, which ordered them to sail "along the land which lies to the north," and in the lack of an explanation by Bering in the "Brief Relation ..." that the expedition had not sailed along the northern coast of Chukotka, but located it on the map on the basis of old sketch maps. Incidentally, on several examples of the expedition's map there is a notation along the northern coast of Asia that "this part of the Shelagsk and Chukotsk lands are entered here on the basis of earlier maps and information."

Was it by chance that in the "Brief Relation..." there was no note as to the longitude they reached, no mention of the fact that during the next sixty-two hours the *Sv. Gavriil* sailed far off the coast, no mention of other facts that Dall referred to? We do not have the material to answer that question.

But the most important basis for the mistake was the misplacing of the northeastern corner of Chukotka by one entire degree to the north on the expedition's final map.

In literature one often comes across designations not only of the latitude they reached but also the longitude. Thus on a map prepared under Müller's guidance in 1754, along a line indicating the expedition's route there is the notation, "The voyage of Captain Bering in 1728 to 66°30'." The same thing was repeated in the final variation of his map in 1758, and on the "Maps of Lieutenant Sind," published in Russian and French in the 1760s.

At the end of the nineteenth century Dall expressed doubts about the accuracy of the coordinates the expedition had reached. Through speculation he came to the erroneous conclusion that the *Sv. Gavriil* reached 67°24' northern latitude and 193°15' eastern longitude, east of Greenwich. In our own time Divin made a major error in declaring that "thanks to the efforts of Chirikov and Chaplin a description was given of a significant part of the coast from Kamchatka to 67° northern latitude" |61, p.57|. But in fact the coast of northeast Asia at this latitude lies 3° west of the longitude that the expedition reached.

Why was Bering in such a hurry to leave the area of exploration? Some scholars are inclined to believe that Bering acted correctly in turning back, while others hold the contrary point of view. Bering himself was the first to try to explain his premature exit from the north. He wrote of this three times in various documents, each time differently. The first explanation is to be found in his decision, written on 15 August 1728, on the eve of the day he gave the order to turn onto the return course. As we will recall, it was not altogether convincing, although at that moment it seemed sufficiently sound to the captain himself. Perhaps afterward his reasoning seemed to him less well-founded than it had at the time. In any event, in St. Petersburg, feeling quite restrained about the results of the expedition, Bering decided not to refer to the difficulties and dangers of the voyage in his report to the Admiralty College. These would not impress the "sea wolves" sitting in the College. In his report, drawn up in the capital on 10 March 1730, he spoke differently of his decision to turn back. He now gave prime importance to the words of the Chukchi, actual and invented.

There is no doubt that the accounts of the Chukchi materially influenced Bering's thinking on the voyage and his subsequent activity. They engendered in him the conviction that the strait had been discovered and that he should therefore turn back. Along with his description of meeting with them on 8 August, Bering also began his second explanation in this report.

The essence of the Chukchi accounts was known through the "Brief Relation..." in the eighteenth century, and excerpts from the report of the Admiralty were published by A.S. Polonskii in the mid-nineteenth century. Unfortunately, however, these are not identical nor is either one identical to the transcript of the interrogation of the Chukchi. Comparison of these leads to an important conclusion.[68]

Recall that the protocol notes of the conversation with the Chukchi were taken down right at the time of the conversation and signed by the three officers, whereas the other two sources represent Bering's own interpretation and were drawn up more than a year and a half later. It is clear that the original transcript must be considered the true source. We will recall that in the first transcript the following Chukchi reply was taken down: "We do not know the Kolyma River. . . ." It is true that they had heard of some river or other, but "whether that river is the Kolyma or not, we do not know." Several other replies were given during the second meeting with the Chukchi, but at this time, to the direct question as to "whether there is a sea route from here to the Kolyma," they replied, "We have never gone by sea from here to the mouth of the Kolyma." In regard to how far the sea extends in the direction of the Kolyma, and how much "beyond" their tribesmen inhabited the coast, there is not a word in the Chukchi's testimony.

Since he had not taken the suggestion Chirikov had made at one time, to sail on to the mouth of the Kolyma, Bering could not subsequently yield to the wisdom of his suggestion. In any event, when he was reporting on his activities before competent judges in St. Petersburg, Bering in his report arbitrarily ascribed the following words to the Chukchi: "Their land forms two bays and *turns toward the mouth of the Kolyma River, and the sea skirts the land everywhere* . . ." [italics added] |49, l. 98|. Precisely which two of the many bays that indent the northern coastline he had in mind it is difficult to say, and not important. Something else is far more important: Bering ascribed to the Chukchi things they did not actually say, which do not appear either in the transcript of the interrogation or in the watch journal.

The resulting report was smooth and convincing: if the sea skirted the land all the way to Chukotka and farther to the west, to the Kolyma itself, then this indicated that Asia was not joined to America. However, in amplifying and altering the Chukchi statements, using his own discretion, Bering overlooked one detail: farther on in the text he retained the actual words of the Chukchi about the fact that they "had never gone" to the mouth of the Kolyma by sea. If the Chukchi had never gone to the Kolyma by sea, how could they have known that the sea lies next to the northern coast of eastern Asia all the way to the Kolyma? One simply cannot imagine that the Chukchi, knowing of a convenient inland sled road to the Kolyma, would have behaved like explorers and used reindeer to make their way along the ruggedly broken coastline of the Arctic Ocean or the hummock ice along the shore that extended for a thousand kilometers in order to prove that "the sea skirts the land" everywhere.

The distortion of the words of the Chukchi went unnoticed, primarily because the Chukchi accounts were not accorded any great significance, since they could not serve as evidence of the existence of a strait. Anything the local inhabitants said were only words that needed to be verified and checked.[69] Information such as that received from the Chukchi could have been obtained from Iakutsk servitors without Bering ever leaving the capital.

Having set forth in his account first of all what the Chukchi "had said," Bering later wrote, "On 15 August we reached a northern latitude of 67°19' and we were 30°14' distant from the mouth of the Kamchatka River.[70] We did not sight land to the right of our course from the island; land does not extend farther to the north, but turns to the west. Therefore I reasoned that I had fulfilled the ukaz given to me, and I turned back." It stands to reason that it was safer to explain his return by saying that the expedition had discovered the strait, rather than by referring to the dangers of sailing farther. The members of the Admiralty College at worst could have doubted that the strait had been discovered, but who could disprove Bering's conclusion relating to the strait without having gone where the expedition had been?

In the extract of Bering's report that was submitted, there was another inaccuracy in the assertion that supposedly "the land [Asia] does not extend farther to the north." He could not have known that, since the ship did not go west of Cape Dezhnev, and the visibility with no fog did not exceed fifteen to twenty miles. However, on contemporary maps, from the northeastern extremity of Chukotka the coast ascended almost 3° to the north, receding to the west at the same time. The coastline turned northwest at approximately the same angle as it did from the mouth of the Kamchatka River to the northeast. And the latter direction, both in Peter's instruction and in the documents of the expedition, is generally considered the order to the north.

This is how it was on contemporary maps. On the final map of the expedition the northern coast of Chukotka turns sharply to the north and swings even to the northeast, ascending above the latitude of the northern coast of Wrangell Island; that is, it extends from the northeastern corner of Asia to the north not for 3° but for nearly 6°.

The third document wherein the reasons for the departure from the north are set forth is the "Brief Relation..." prepared for the Tsaritsa. Bering arrived in gold-domed Moscow and probably realized that the court was busy with other matters and that there would not be a close interrogation of him. Furthermore, in contrast to the naval authorities in St. Petersburg, here both Anna and her immediate advisors understood little of scientific and naval matters. Perhaps because of this the third variation of the explanation made its appearance. At first Bering repeated in his account the motive that he had set forth in his report to the Admiralty College: "On 15 August we were in 67°18' northern latitude, and I concluded that judging from all the evidence the instructions had been carried out, for land did not extend farther to the north, there was no land whatever beyond Chukotka or the eastern point, and thus I turned back." But whereas in his report in speaking of land east of Chukotka he precisely stated that fact ("I did not see the land ... to the right of our course"), here he stated categorically that there *was* no land beyond Chukotka.

Farther on in the "Brief Relation ... " he advanced reasons from the conclusions of 15 August 1728: "If we had proceeded still farther, and there had happened to be contrary winds, then we could not have returned to Kamchatka that summer. There would have been no justification for spending the winter in that land, because there is no forest, the local natives are not under the sovereignty of the Russian State, and they have no intercourse with our iasak-paying natives" |53, p.94|. We have already observed that these arguments are not convincing.

V. Berkh was the first of the Russian scholars to accept Bering's explanation *in toto* on faith.[71] Academician K.M. Baer was more emphatic in this point of view, surpassing even Bering, since Baer considered the main reason for leaving the north to have been the danger of becoming ice-bound, something Bering had not even mentioned.[72] The Dane P. Lauridsen also defended Bering's actions. He wrote,

> It is entirely possible that we may feel inclined to blame Bering for his haste. Why did he not cruise about in the

region of 65° to 67° north latitude? A few hours' sailing would
have brought him to the American coast. This objection
may, however, prove to be ill-founded. Bering had no inkling
of the nearby continent ... hence in the nature of things he
could not be expected to search for land of which presumably
he knew nothing. We must also take into consideration his
poor equipment. His cables, ropes, and sails were in such
poor condition after three years' transport through Siberia
that he could not weather a storm. His stock of provisions
was running low and was so scant that it precluded any in-
clination to go beyond his main objective, and this is the reason, as we see, that he did not intend to explore the American
coast and resolve the question as to whether Asia and Amer-
ica are joined |75, p.37|.

It is not possible to accept Lauridsen's conclusion that Bering
did not know where the American coast was and therefore did not
discover it, and that he did not intend to resolve the question as to
whether Asia is joined to America. If the location of the American
coast had been known, then it would not have been necessary for
him to discover it. And in regard to whether there was a "joining"
of continents, resolving that question was precisely the purpose
of the whole expedition.

The second part of Lauridsen's reasoning is also erroneous. Although the rigging and sails were in less than ideal condition, neither Bering nor Spanberg mention their dilapidated condition as
one of the reasons for leaving the area of exploration. Furthermore, Ivan Fedorov and Mikhail Gvozdev later sailed in these
waters in the Sv. Gavriil until the end of September using the
same sails and rigging, but in even worse condition. With regard
to the supply of provisions, recall that the vessel had taken on a
cargo of provisions enough to last an entire year, and by 15 August it had been at sea scarcely more than a month. The American
scholar Raymond Fisher evidently overlooked this. For some reason he refers to Sven Waxell, who did not take part in this expedition, as his source for stating that the seafarers "suffered from a
shortage of provisions and other necessary items" |113, p.103, n.
49|. Fisher also mentions Bering's possible worries over the water
supply and his "concern lest he be trapped by adverse winds" |113,
p.97|. But twenty barrels of water were sufficient for the seafarers

for twenty-five days, and on 7 and 8 August they had renewed their supply of fresh water and by 16 August they had used only seven of the twenty barrels. In regard to the wind, as is evident from the notes in the watch journal from 14 to 16 August, it was calm, moderate, average; the 14th was even still, and the ship drifted for several hours on the current to the southwest.

This premature departure from the north has generally been given insufficient attention in scholarly literature. Those authors who have touched on it have accused Bering of indecisiveness and a lack of the explorer's spirit and have expressed regret that he did not proceed on to the Kolyma and discover America, but at the same time they have justified his actions. The widely held version is that Bering acted in accordance with the government's interest and instructions. Andreev |17, p.10| was the first to express this point of view. Explaining Bering's instructions to return he wrote, "the fear of violating the 'state interest,' of losing the ship and its men, led him to make the decision, the implication of which was completely clear to him." Lebedev, Grekov, and Divin share this view.

Obviously, if Bering acted according to his instructions, then Chirikov's proposal was counter to the instructions. But no one is prepared to state this. Then what actually was the case?

The second point in the Tsar's instructions directed Bering to sail "near the land that extends to the north." Up to the time of sailing to the southeastern corner of Chukotka this order had been strictly adhered to. But farther on, in defiance of the instructions, Bering twice, at Capes Chaplin and Dezhnev, gave orders to sail northeast, thus moving away from the coast. It was precisely so as not to disobey Peter's ukaz that Chirikov suggested that they proceed along the coast toward the mouth of the Kolyma, "to the place indicated in the aforesaid ukaz of His Imperial Highness." Chirikov was not simply expressing an opinion, but rather a scientifically founded proposal, in order that the instructions be faithfully carried out. The third time the instructions were disobeyed was when the ship turned back along the same track instead of proceeding along the northern coast of Chukotka to the northwest.

Thus, Chirikov's point of view in opposition to Bering's came about during the voyage itself. Müller later subscribed to it.

It stands to reason that neither Müller nor, particularly, Chirikov—a contemporary of Bering's and his subordinate—could completely explain the actions of the leader. Dall evaluated these actions more fully at the end of the nineteenth century when he maintained that vast amounts of energy, time, and money had been expended in order to reach Chukotka, but Bering, after having been in the area barely twenty-four hours, "ceased exploring and turned back," although natural conditions would have permitted them to sail on for another six weeks; "... where is there anything adventurous, daring or heroic in such conduct?" queried Dall |70, p.163|.[73]

Another American scholar, Frank A. Golder, amplified this characteristic. "Bering did not appreciate sufficiently the fact that ... his arguments needed scientific demonstration.... Why did he fail to search for land opposite Chukotski Cape? Why this great hurry to get away? Navigation in these waters was open for at least six weeks more" |31, p.148|. It is difficult not to agree with these conclusions.

The Soviet historian M.I. Belov |65, p.256| justly calls Bering's premature departure from the northern latitudes an ill-advised action and suggests that some role in this was played by the relationship between Bering and foreign diplomats in St. Petersburg. Such a suggestion seems quite improbable to us. N.K. Chukovskii expresses a different point of view. He maintains that Bering supposedly received news in the spring of 1728 (prior to setting out on his voyage to the north) of the death of Catherine I and of the accession to the throne of Peter II. Knowing that the new Tsar might well be opposed to the Kamchatka Expedition, and uneasy about his own future, Bering hastened home |48, p.33|. This version is readily refuted by the facts. The seafarers, when they set off for the north, did not know of the death of the Tsaritsa and the change on the throne; they received news of this only a month after they returned from their voyage, on 2 October 1728.

In the northern latitudes Bering made a series of miscalculations that surprised his contemporaries and even now, more than two and a half centuries later, give rise to arguments among geographers and historians.

The fact is that Bering disobeyed his instructions in not sailing along the shores of Chukotka to the northwest, and that he did not follow Chirikov's suggestion. For the first time in history Russian seafarers had reached an area north of 67° northern latitude in this region. Ahead of them lay boundless ocean spaces. Thirty-two rhumbs fanned out on the compass card. Imagination indicated many possible directions, and each was mysterious and unknown, except for one—the one by which they had come. It was not too late to proceed west. This route would have taken them to the northern coast of Chukotka. They could have sailed farther north. By this route they would certainly and no doubt quite soon have come upon ice and thus would have been convinced of the existence of a strait. Any eastern compass point would have led them to the shores of Alaska. But of all possible directions, Bering chose the very least advantageous, the same one by which he had sailed north. He thus broke the tradition of the naval explorer never to make both legs of a voyage by the same route. It was not by chance that in the draft of the ukaz from the Senate of 28 December 1732 concerning organizing a new expedition, the directions were to return by a different route. On its return voyage the ship had only to turn from its previous course to the left, and it would have found itself at Cape Prince of Wales, the westernmost point of America. They would not have encountered ice, and very soon the diminishing depth would have indicated their proximity to shore.

When they were on their return voyage on 16 August, sailing with a favorable northwest wind at a speed of about seven knots, they sighted an island (Ratmanov) at a distance of sixteen miles from the ship. It would have taken at most two and a half or three hours to circle the island, or at least to approach it. Then inevitably they would have discovered a second island, and circling that, the ship would have found itself so close to the coast of America it would have been impossible not to sight it. The orders Bering gave are all the more difficult to understand since he had learned from Petr Tatarinov of the proximity of Bolshaia Zemlia (America). Chirikov had reminded him of that when they were in the strait, and Bering could see this on L'vov's map, of which a sketch copy had been made in Iakutsk for the expedition, and on other maps.

The most serious miscalculation was of course that Bering did not heed Chirikov's proposal to sail west.

The reasoning of the threat of becoming ice-bound and of bad weather is disproved by the simple calculation of days with good and bad weather (according to the watch journal). Of sixteen days, that is, eight before turning back and eight after, twelve had light winds, two had no wind, three had fresh wind, and only one had heavy wind. Although overcast weather prevailed, there was fog only four times in all, and many clear days were noted. It rained only once.

Did the season and weather conditions permit sailing west? In order to present the natural conditions of the region more clearly, let us examine certain contemporary information. The Chukotsk Sea is one of the warmest of the Arctic seas, due to an influx of warmer water from the Bering Sea. The temperature of the water in the region of the strait at the end of August reaches 14° centigrade. Farther to the west, along the northern coast of Chukotka, it falls to 7° and even to 4°. In the southern part of the sea in summer, south and southeast winds prevail. Toward the end of the season there is a prevailing northwest wind. In summer the edge of the ice retreats to the line of the northern tip of Wrangell Island, Cape Barrow. Generally there is little ice from the second half of August to the first half of October. Only at the end of September does new ice appear, and from late October to early November the temperature of the water is near the freezing point.

In the East Siberian Sea, where Chirikov proposed sailing, ice generally forms between the end of September and early October, while in the eastern part the ice cover forms ten to fifteen days later |77, p.157|.

True, in the first half of the eighteenth century in the Arctic, particularly in the northeast, there was some drop in temperature. However, in the eighteenth and nineteenth centuries Russian seafarers sailed both in the Arctic and in the Antarctic in the fall, and in this same region the English explorer James Cook sailed,[74] as well as Russians who were contemporaries, and more importantly, predecessors, of Bering. Dezhnev had navigated the strait in the month of September, as Kurbat Ivanov did later, in 1660, when he went to Chukotsk Cape after 8 September and did not head south until 18 September. It is interesting that Fedorov and Gvozdev sailed this same vessel, the Sv. Gavriil, four years later, in 1732. At that time the vessel and its rigging, masts, spars, and sails had all become dilapidated; Fedorov was the only experienced seaman aboard and he was ill; they took fewer provisions than Bering had; yet they managed to reach Alaska on 21 August and return to Kamchatka on 28 September, at the urging of the crew, not the commander. Sind also sailed in the strait in the autumn of 1766 with nine of his crew seriously ill.

In scholarly literature one may find strange contradictions. Everyone acknowledges Chirikov's proposals as sound, but at the same time some authors hold that Bering refused to follow them out of prudence.[75] Is it possible that the lieutenant's proposals, which were essentially sound, concealed certain dangers, and were therefore unworkable? No one suggests this. The problem falls into a labyrinth, which we shall attempt to unravel.

Compromise is certainly possible in disputes. Chirikov advised sailing to the mouth of the Kolyma or to the first sign of ice, but it is possible that if his counsel had been followed they would not have gone near ice. Further, the lieutenant allocated twelve days for sailing northwest and searching for harbor. If Bering had reserved more time in order to assure a successful return, but still had accepted the lieutenant's wise suggestion, there would then have been good reason for considering the captain prudent.

Bering was right in not accepting Chirikov's idea of spending the winter in the northern latitudes.[76] He may have felt he did not have enough provisions, and he may have feared for the safety of the ship and the health and lives of his men. Objections to a winter stay in the north were especially well taken because the suitable base at Nizhnekamchatsk was fifteen days away. In fact it would have been reasonable to return to that base at the beginning of June, almost a month and a half earlier than in 1728, and set out to sea again so as to complete the exploration under ideal navigational conditions. In that case it would have been possible to spend not just twelve days but an entire month studying the polar regions, and still have time to return to Nizhnekamchatsk in early August and reach Okhotsk before bad weather in the fall.

Only if a second voyage had been planned for the following year could one regard the departure from the north as a manifestation of wisdom and prudence. But not one of the documents mentions that Bering advised returning to the area of exploration the following year. This means that he should have taken advantage of his presence there to study the region even if only for part of the twelve days Chirikov proposed.

As we know, however, this did not take place, and therefore the word "prudence" as applied to Bering's actions has an empty ring.

Relying on the words of the Chukchi as he understood them, Bering did not take a risk and considered it unnecessary to obtain any "supplementary" evidence of the existence of a strait between the continents. Perhaps it was difficult for him to forget the official slight of long ago, which had caused him to retire from service in 1724. Recalling his desire to spend his old age living quietly in one place in his own home, one might feel this hardly predisposed Bering to take risks.

Furthermore, Bering had a very narrow comprehension of the problem of the strait, since he conceived it as a strait between Chukotka and land opposite, rather than between whole continents. It was not by chance that after having asked the officers to submit written replies on 13 August he himself wrote, "The cape of the land of Chukotka, concerning which an opinion has been held that it is joined to America, is separated from it by the sea." It is not necessary to reiterate that Peter's instructions speak of Asia being joined to America, not just the Chukotsk peninsula. Bering properly considered he had solved this narrowly interpreted problem; at least up to 67°18' there was no land connection revealed between the continents. But Bering could not definitely say whether they were not joined somewhat farther north and whether the sea by which they had sailed to 67°18' northern latitude was not a large bay, bounded on the north by an isthmus and by continents on the east and west.

In all, he had seen only a few miles of the northern coast of Chukotka, which appeared to lie in a northwesterly direction, although he did not encounter any ice nor did he, from the northernmost point of his route, sail west, north, or east. He did not circle Diomede Island nor pay heed to Tatarinov's information about Bolshaia Zemlia. Bering thus turned the ship back and almost without deviating from his previous course, sailed back to Kamchatka. On his return voyage he again encountered Chukchi, talked with them, and obtained almost the same information as before. Bering added this to the former information in order to convey it to the capital as proof of the existence of a northeastern sea passage.

This is completely incomprehensible. The expedition had spent more than three and a half years on this journey, leaving St. Petersburg with the necessary materials and instruments to travel halfway around the world, build fifteen river boats and two sea-going vessels, prepare provisions in Siberia and transfer them to Kamchatka, and on the new vessel with enough provisions for a year, to set out to sail where Peter had sent them. The expedition had spent an enormous amount of money and had paid with the lives of fifteen men. And for what? Having reached the assigned region, Bering, despite instructions, moved away from the coast and after proceeding only sixty-six miles farther, decided that all his goals had been fulfilled, broke off the voyage to the north, and left the polar waters.

Not only Chirikov but many contemporaries and especially such high government bodies as the Senate and the Admiralty College considered Bering obliged to have done more. It was not without reason that two years after the expedition an ukaz from the Senate clearly stated that Peter the Great "had sent [Bering] to determine from both shores whether the American coast is joined to the Asian coast." In other words, by the very intent of its instructions, the expedition was to have explored both shores. This is also confirmed by the fact that even in 1719 Peter had ordered Luzhin and Evreinov to clarify "whether America is joined to Asia, and to do everything necessary very carefully, going not only south and north, but east and west as well" |17, p.5|.

Thirty-five years after the first voyage of the *Sv. Gavriil* Lomonosov wrote, "... it is too bad that on his return voyage Bering took the exact same route and did not go farther to the east, by which route he of course might have perceived the northwest coast of America" |23, p.451|.

Strictly speaking, the expedition, having established that Chukotka is surrounded by sea on the east, could not have proved whether a strait exists, even between this peninsula and America. Indeed, the concept of a "strait" does suggest the presence of two shores opposite one another. But Bering's expedition did not reveal the position of the American shore opposite. And since no one had any precise information at that time as to where it was located, it could have been suggested that the shore lay at a great distance from the Chukotsk peninsula and extended considerably farther south than was depicted on certain maps of that period, as Bering himself thought in 1729 when he tried to find America east of Kamchatka at no great distance. But it goes without saying that in that case one could not speak of a strait along the shores of Chukotka.

That North America was near Chukotka was proved later, but not by Bering. No one doubts that the *Sv. Gavriil* was in the strait in 1728. But Bering could only suppose that he was in a strait, and supposition is not proof.

Returning from the north the sailors outfitted the *Sv. Gavriil* and the *Fortuna* for the winter stay. They unrigged the ships, put the rigging and sails into the cabins of the boats, and placed both vessels in the care of the local administrator.

At the end of September Chirikov and part of the crew and then the rest of the members of the expedition separated to their winter quarters. Spanberg, the geodesist Putilov, and one soldier were ill, and the latter soon died. Apparently Putilov also was seriously ill, for the journal mentions that "the geodesist is completely out of his mind."

On 2 October 1728 the sailors from Bolsheretsk arrived in Nizhnekamchatsk, sent by the navigator Enzel with a manifest concerning the death of Catherine I and with Enzel's report. Enzel advised that all the materials had been taken from the Gorbeia zimov'e and had been put in Iakutsk, but that the flour and other provisions remained on the Gorbeia River, because there were not enough men to move them. In the spring of 1728 Enzel again sent the sailor Ivan Belov and several soldiers to the Gorbeia zimov'e. They handed over the provisions to the representatives of the Iakutsk officials and went up the Iudoma River to Okhotsk, picking up the cargo that Spanberg's detachment had left there in 1726. At Iudoma Cross they waited for Enzel who was transporting provisions from Iakutsk on seventy-seven horses and had been sent to Okhotsk with them. Further on in the report he advised that when the old vessel reached Okhotsk from Kamchatka, it absolutely "reeked of incense" (was ready for the undertaker). The navigator ordered the vessel to be repaired once again and on 5 August they put out to sea, but contrary winds forced them to turn back. A week later they set out again, and at the end of the month they reached Bolsheretsk with various provisions and materials and cases from Raguzinsk. In his report Enzel alarmingly warned of the inadequacy of provisions for twenty-two servitors, and of the illness of the apprentice Endogurov. Bering sent enough provisions for two months to Bolsheretsk and ordered them to send the ailing Endogurov to Nizhnekamchatsk.

In October of 1728 the seafarers Kondrattii Moshkov and Ivan

Butin returned to Bering with a request to be issued the salary they had not yet received; this would be their first salary issue since 1726, and only the second since 1723. They assumed that such a long wait for their pay was due to the fact that they had never requested it, since they had been sailing continuously across the Sea of Okhotsk. Bering ordered that the sailors be paid for 1727, although the money was not actually issued until 1728.

Once they were settled into their winter quarters, when the weather was good the men busied themselves with their apprenticeships, repairing the rigging, and other tasks.

Winter was near. Frost came in October, and by the end of the month the river had frozen over in some places. In February Enzel arrived in Nizhnekamchatsk from Bolsheretsk with the sailors and soldiers.

On 3 February at 5:00 A.M. the seafarers observed an eclipse of the moon for the third time during the expedition.[77]

ELEVEN

The Voyage of 1729 and the Return to the Capital

W ITH THE APPROACH of spring the members of the
expedition undertook to repair the *Sv. Gavriil* and
make it ready for sailing.

At the beginning of May the ice in the river broke up and they
brought the materials, rigging, and provisions to the ship. On 31
May the crew arrived. They were ready to put out to sea. Forty
men set out on the vessel including Bering, Chirikov, Enzel, the
physician Butskovskii, Chaplin, fourteen sailors, seven soldiers,
seven admiralty servitors, and two interpreters. In April the ailing
Spanberg had been sent overland to Bolsheretsk. The rest of the
men sailed on the *Fortuna*, including Kozlov, Endogurov (who
was ill), the geodesist Putilov, seven soldiers, and the navigators
Moshkov and Butin. Kozlov was senior officer; his mission to
take the vessel around Kamchatka was made easier by the fact
that the seafarers had previously made this voyage in 1728.

Before setting out on this venture Bering on his own authority promoted the sailor Ivan Belyi to mate.

On 5 June first the *Fortuna* and then the *Sv. Gavriil*, taking advantage of the tide and the current, put out to sea. The *Fortuna* made its way to Bolsheretsk. But where did the *Sv. Gavriil* go?

At Nizhnekamchatsk Bering had heard from local inhabitants that "on clear days they could see land across the sea" east of Kamchatka.[78] The captain concluded that this was America, and resolved to verify the mysterious report. Since he had not found the American continent to the north, he hoped to discover it near Kamchatka.

G.F. Müller wrote that by the summer of 1729 Bering had devised an entire system of proofs for "verifying" the proximity of America to Kamchatka. The principles were as follow:

On Karaginsk Island they had met a native who told them that in his native land large pines and firs grow (and there are none on Kamchatka). And in fact, the trunks of these trees actually had been found quite often on the island, carried there by the sea, and in spring they found footprints on ice floes. Furthermore, from the east every year many migratory birds flew to Kamchatka. Among other arguments that seemed convincing to Bering was the observation that the waves on the sea on which he had been sailing were not as high as on other seas. But lower waves also occurred in narrows in the north, in Krest Bay, in the strait between the continents. Likewise, a reference to the negligible depth of the sea was not convincing, for when it sailed north the *Sv. Gavriil* did not go any great distance away from the coast of Kamchatka, and on the return voyage when they were passing Chukotka, and when they did sail far out from shore, either they did not measure the depth or when they took sounding they did not reach bottom.

Bering's other arguments, especially the Chukchi account that bearded people live east of the Chukotsk peninsula and bring them marten furs to sell, is not pertinent, since they were speaking of the north, and their tales could only be verified in the region of Chukotka where the bearded strangers brought the furs.

Why then did Bering decide to sail east anyway, in order to look for America near Kamchatka? Why did he at that point not dismiss all these reports about the proximity of a neighboring con-

tinent, as the previous year he had ignored reports of the proximity of Bolshaia Zemlia to Chukotka?

It may be suggested that considering the outcome of his venture to the north in 1728, Bering came to the conclusion that the
Admiralty would not be completely satisfied. Apparently these
misgivings led him to undertake yet another voyage, thus perhaps
compensating for what he had not accomplished in the north.

This voyage was of secondary importance to Bering. He did not
attach any great significance to it and later tried not to bring it up.
It was no accident that in his final report he did not even manage
to find room to mention it.[79]

Thus early in the morning of 5 June 1729 the *Sv. Gavriil* raised
sail and maneuvered out of the harbor and set course for southeast by south. There was a light wind on 6 and 7 June. At night
the wind grew stronger; the foresail ripped, and they proceeded
under the mainsail. The following day there was still a strong
north wind and the day was overcast. The compass variation was
one and one-quarter easterly. They had already made more than
one hundred miles, and there was still no land in sight. Then at
2:30 P.M. on 8 June when the ship had reached 55°32' northern latitude and 166°25' eastern longitude, Bering lost hope of discover-
ing America and gave orders to turn back.

But off to the south, quite near, there was land, the island on
which Bering died several years later, which to this day bears his
name.

In historical literature the opinion has been that the voyage was
cancelled because of heavy winds that raged for some two days.
The watch journal indicates, however, that by 1:30 P.M. on the return voyage the wind died down and for the next ten days was
light with occasional periods of total calm, and the weather was
clear. It was summer, home base was nearby, it was hardly dangerous to sail in this region, and Bering could easily have turned
around and spent several days searching for land, which was the
whole purpose of this voyage. But he did not return.

It should be noted that on Berkh's map, the only map of
Bering's 1729 voyage, the track of the *Sv. Gavriil* is incorrectly
shown. Berkh ended the track of the ship west of Bering Island
and did not extend it up to the island. In fact the ship went north
of the island and beyond it. This is borne out both by deducing

from the above coordinates, and by Chirikov's precise notations as to the rhumb of the location reached at noon on 8 June—east-southeast 8°06′ east of the mouth of the Kamchatka River. According to Bering's figures they sailed some two hundred versts to the east in all.

The voyage of 1729, nearly a month in length, is not of interest to us. It was notable for its many changes of course and tacks, sometimes because of contrary winds, sometimes because of the proximity of shore, which was now and then unexpectedly glimpsed through the fog. The impression has even been held that Bering for some reason was in no hurry. Perhaps he was searching for the mythical "Yezo Land" or "De Gama Land," which at that time were shown on certain maps.

On 1 July they rounded the southern tip of Kamchatka and two days later were in the mouth of the Bolshaia River. At Bolsheretsk and also at Nizhnekamchatsk they had left part of the powder and shells and some eight hundred puds of flour, groats, dried meat, and salt. The *Fortuna* was already there.

On 14 July both vessels put out to sea and ten days later reached Okhotsk. The naval campaigns of the expedition were concluded. From Okhotsk the navigator Enzel, the sailors, and four soldiers immediately set out for Iakutsk, so that they could prepare a vessel to sail down the Lena and dispatch supplies onto the Aldan to meet up with the expedition.

They unrigged the vessel and transferred it into the possession of the Okhotsk authorities, together with the rest of the provisions (more than 2,600 puds), the sails, rigging, and various materials. They gave certain items such as anchors and cables to Moshkov on the *Fortuna* and Treska on the old vessel. On 29 July they set out from Okhotsk with seventy-eight horses and on 8 August reached Iudoma Cross. They decided to use lodkas and rafts to reach Iakutsk, going by way of the Iudoma, Maia, and Aldan rivers. They spent two days going down the Iudoma. (Berkh |73, p.84| mistakenly stated that Bering "went overland" to Iakutsk.) Bering observed in his report that they traveled in four lodkas, "and the rest of the servitors went on rafts, because there was no room for them in the lodkas."

On 29 August the first party reached Iakutsk. En route there was an unfortunate accident: the raft that was carrying the two seriously ill men, the geodesist Putilov and the apprentice

Endogurov, was caught in the current and dashed against an island where it capsized. It was with great difficulty that they
rescued the invalids for whom there had been no room in the
lodkas. A great deal of ammunition and other goods were lost.

In Iakutsk, Bering received ukazes from the Admiralty College
concerning approval of the promotion of Petr Chaplin to the rank
of midshipman "for his work in the Siberian expedition," and regarding Kozlov's promotion to apprentice and Endogurov's raise
in pay |49, ll. 246,247|.

Endogurov requested that Bering leave him in Iakutsk until he
had recovered, issue his salary, and assign a man to care for him.
Bering consented.

On 10 September, not waiting for the eighteen men from Okhotsk who were crossing the Sea of Okhotsk on the old ship, they
proceeded up the Lena in two doshchaniks. With few exceptions
they sailed night and day. But the cold season was already commencing. On 30 September there was ice in the river, and all
night long they broke through sheets of ice. They finally reached
the settlement of Peledui and organized themselves there to
await winter travel conditions.

In October the last member, the exiled Captain-Lieutenant
Vasilii Kazantsev, very belatedly joined the expedition.

On 23 October after snow had fallen and the Lena was ice-
bound, they set out along the ice of the river on horses. On 14 November they reached Ilimsk. En route Bering received an un-
welcome ukaz from the Admiralty College concerning the fact
that they had recommended discontinuing the issuance of funds
to his wife.[80] Recall that the instructions of General-Admiral
Apraksin required Bering to report on the activities of the expedition on a monthly basis. At first he kept to these dates, but then
he began sending reports less frequently. It was possible to send
mail out from Kamchatka only once a year, when the old vessel
made the voyage to Okhotsk. And Bering sent his reports even
less often. He did not send a single report to the College about the
1728 voyage. The matter of financial reporting was even worse.
Having entrusted midshipman Chaplin, commissar Durasov, and
the sailor Belyi with the financial accounting for the chancellery,
the leader did not inquire very closely into these matters, and
thus did not send reports to the capital. Judging by the length of
time it took to investigate the report after it was received, it must

have been considerably muddled. And since huge sums of money had been spent on the expedition, the College, having received no word from Bering for two years, manifested their extreme concern through issuing this ukaz.

A more conservative group of feudal aristocrats had come into power at the court of Peter II, who had acceded to the throne after the death of Catherine I. The Bering Expedition, as well as some of the other enterprises of Peter the Great, lost popular support, and objections were raised over unreasonable expenses of the expedition. Under these circumstances the Admiralty College had recourse to economic sanctions.

On 5 December the men traveling on the ice of the Angara and the Enisei reached Eniseisk, and after sixteen days spent crossing the steppe and traveling by sled on the Chulym they reached Tomsk. Finally on 11 January 1730 they reached Tobolsk via the Barabinsk steppe and the Irtysh River. Here they were all immediately summoned to the custom house where, as Chaplin reported, "they went through our effects, listed everything, and imposed duty." In his words, there was not a "post station [to change horses] from Peledui to Tobolsk, and we paid our travel expenses in cash, by the verst, for each wagon."

In Tobolsk, Bering belatedly received an ukaz from the Admiralty dated 27 November 1729, ordering him to "make new descriptions of Kamchatka Nos, both the interior and the coast, with the indications of towns and important places and settlements, and when you have completed the map, send it to the College as quickly as possible. Although there is a map of this Nos in the College, it does not indicate towns and important places and settlements" |39, l. 282|. This document indicates the College's lack of information. The expedition had already made a map of the Kamchatka peninsula and included it in the final report. True, it was not as detailed as the College had wished. However, it did show the rivers and large harbors and some of the populated places. The members of the expedition personally took this map to St. Petersburg.

The soldiers who had joined the expedition in the capital of Siberia five years earlier remained there. To the great honor of the Siberian troops it must be stated that they had performed the most difficult labor alongside the sailors, and at times were entrusted with important assignments. They displayed a fine understanding of their duty and a rare fortitude.

On 24 January 1730 the expedition moved along the same route they had taken from St. Petersburg to Tobolsk in 1725, and on 5 February they were in Solikamsk, and in another thirteen days in Vologda.

On 23 February Bering and four members of the expedition went on ahead. After several days the expedition's line of sleds passed Staraia Ladoga, and at 8:00 A.M. Sunday, 1 March, they reached St. Petersburg, where their leader awaited them, having arrived there on 28 February.

Thus this five-year heroic epopeia was concluded—the first large-scale scientific naval expedition in the history of Russia.

Upon his return to the capital Bering submitted to the Admiralty College the two final reports, one on 10 March and the other on 12 March |49, ll. 98–100,104|. In the first he made a general statement on the activities of the expedition, dwelling at some length on the main events. He singled out the seaman Ivan Belyi for commendations. In his second report Bering detailed the work of the expedition and the hardships they had experienced and recommended the participants for rewards. This document recognizes the outstanding role of the participants of the expedition, including the men of the rank and file. It reads as follows:

> I humbly submit that in my estimation those men, senior and junior officers and rank and file, who served with me on the Siberian expedition, are deserving of rewards for their devotion to duty and for overcoming the great hardships attendant upon that expedition, which were on a scale that rarely occur. I append a detailed list of these deserving men who expended great effort on the journey. In 1725 they traveled by rivers, up the Ob, Ket, Enisei, Tunguska, and Ilim; in 1726 they built vessels on the Lena River near Uskut and succeeded in going up the Aldan, Maia, and Iudoma; in 1727 they proceeded, without horses, to carry on their backs all the supplies for the boats, cable, anchors, munitions, and other equipment, and to ferry it from the Gorbeia River to the sea, across a great expanse of deserted land. Had it not been for God's help they would never have survived

the hardships and shortage of provisions. All the livestock
perished. From Iakutsk to the sea they ferried provisions
overland across mire and marsh and built ships at Okhotsk
ostrog. . . . They also ferried provisions and other goods
across the land of Kamchatka from Bolsheretsk at the
mouth of the Bolshaia River to Nizhnekamchatsk ostrog.
They built a boat on Kamchatka, and in 1728 they crossed
the sea to unknown places where the features of the local
landscape provided additional severe hardships. One of the
problems on the voyage was the fact that because of the
shortage of sea rations none of the servitors received his full
issue, nor did the senior officers receive any funds for their
share. In 1729 upon our return by sea around the southern
tip of Kamchatka, and during the entire expedition we experienced considerable hardships and for most of the time
were in need. To explain this in detail would require a long
description. But in brief, I humbly request the State Admiralty College to grant the following rewards:

ADVANCEMENT IN RANK	Captain-Lieutenant Martyn Spanberg
	Lieutenant Aleksei Chirikov
	Navigator Rykert Enizel [sic]
INCREASE IN PAY	Physician Butskovskii
ADVANCEMENT TO RANK OF NAVAL SECOND LIEUTENANT	Midshipman Chaplin
ADVANCEMENT TO FIRST CLASS	Quartermaster Borisov
TO BOATSWAIN	Dmitrii Kazachinin
	Vasilii Feofanov
	Grigorii Shiriaev
TO SEAMAN'S MATE	Afanasii Osipov
[ILLEGIBLE]	Savelii Ganiukov
	Elisei Selivanov

Nikita Efimov
Prokopii Elfimov
Nikifor Lopukhin

TO QUARTERMASTER   Grigorii Barbashevskii
Afanasii Krasov
Aleksei Kozyrev

ADVANCEMENT IN RANK   Apprentice Boatman
Fedor Kozlov

TO CHIEF CARPENTER   Carpenter-Desiatnik
Ivan Vavilov

TO CARPENTER-DESIATNIK   Carpenter
Gavrilo Mitrofanov

TO REGULAR RANK   Aleksei Ivanov
Nikifor Khleskov

TO REGULAR RANK   Caulker Vasilii Gankin
Sailmaker Ignatii Petrov
Blacksmith Evdokim
Ermakov

ADVANCEMENT IN RANK   Apprentice Mastsetter
First Class Ivan Endogurov

Then Bering handed in the list of the participants in the expedition and asked that his subordinates be issued uniforms for all the previous years or money for the same, "since money was deducted from their pay all during the expedition for uniforms."

In regard to the service of the participants and their rewards, Bering personally expected to receive the rank of Rear Admiral. However, it was only the rank of Captain-Commander that was conferred upon him in 1730, a rank between Captain First Class and Rear Admiral. But as it happened, he was supernumerary in that rank, and he was given the old rate of pay. Bering considered this a grievous insult and asked for a raise in pay, salary in accord with his new rank, and asked to be made "senior in rank to my

brother officers." In December 1731 the Admiralty College requested the Senate to grant him twice the usual salary "because
of the hardships Bering has experienced on the Siberian expedition, and for the extended length of his expedition." The request
was granted and he received one thousand rubles instead of five
hundred |15, Part VII, pp.307–8|. However, this did not satisfy
Bering, and early in 1733 he presented another request in which,
reminding them of his financial hardships during the expedition,
his "huge debts," his many years of service, and the fact that he
was again to go on an expedition of some years' duration, he asked
that he be promoted to Rear Admiral.

Despite their reservations as to the value of Bering's service,
the College acceded to his request and passed on his petition for
the Tsaritsa's review. She did not advance the Commander to the
rank of Rear Admiral, evidently because she did not consider his
financial difficulties and length of service as a basis for such an
advancement. She likewise considered his previous service and
duties as leader of a future expedition insufficient reasons for
promotion to the high rank. However, Bering was paid the salary
of a Captain-Commander from the moment of his promotion to
this rank, and as of January 1733 he was issued double salary, as
also were the rest of the members of the Second Kamchatka Ex-
pedition |15, Part VII, pp.450–51|.

Chirikov and Spanberg were advanced in rank. In connection
with his assignment to the Second Kamchatka Expedition,
Chirikov was appointed Captain of the Third Rank ahead of
schedule, in 1732. A year later he was made Captain of regimental
rank. His work was again highly esteemed. In the journal of the
Admiralty College we read, "On this expedition ... he proved
himself thorough and industrious, as befits an able naval officer."
The College recognized his service, noting "... Chirikov, by
virtue of having been sent on this expedition, greatly strength-
ened it with his skill ... he zealously advised Captain-
Commander Bering on all sailing matters during general council
sessions" |15, Part VII, pp.520–21|.

It is not by chance that the Second Kamchatka Expedition is
often called the Bering-Chirikov Expedition.

TWELVE

The Scientific Results and the Significance of the Expedition

THE QUESTION of the scientific results and the significance of the expedition also has been insufficiently examined in historical literature.

For an analysis of the scientific accomplishments of the expedition one must begin by considering whether the primary goal was accomplished. From all accounts it appears that to the very end the seafarers did not carry out their main assignment; they did not bring back incontrovertible proof of the existence of a strait between Asia and America. And although Bering, relying on "corrections" of the Chukchi's accounts to him, denied it, to the members of the College it was clear that he had violated his instructions and had not proved the existence of a strait between the continents, and that he had operated on the basis of reports of aborigines, which should have been verified on location. The article in the *Sankt-Peterburgskaia Vedomost* did not help, which communicated legendary reports of the arrival of a ship in Kamchatka from the Lena River some fifty to sixty years earlier. It has already been mentioned that even as late as 1737 Bering doubted that persons had sailed from the mouth of the Lena to the Kolyma. In regard to Müller's report about Dezhnev's voyage around Chukotka he wrote, "the information is not very reliable." Finally, if Bering had actually heard about such a voyage he would not have failed to mention it in his final report.[81]

It is impossible to agree with Grekov, who assumes that the newspaper article could not have appeared without the knowledge of some government body, and concludes that "evidently the opinion about Bering's discovery of a northeastern passage was at first disseminated in official circles" |42, pp.39,334|, and that only later were people's eyes opened by the notes on the final map. The fact is that this map, presented to the College at the same time as the report, was studied there in detail |49, l. 100|, and the members of the Admiralty College immediately disbelieved Bering. This was referred to somewhat later in one of the College ukazes: "Above the latitude of 67°18', those places that Bering located on the map north and west of the mouth of the Kolyma River were located on the basis of previous maps and oral accounts. We are thus firmly convinced that *his reports about the continents not being joined are untrustworthy and unreliable*" [italics added] |78, l. 1059|.

This idea was even more positively expressed in one of the Senate ukazes: "The Emperor Peter the Great, out of curiosity sent [the expedition] out to investigate from both shores whether the American coast is separate from the Asian coast; but this was not actually carried out" |79, p.1004|. The twenty-second point in the instructions for the Second Kamchatka Expedition was equally clear: "*It may be that there is an open sea passage from the mouth of the Lena to Kamchatka that is presently unknown*" [italics added] |27, l. 178|. This indicates that even in 1732 the existence of the strait between the continents was still not known.[82]

Was it possible after this to affirm that Bering "with documents in hand persistently proved to the scholarly world of Europe the truth of his beliefs" |19, p.54|? Bering had documents that confirmed the absence of an isthmus only between Chukotka and America, and that only as far as 67°. For the rest he relied on the Chukchi accounts that he had revised.

Apart from the documentary information known to us, there are other forcible arguments that the existence of a sea passage between the continents had not been proved—both facts and solid evidence.

Through such information it appears, for example, that in the composition of the next expedition a special section was created with Dmitrii Laptev in charge, which was to go around Chukotka from the mouth of the Kolyma to Kamchatka in order to finally resolve, in addition to other matters, the question of a strait between the continents. A Senate ukaz of 28 December 1732 acknowledged that the presence of a strait or of an isthmus were equally probable, and stated that "if they *do not find* such a union with the American land, then rather than turn back, they are to proceed around the point and go to Kamchatka. . . ."[83]

I.K. Kirilov affirmed this in his project of 1734, giving priority to the matter of resolving the question of a strait among the tasks of the second expedition. He wrote, "The justification for this important expedition lies in various investigations: first, to ascertain positively whether one can proceed via the Northern [Arctic] Ocean to Kamchatka or to the Southern Ocean. . . ."[84] Kirilov, Secretary of the Senate and an important scholar of that time, in the opinion even of Bering's most fervent advocates, was almost the only supporter of Bering.

For the next 250 years there were two points of view: some scholars considered that Bering had not proved the presence of a strait between the continents; others maintained the opposite. In our own time the proponents of the first point of view have been such scholars as L.S. Berg, A.I. Andreev, M.I. Belov, D.M. Lebedev, and others. Andreev has been the most outspoken. He has declared that the question of the strait was not settled, and that "the members of the expedition themselves, Bering in particular, clearly realized . . . that they had not fulfilled the assignment given them" |80, pp.11–12|. Belov also expressed himself very decisively. Calling Bering's premature departure from the area of exporation ill-advised, he wrote that the expedition, having reached the strait and finding itself close to its goal, "through the fault of Bering and Spanberg was not in any position to attest to the existence of a strait" |65, p.256|.

It is true that Belov later declared that Bering "did everything so that the world would learn that Asia and America were not joined, and that it was entirely possible to go by sea from Kamchatka to the mouth of the Lena River" |19, 53|.

The first point of view was also held by the Americans W.H. Dall and F.A. Golder. Dall's opinions are especially interesting. He wrote that Bering returned without having resolved the aims set for him. "As it was, he left the question in a state so unsettled as to be a subject of debate for nearly half a century; even an authority such as Campbell, who was well disposed toward Bering, asserted with great confidence that Bering's conclusions as to the separation of the two continents were erroneous" |70, pp.163–64|. However, both American scholars, following the example of K.M. Baer and A.P. Sokolov, mistakenly maintained that James Cook was the first to establish the existence of the strait and its width, whereas it is widely known that in 1732 Fedorov and Gvozdev discovered the western extremity of America in the strait, and that four years later Müller demonstrated through documents that Dezhnev had put out from the Kolyma and proceeded by sea around Chukotka, thus proving the existence of a northeastern sea passage. These discoveries, from this time on, were reflected on many Russian maps.

In the nineteenth century V.N. Berkh, K.M. Baer, and the Danish scholar P. Lauridsen defended the second point of view, which Bering fathered.

Baer felt that Bering's contemporaries distrusted his basic conclusions because the members of the Admiralty College were not well disposed toward him; that the maps of the cossack colonel Shestakov, which showed Bolshaia Zemlia, created an unfavorable impression of Bering; and that he was ill-served by the intrigues of the Frenchman Joseph Delisle who was a member of the just recently founded Russian Academy of Sciences. In actuality the causes for mistrusting Bering's conclusion lay in the results of the expedition. Lauridsen repeated Baer's version about unfair attitudes toward Bering and stated emphatically that Bering never made conclusive statements unless he had definite knowledge. This would apparently mean that if Bering declared he had proved the continents were separated he should have been believed unconditionally.

Among Soviet geographers and historians one of the first to accept this point of view was M.S. Bodnarskii; A.V. Efimov was also a strong proponent in his time. "The first expedition," he wrote, "not only proved the separation between the Asian and American continents, but ... established the relative proximity of Bolshaia Zemlia, or America" |29, p.163|. No one, including Bering himself, ever seems to have claimed more. In justice to the scholar one must add that he later reappraised his position and stated that since the expedition had not reached the mouth of the Kolyma, the question of the existence of an isthmus between the continents was unresolved |1, p.ix|. But in the most recent edition of his study (1971) Efimov repeats, "The question of whether America was joined to Asia was essentially resolved prior to the beginning of the second expedition..." |5, p.235|.

Some authors avoid this question. Divin, stating the opposing views of various scholars, does not divulge his own position. But he does make an unexpected observation. "The collected materials from the expedition have shown that the width of the strait was not significant." Bering considered certain facts, such as the flight of birds and non-native trees that were carried by the sea to the shores of Kamchatka, as proof of the proximity of America, not to the Chukotsk peninsula, but to Kamchatka. And it was just there that he searched for the American continent in 1729 |25, p.62|. But Kamchatka is a vast distance from America.

To summarize: there is no question but that the truth lies with the proponents of the first point of view. However, in spite of the fact that the First Kamchatka Expedition did not completely fulfill its principal aim, it did accomplish great scientific work and had enormous significance.

The expedition did not prove that the continents are separated, but it did establish that Chukotka is washed by the sea on the east. This was an important discovery for that time, since people generally held the opinion that the land was joined to America. And it was soon afterward shown (in 1732) that the watery expanse lying east of the Chukotsk peninsula was a strait between the two continents.

The cartographic work and the astronomical observations of the expedition were of exceptional importance, and the results of these appeared on the final map and table of geographical coordinates of various points along their route. In addition, the distances between many points of land were determined as well. The map and the table are valuable in and of themselves, because this was the first time such observations had been carried out in Eastern Siberia.[85]

We know that maps, one of the primary goals of geographical explorations, are an indication of the knowledge of one region or another and are important historical sources.

From the documents of the expedition it is clear that the five years of work by its participants produced four maps. One was the copy of a map found in the instructions for the expedition.[86] A second copy, as noted earlier, was made in the spring of 1726 for Savva Vladislavich Raguzinskii. The facts indicate that Bering had unique maps, such as even the head of a diplomatic mission did not possess.

The second map likewise appears to be a copy made from an old map that Bering obtained in Irkutsk. The Iakutsk inhabitant Ivan L'vov copied it.[87] Unfortunately, it is not apparent from the documents precisely which map they refer to. At least two copies of this map were made, one of which had already reached the capital by the end of 1726 or the early part of 1727, tentatively titled, "Captain Bering's map of Russia" |28, pp.36–37|. Here it was examined in the Academy of Sciences, according to the protocol of the conference of the Academy dated 17 January 1727.

A third map traces the route of the expedition from Tobolsk to Okhotsk. On it are indicated a degree grid, the rivers along which the travelers moved, and also the main tributaries and the nearby mountains. Petr Chaplin was thought to be the compiler of this map. In accordance with the tradition at that time there is no indication of this except for the fact that his signature is on the map. But he was the best graphic artist on the expedition, and his signature at least indicates that he executed this particular copy and was responsible for the accuracy of the copy. The signatures of the actual compilers would have been on the originals, which have vanished without a trace. However, Chaplin could not have been the compiler of the original map because in the instructions given to him when he was sent on ahead of the expedition from Tobolsk there is no mention of his making a survey or keeping a journal, as was the case in analogous circumstances. Furthermore, he was not issued the instruments that would have been necessary.

As to whether Chirikov was the person who compiled the map from Tobolsk to Okhotsk, the following detail is evidence. In his journal Chaplin repeatedly refers to one of the tributaries of the Aldan as the "Amga," whereas Chirikov in his journal calls it the "Mga," and this is how the name of the river is spelled on the map |58, ll. 55, 73|. Our conclusion is confirmed indirectly by the fact that during their eight months' stay in Okhotsk, Bering and Chaplin several times sent reports to the College but never sent a map of their route. Chirikov would have had to arrive in Okhotsk soon after such a map had been dispatched to the capital.[88]

Late in 1728, President Bliumentrost, of the Academy of Sciences, acquired a copy of this map, which had been sent to the Academy upon the recall of Delisle |52, pp.131–132|. Andreev mistakenly supposed that Delisle had analyzed the journal of the expedition and that in one of the letters he meant the map of "Bering's voyage," not the route from Tobolsk to Okhotsk.

Lastly, the fourth and final map was delivered to St. Petersburg by the members of the expedition themselves.[89] The original version of the map was later sent to the Senate, and the College kept the copy that had been especially made for it, as well as the copies of the journal and other documents. Bering presented the original journal to the Senate |39, l. 285; 78, l. 1054|.[90]

Thus, all the original documents of the expedition were sent to Moscow, and unfortunately most of them have never been located. However, there are copies in the Admiralty College, and Chirikov's journal is now located in the TSGAVMF.[91]

Turning to the question of the copies of the final map, it is probable that Petr Chaplin made several of the copies. The copies in the TSGAVMF, TSGVIA, and TSGADA have the notation, "This map was compiled on the Siberian expedition under the command of navy Captain Bering from Tobolsk to the point of Chukotka"; the others say, "Drawn by midshipman Petr Chaplin"— not "composed" or "compiled" but "drawn." It is clear that Lieutenant Chirikov did not bother with such technical work.

Chirikov was the assistant to the head of the expedition, but in Lebedev's opinion he was more than an official leader|18, p.95|.[92] It would be more accurate to say that Chirikov's great strength was that he was a scientist, and his role in the scientific work of the expedition is hard to overestimate. In regard to commanding the expedition as a whole, the service of Vitus Bering, in spite of his mistakes and blunders, was, of course, more important; he was responsible for everyone and everything.

For several years Chirikov had been teaching in the highest institution of learning in the navy, the Naval Academy, and had prepared many officers. His activity in the scientific-pedagogical field was highly esteemed.[93]

The expedition would not have been scientific had there been no scientists with it. But where were they to be found? The Academy of Sciences had only just been founded and at the time the expedition was being fitted out it had not actually begun its scientific activity. So they looked to the Naval Academy. The young and able Lieutenant Chirikov was very useful to the Academy, and it was difficult to find a replacement for him, but nonetheless he was sent on the Kamchatka Expedition. It was an altogether fortuitous choice. Chirikov was completely different from some of the foreign scientists in Russian service, to whom everything Russian was often alien. He combined the qualities of a bold seafarer, a passionate explorer, and a fervent patriot.[94]

Soviet historians who value Chirikov's role in the First Kamchatka Expedition highly do not discuss his cartographic work and thus minimize his role in the expedition. In this regard, we note that Chaplin's role is often exaggerated. For example Andreev writes, "Midshipman Petr Chaplin of the expedition not only kept the sailing journal for the ship *Gavriil*, and composed the report of the expedition, but also compiled the map of the entire route of the expedition from St. Petersburg to the Bering Strait" |80, p.40|.[95] Even Grekov, who devotes more attention to the cartographic work of the expedition than other authors, unhesitatingly attributes the compilation of the two most important maps of the expedition (the one of 1727 and the final map of 1729) to Chaplin, and does not even mention Chirikov |42, p.41|. Efimov also attributes the creation of the final map to Chaplin |1, Nos. 63, 64, 66, 67|. The authors of the five-volume history of Siberia also fall into this error |22, p.344|. But Chaplin was taken into the expedition as a naval cadet, and it was only under the tutelage of Chirikov, with whom he had a friendly and sympathetic relationship, that he became an experienced seafarer by the end of the expedition.[96]

Strange as it may seem, even Divin in a special chapter |61| devoted to Chirikov's scientific merit, says nothing about his role in the First Kamchatka Expedition, and in a later work |25, p.66|, he credits Chaplin with making all the maps of the expedition.

Yet Chirikov, as Belov rightly observes, was the most active and learned man on the expedition. He was remarkable for his modesty and his enormous capacity for work, and he proved himself an outstanding organizer and a splendid scientist |65, pp.252–3|. He not only had a firsthand part in the compilation of all the maps, but he actually directed the work. His subsequent activity in the Naval Academy testifies to this; remarkable maps were drawn up under his direction.

In Chirikov's journal one may find confirmation of the fact that he was the one who directed the scientific observations. The lieutenant took down narrative accounts from the individual participants of the expedition and used plural pronouns, "we observed," "we reckoned." Only once, 14 August 1728, did he "let the cat out of the bag": "And for that date I [emphasis added] reckoned our distance for the day at eight and three-quarters miles." Chaplin, transferring this entry into the general journal, uses a plural pronoun "And for that date we reckoned...."

As previously stated, the watch journal, which Chaplin has been credited with keeping, was actually kept by both Chirikov and Chaplin. Chirikov's entries are usually more detailed. Thus, from 30 July to 12 August Chaplin almost never mentions the distance to coastal points, whereas Chirikov always gives this when the shore is visible. It is customary to suppose that Chirikov kept his journal for a rather short period of time. Actually his journal includes entries made from 22 April 1725 to 28 February 1730. His journal is not simply a repetition of the ship's log; there is additional material in it. This is borne out also in the fact that later, when the Admiralty College was interviewing him, Chirikov's journal was sent over to the Senate, then returned to the College for safe keeping.[97]

In L.S. Bagrow's compendium of the copies of the final map, there is a list of fifteen copies. All of these are preserved in archives, libraries, and museums of various countries. Ten of the maps are outside the Soviet Union: five in Sweden, three in France, one in Denmark, and one in England. All the copies are similar in basic outline but different in detail, providing additional information on ethnography, the distribution of forests and mountains, and other details.

Regions where the expedition did not personally travel are copied from earlier maps, as indicated in inscriptions on copies of the final map deposited in the Library of the Academy of Sciences of the USSR and the Archive of Ancient Acts. Information was taken from the maps of the geodesists P. Skobeltsyn (a member of Putilov's expedition), P. Chichagov, V. Shatilov, and others.

The compilation of the original final map was concluded between the latter part of 1728 and the first half of 1729.[98] The copies of this map were probably made in 1730; the copy in the British Museum is dated 1729, but this could mean the year in which the original was compiled.

The final map is fundamentally different from all maps of the eastern countries of the seventeenth and eighteenth centuries. The old maps, particularly those without degree grids, could not give a notion of the outlines of the countries. The view of the continents sometimes accommodates itself to the shape of the sheet of paper. All the old maps show Siberia incorrectly, drastically compressing its extent from east to west. Thus, even on maps that are comparatively correct in this regard, such as those of A. Vinius (1678–83) and F. Stralenberg (1730), Siberia, from the mouth of the Ob River to Cape Dezhnev, extends only to 95° rather than to 117°; on the map of Evreinov and Luzhin the extent of Siberia is reduced by half; on the map of Izbrandt Ides (1704), it is reduced by more than half, extending only to 57° |42, p.42|.

Only through the use of instruments, the observation of lunar eclipses, the systematic determination of geographical coordinates, and the strict calculation of distances could the expedition produce this first correct assessment of the length and breadth of Siberia. Furthermore, the members of the expedition, in contrast to many earlier cartographers, personally traveled the entire country from St. Petersburg, covering in all an extent of more than 160°, or almost half the globe. The depiction of Siberia on the new map was so different that Delisle, for example, expressed his faith in the map as a whole but refrained from giving a definite opinion on the extent of Siberia.

Yet the primary significance of the final map of the expedition is not that it shows the true extent of Siberia for the first time;

this is incidental. Soviet literature emphasizes that on the expedition's map "the northeastern coast of Asia is shown quite accurately" |42, p.41|. The coastline of Kamchatka, and especially the coastline of the Gulf of Anadyr and of Chukotka, previously had been depicted incorrectly. Prior to the First Kamchatka Expedition the only experts who had actually been to the Far East were the geodesists Evreinov and Luzhin; however, of the lands that are of interest here, they visited only Kamchatka, and their map has serious errors.

In evaluating the final map of the expedition, it must first be emphasized that it was not simply relatively correct, but immeasurably more accurate than all previous maps. For a long time the map of the expedition was the only reliable map of this region, and from then a new stage began in the development of the cartography of Siberia.

The main contribution of the expedition to world cartography was precisely this: with the maximum precision possible at the time, it set down the outline of the coast from the southern tip of Kamchatka to the northeastern extent of Asia, revealing two islands near Chukotka. Of all that the expedition managed to accomplish, this was the most important. The naval surveys were part of the work that only such a naval expedition could carry out.

The final map with its important precision provided the contours of the coastline, particularly where the ship sailed close to shore. Those who sailed here later placed great value on this. For example, James Cook wrote, "In justice to the memory of Beering [sic], I must say that he has delineated the coast very well, and fixed the latitude and longitude of the points better than could be expected from the methods he had to go by" |85, p.473|.

The expedition's map contained a number of inaccuracies that were common at that time. For example, the Kamchatka peninsula is too short. The narrowest place on the isthmus is actually only 1.6 times narrower than the widest part, but the expedition's map shows it as four times narrower. The reason for this disparity is that the northwest coast of the peninsula, which the expedition did not sail near, is incorrectly depicted. The east coast of Kamchatka is shown less jagged than it really is. Karaginsk Island has been rotated along the length of its axis; it actually lies southwest to northeast. The Anadyr River is displaced more than 2° to the south and empties into the sea near Cape Navarin, whose outline is also inaccurately shown. The Gulf of Anadyr is depicted as only slightly indenting the shore. St.Lawrence Island is too small and incorrectly oriented. This mistake apparently was made because the west coast, where the expedition only touched, was assumed to be the long side of the island. The southern extremity of Chukotka does not extend as far south as is actually the case. The eastern part of the Chukotsk peninsula is incorrectly depicted. The difference between the southernmost and the northeastern points of the peninsula is shown as exceeding 2°40', whereas on a present-day map this is less than 2°. In this regard, the north-eastern point of Chukotka actually extends 8' north of 66°, whereas on the expedition's map it is mislocated one entire degree to the north.[99]

Some authors maintain that the expedition drew up a map of Chukotka "based not on tales and imagination but on actual facts" |60, p.293|. However, only the southern and eastern coasts were drawn on this basis; the northern coastline of Chukotka and eastern Siberia were copied from earlier maps and incorporated the usual mistakes.

In the USSR there are seven copies of the final map of the expedition, not five as Bagrow thought: One is in the TSGADA |86, No. 7|; another in the TSGVIA (made by Khanykov); a third in the manuscript division of the Library of the Academy of Sciences of the USSR |1, No. 63| (the same map); a fourth in the TSGVIA |1, No. 64| (made by Chaplin); a fifth in the TSGAVMF |67, No. 61; 1, No. 65|; a sixth in the State History Museum |1, No. 66|; and the last also in the TSGVIA |1, No. 67| (copied by Kh. Purpur, with inscription in German). This means that in all there are seventeen known copies, rather than the fifteen Bagrow supposed.

The copies of the final map of the expedition located in the USSR differ slightly one from another. On the copy located in the TSGAVMF the east coast is depicted as mountainous only in part, whereas on the map in the Library of the Academy of Sciences, the mountain chain extends along the entire coast. Almost all the capes on the former are sharp, but on the latter, rounded. On the map in the TSGADA, along the east coast from Nizhnekamchatsk to the northeastern part of Chukotka there is the inscription, "High rocky mountains that are not free of snow in summer, and in many places lie along the sea like a steep wall of considerable height." Along a large part of these shores the depth varies from

ten to thirty sazhens. We also find such information and indications of compass variations at several points on the copy of the
final map in the Library of the Academy of Sciences. The Anadyr
River on the second map is shown almost as a closed loop,
whereas on the first it is more of a straight line. On certain copies
in the USSR, as well as on copies held in other countries, figures
have been drawn of Kamchadal, Koriak, Kuril, and Chukchi natives. Some of the drawings were done by experienced artists, but
give an unrealistic picture of the characteristics and dress of the
inhabitants of Siberia. The artists for most of these drawings were
not members of the expedition. Further, the placement of the
drawing on the map is done in a rather haphazard fashion, so that
they do not actually correspond to the regions inhabited by these
or other peoples.

For these reasons it is not possible to agree with Berg, Grekov,
or other scholars who attribute great ethnographic significance to
the final map of the expedition. To look, as Grekov does, for proof
of such significance in the inscription on the back of the map in
the TSGADA (which reads, "A map showing the nomadic territo-
ries of the Ostiaks, Tungus, Iakuts, and other natives") in our
view is a mistake, since the wording of the inscription is indica-
tive of the fact that it was written later, by a person who did not
understand the true significance of the map and who titled it on
the basis of the first thing that struck his eye.

One of the 1732 Senate documents offers convincing corrobora-
tion of this. "You are to make observations . . . and on the basis
of these, make an accurate description of the local natives and
their customs . . . which no one has yet done, neither Bering on
his first expedition, nor anyone since then. . ." |27, l. 98|.

The remarkable final map of the First Kamchatka Expedition
immediately gained recognition in both Russian and world
cartography. For the next one hundred years it was almost the
only text for scholars and seafarers of all countries, and it became
as widely known as a reference throughout the world as did the
collected maps of D. Harris, which were published in London in
1764. The map not only had an impact on European cartography,
but was the basis for depicting Northeastern Asia on all more or
less reliable Western European maps.

Joseph Delisle was the first person in Russia to use the final
map. He utilized it as a basis for showing Northeastern Asia on

his maps of 1731 and 1733.[100] The first reprint of Kirilov's map is also related to the 1733 map; it fully utilizes the information of the expedition's final map. A year later this map appeared in Kirilov's atlas under the title "A General Map of Russia." In 1745 it was included in the "Atlas of the Russias" published by the Academy of Sciences. The following year Chirikov used the information from the expedition in drawing up his maps for the Naval Academy |1, Nos. 93, 109–111, 117|. Between 1754 and 1758 the Academy of Sciences published Müller's map which was also based on the information from the final map of the First Kamchatka Expedition.

Abroad, the final map was first published in Paris in 1735 by the French Jesuit Jean Baptiste Du Halde, then later by d'Anville. It was published in London in 1736 in an English translation of Du Halde's work. D'Anville published it again in 1737. The map was compiled in 1732 by means of a copy that Delisle had secretly sent from St. Petersburg to Paris |87, pp.247–9|. Belov documents the fact that Bering gave to the Dutch envoy in St. Petersburg the final map of the First Kamchatka Expedition, which the government published secretly.[101]

In 1743 the information from the final map was reflected on the map of Hazius |42, p.37|. In 1750 and 1752 Delisle again availed himself of the data |29, p.203|, as did d'Anville in 1753 |89, p.23|. The 1754–58 map compiled by Müller was supposed to refute Delisle's falsification of 1752. In the opinion of F.G. Gnuchev, Ivan Truscott made the map. Andreev maintains that Müller himself compiled it. Müller wrote that it was made "on the basis of my data and under my supervision" |90, p.151|. Northeastern Asia on this map was drawn with regard for all the information collected by the First Kamchatka Expedition, but certain parts, such as the base of the Kamchatka peninsula, are more accurate than on the 1746 maps of the Naval Academy. Dezhnev's route of 1648 is shown, albeit rather tentatively, as well as the track of the *Sv. Gavriil* in 1728; these are not shown on the general maps of the Naval Academy. Northern Siberia is depicted relatively accurately. In brief, Müller's map of 1758, intended as an unrestricted publication, contained much data that before then had been kept secret.

The 1758 map has never been properly appreciated. Müller did not have original material of his own, but his map nevertheless holds an important place in world scholarship, because for the first time it summed up the geographical discoveries and explorations of Russian seafarers and made this information available to the entire world. Henry Wagner, for example, regards it as the first map to show the discoveries of the Second Kamchatka Expedition and the track of its vessels across the Pacific Ocean |91, p.337|.

Thus, the information gathered by the First Kamchatka Expedition began to come into the "golden [archival] fond" of Russian and world cartography in the 1730s. We cannot agree with Bagrow who feels that Bering's work was not much used abroad. It is true that occasionally maps appeared that failed to take into account the new achievements of science. And unfortunately Russian popular publications sometimes were misleading. In one such anachronism Northeastern Asia appears on a map from the *Atlas Compiled for the Utilization and Use of Young Persons and of All Readers of Records and Historical Publications*, published in 1737 in St. Petersburg. On one of the maps in this atlas both Chukotka and Kamchatka are incorrectly depicted |29, p.120|. Cape Lopatka is dropped to almost 40° northern latitude and the northeastern point of Chukotka does not even reach to 56°. We find an even more erroneous depiction of Northeastern Asia in the same atlas on the map of the eastern hemisphere |29, p.122|. Here Cape Lopatka extends to almost 30° and Chukotka is only hinted at. Therefore, we perceive Efimov's remarks as rather dry irony, that this map gives "some notion of the Chukotsk peninsula."

The maps of Skobeltsyn, Svistunov, Baskakov, and Shatilov of 1742 are far from accurate in their depictions of Kamchatka, the Anadyr region and Chukotka, as are Lindenau's map of the same year, Perevalov's sketch map of 1744, Shekhonskii's map of 1749, that of Colonel Fedor Kh. Plenisner of the second half of the eighteenth century, and Daurkin's maps of 1765 and 1771 |1, Nos. 77, 122–6, 128, 130|. On these maps and field sketches the data of the First Kamchatka Expedition are not used, and these areas are depicted in the old popular tradition of cartography.

Seemingly the final repercussions of the cartographic errors in Russia are encountered on a map published in St. Petersburg in 1773. On this, the narrowest part of the Bering Strait extends over 20 degrees |31, p.148|. From this fact Golder, consigning to oblivion the expedition of Fedorov-Gvozdev, came to the conclusion that right up until Cook's voyage the world did not know how close the continents are to one another.

On the maps of Doppelmeier of 1733 |1, No. 75| and Seuter of 1739 |89, p.20| there is not even a suggestion of familiarity with the final map of the expedition.

In the present time Sergei E. Fel's underestimation of the work of the First Kamchatka Expedition is astonishing and incomprehensible |92, p.160|. He not only refuses to acknowledge the maps of the expedition, but leaves out of his reckoning all the astronomical determinations of points in Siberia, and there are twenty-eight of these in the expedition documents. In referring to Kirilov's maps he does not mention the fact that the maps of the First Kamchatka Expedition are the only places where Kirilov could have found both the true extent of Siberia and particularly the depiction of the coastline from Cape Lopatka to the northeastern extremity of Chukotka.

In addition to the maps, as we know, the expedition compiled a table of coordinates.

The geographic and ethnographic observations and notes made by members of the expedition are of great interest. We find in Chirikov's journal clear and precise descriptions of rivers, shorelines, fish, and forest resources. A keen scholar, he ascertained much information on the weathering of rocks, volcanic activity, lunar observations, and various meteorological occurrences. On the basis of accounts by local persons he described epidemics, earthquakes, and the like. His journal contains extremely rich material—observations made during the voyages concerning compass variations, depths, currents, sea fauna, shore relief, and weather conditions.

In the journals and particularly in the numerous documents from the expedition's correspondence, there are many notes on the administrative organization of the vast Siberian lands and the economy, the still very poor development of productivity, the terrible lack of roads, the depressed condition of the local inhabitants, the tyranny and abuses in many places, and much more. There are also ethnographic observations, of course, but these are often overvalued.

As the Russian government became acquainted with the eastern lands, plans were proposed for furthering their development.

In order to render an accounting before the Senate, Bering set out for Moscow at the end of March. Traveling with him were midshipman Chaplin, commissar Durasov, and other members of the expedition. In March of 1730 Chirikov was given leave "to attend to affairs at home until 1 February 1731" |93, l. 95|.

In Moscow, Bering was to have handed over the financial and other documents. But evidently he was not immediately received in the Senate. At that time Moscow was busy with other important affairs of state: the new Tsaritsa had only just ascended the Russian throne as autocrat. It was not until August that Bering was summoned to the Senate and could present all the documents, including the journals of Chaplin and Chirikov |27, l. 4|. At the request of the Senate he shortly afterward wrote for the Tsaritsa the previously mentioned "Brief relation..." together with his report on the work of the expedition. Further patience was in order since it was a very slow process for matters to be considered in Moscow. At the end of the year Bering received orders to present "the news that Siberia and the eastern region are recognized to be of value to the state,"[102] and he quickly began to compose his report.

The fifty proposals that he drew up embraced a rather wide range of matters.[103] They were all related to questions of land, the organization of services for the region; the assimilation of Kamchatka; development of industry, agriculture, seafaring, and trade; increase of state revenues; and improvement in the way of life of the indigenous population. One may suppose that Bering was prompted to give a practical aspect to his proposals by the Over Secretary of the Senate, Kirilov, who was involved in all matters and was himself at that same time working on a project for putting the administration of the eastern regions into good order and developing the lands.

Bering raised the question of spreading Christianity among the Iakuts and of teaching them to read and write. He recommended developing several kinds of enterprises such as smelting iron from ore deposits located along the Angara, and near Iakutsk and in other places, so the metal would not have to be transported from Tobolsk. He suggested manufacturing tar in Kamchatka and setting up shipbuilding facilities there. He advised educating sons of cossacks in seamanship so as not to have to send seamen there from the capital. He considered it necessary to settle more artisans in Kamchatka. Bering also urged the development of agriculture in the east. He suggested settling a number of Iakut families in Okhotsk and Kamchatka where they would breed fine cattle and horses—since there was plenty of good forage in those places—and would grow cereal crops and garden produce.

Bering wrote about the ruthless exploitation of the local populace by the iasak collectors and urged sending an administrator to Kamchatka for several years who would look after the natives, someone who would be just and not oppress them. He recommended that salaries be paid to all servitors, which he felt would double government profits.

To augment state revenues Bering considered it necessary to establish a state monopoly over the sale of spirits, which was making merchants fabulously rich and ravaging the local populace; he would put the entire liquor trade under state control. In order to develop trade in Kamchatka he recommended establishing a firm rate of pay for the transport of merchants' goods across the Sea of Okhotsk.

He proposed allowing the local population to pay their iasak in whale whiskers. He felt an ostrog should be built in Oliutorsk Bay to protect the Koriaks and Iukagirs from the Chukchi.

In 1729 when the *Fortuna* sailed around Kamchatka to Okhotsk, the men on the ship saw several Japanese on shore. At that time Bering ordered the local administrator to find the Japanese, outfit a special ship, and send them back home so that this opportunity could be used to initiate trade relationships with Japan.

He advised future voyages to use reindeer meat, fish oil, and spirits distilled from grasses instead of the usual provisions. In one of his proposals Bering strongly recommended that the Kamchadals be "firmly ordered" to desist from the "inhuman" customs and to teach their children to read and write, at least those children of the leaders.

The Senate was not satisfied with the captain's proposals because they did not mention future exploration. They asked Bering to make additional recommendations concerning the study of the eastern lands and the Pacific Ocean.

Bering drew up five more proposals |27, ll. 83–84|. Based on the facts that supposedly "the ocean waves are lower as one goes farther to the east" and that fir driftwood had washed up on Karaginsk Island but that fir does not grown in Kamchatka, Bering declared that America was not more than 150 to 200 miles from Kamchatka. Using his supposition as actual fact, Bering proposed "establishing trade with the indigenous population," for which purpose it would only be necessary to build a ship. Kamchatka was the most logical place to build a ship, for there were large forests there with timber of fine quality, provisions were readily available, aid would be more easily obtained from the local people than in Okhotsk, and the ship could be taken out across the mouth of the river. Bering advised investigating the possibility of "water transport to the mouth of the Amur and beyond, to the Japanese islands," in order to negotiate trade with Japan. In his last point he recommended following the northern coastline of Siberia from the Ob to the Lena either by boat or overland.

From the point of view of the history of geographical knowledge, these additional proposals are, of course, of great interest; however, their importance is sometimes exaggerated. Efimov, for example, considered that the expedition had actually established the proximity of American to Kamchatka, by reason of the driftwood that had washed up at Karaginsk Island |5, pp.215–16|. In stating his theory about the proximity of America, Bering had suggested that there might be "other land located between," and had stated emphatically, "and if this is true, then trade could be established. . . . " On the basis of this, Efimov maintained that the expedition had in fact established the proximity of America.

Some historians consider that Bering's proposals included the entire plan for the Second Kamchatka and Great Northern expeditions, and that Bering had personally set their goals. Andreev speaks of "the grandiose goals that *Bering set*" |17, p.13|. B.G. Ostrovskii |82, pp.106, 114, 117| considered that Bering was the initiator of the Great Northern Expedition. Actually the plan for exploring the Northern Sea Route, and also the extension of this route across the Pacific Ocean, had been developed by Saltykov in the early part of the eighteenth century. Furthermore, the actual fulfillment of the Second Kamchatka Expedition's program of investigations was considerably broader than Bering's conception.

It is sometimes suggested that in Moscow Bering worked very energetically to show the necessity for taking various measures to develop the Eastern lands.[104] Under the conditions of autocratic Russia at that time, however, this would have been quite impossible for Bering. He was a very small figure. In reality Bering's mission consisted of making his proposals and waiting. And he had a very long wait.

It was not until 31 December 1730 that the Senate reached its decision. The Kamer-College was to spend a month reviewing Bering's report with him; however, even after an entire year the report was still not finished.[105] All during this time he was on half pay, which in his words caused him to suffer "unjust injury; I was in great need." Bering also stated that he and his colleagues while in Moscow "are living in idleness and are in Her Imperial Highness' Service, but are performing no service" |95, 1. 8|. In his petition, which was presented to the Senate, Bering asked that he be sent to St. Petersburg, since his assistants were drawing up accounts of income and expenditures during the period of the expedition, and Moscow was awaiting the completion of his account. On 26 December 1731 the Senate decided to comply with Bering's request.

Kirilov indicates that the seafarer's project was not immediately taken under consideration. "Although Captain Bering had made his proposals, they had still not been acted upon by 1732" |29, p.290|. Only in March of 1732 did the cabinet instruct the Senate to examine the proposals, and on 17 April of that year the Tsaritsa signed an ukaz concerning the Second Kamchatka Expedition. While Bering's proposals lay gathering dust, Kirilov's project was examined at the highest levels, referred to the Senate on 27 February 1731 and quickly confirmed.

The significance of the First Kamchatka Expedition is that by demonstrating the colossal difficulties in transporting cargo from the European part of the country to Okhotsk and to Kamchatka, it thus furthered the advent of the first Russian projects for circumnavigation. The problem of transport was of especially great interest in regard to the forthcoming Second Kamchatka Expedition. Soon after the publication of the ukaz regarding the expedition, the members of the Admiralty College were summoned to the Senate where they "proposed that ships could be dispatched from St. Petersburg to Kamchatka to carry out our plans there, and for this purpose experienced naval officers should be sent" |97, 1. 74|. All the documents from the First Expedition were sent over from the Senate to the College, with instructions to draw up a detailed opinion on transport and to present it to the Senate. It was in regard to carrying out this instruction that the first Russian projects

for circumnavigation came into being. One was made by Admiral
N.F. Golovin |98, ll. 1–8|,[106] President of the Admiralty College. A
second proposal was made by a member of the College, Vice Ad-
miral T. Sanders |99, ll. 132–8|.[107] The two projects were related
and differed only in details. Unfortunately they were not imple-
mented at that time. The first circumnavigation by Russian seafarers was not accomplished until seventy-one years later, by I.F.
Kruzenstern in 1799 |26|.

The difficulties of transporting cargo, brought to light at the
time of the First Kamchatka Expedition, prompted the thought
that they must find a better overland route to the Sea of Okhotsk,
which would bypass Iakutsk and Okhotsk. In accordance with an
ukaz, this was written into the instructions given Bering regard-
ing outfitting the Second Kamchatka Expedition |7, pp.132,138|.[108]

The search for a better route to the Sea of Okhotsk continued
through the eighteenth century. Later they tried also to find a better port than Okhotsk on this body of water. They likewise
searched for new routes on which to build cart roads to the coast
of the Sea of Okhotsk at the end of the eighteenth century. But all
of this was unsuccessful.

In speaking of the significance of the First Kamchatka Expedition, one must not neglect to mention the invaluable experience
that it gave Russian seafarers and scientists. They used this experience in fitting out the Second Kamchatka Expedition and other
later expeditions, including circumnavigations.

The First Kamchatka Expedition was very useful in many ways
in the organization of similar undertakings. The personnel of subsequent expeditions was composed, as it had been in 1725, of
volunteer sailors from various ships in the Baltic Fleet, with pref-
erence being given to the healthiest and heartiest.

Heeding the unfortunate experience of the First Kamchatka Expedition, the participants of the Second and of other later expeditions began to dispense double rations of food and money. In addition, each member of the Second Kamchatka Expedition received
annual salaries, and all the geodesists were given military rank.
Finally, it was decided to issue all the participants of the expedition a year's salary in advance in the capital, and then again in either Tobolsk or Iakutsk, whichever they preferred. It became a
permanent practice to pay double maintenance to those sent to
the Far East.

The Second Kamchatka Expedition employed the same method of procuring provisions and transport by using avant garde parties with officers in charge, and they used the river route between Iakutsk and Okhotsk more than did those in the First Expedition. From Iudoma Cross to Okhotsk they built warm izbas every two miles. In winter, according to Waxell, they posted permanent sentries in these izbas so that incoming transport carts were assured warm lodging at all times. The experience of building ships and carrying out ocean-going voyages was also invaluable. In particular, future sea expeditions set out not one but two vessels. Very often, seafarers sent to eastern Siberia were supplied with excerpts of reports from the First Expedition.

In addition to its scientific importance, the expedition had an important political significance. It ascertained the limits of possible advancement east into Asia, and located the maritime boundaries of northeastern Asia on the map. By these means, on the basis of true first discovery, lands beyond (European) Russia were secured once and for all and placed within her boundaries.

The First Kamchatka Expedition, conceived in the course of the economic and political development of the country, utilized the experience of courageous Russian overland explorers and seafarers and played an important role in the further exploration and development of the Siberian Far East, of the NorthPacific, and later of Northwest America. Thanks to the expedition, interest in this region grew still greater, and a new stage of geographical exploration began. Explorations were better organized and more systematic; they took on state significance and the leadership passed directly into the hands of the central government. The First Kamchatka Expedition was the first large-scale Russian scientific naval expedition.

Epilogue

THE FIRST KAMCHATKA EXPEDITION served for a long time to rivet the attention of scholars on the Siberian Far East. Even while it was under way, the Shestakov-Pavlutskii military expedition was organized and dispatched. Shestakov, assigned as "commander-in-chief of the northeastern regions," was in Okhotsk in 1729 when Bering returned from his voyage. It was to Shestakov that Bering handed over his ships and remaining provisions. One of the crew members of the new expedition under the leadership of Ivan Fedorov and Mikhail Gvozdev also discovered the northwest coast of America in 1732.

After Bering's return to St. Petersburg, planning began for the projects of the Great Northern (Second Kamchatka) Expedition. This expedition lasted more than ten years. Some one thousand men took part in it, and if one counts the persons who were involved in transport as well, the number is close to ten thousand.

An early 20th century view of the stark memorial to Vitus Bering located in Petropavlovsk. Captain Charles Clerke, who succeeded to Cook's command of the Third Voyage, was later interred here and his memory honored, together with other unfortunate sailors of the North Pacific. (Published with permission of VAAP, Moscow.)

Bering was named leader with Chirikov as first assistant and Spanberg as second. Chirikov was the leading spirit of the expedition. Many rank and file members of the First Expedition took part, including Ivan Belyi, Kondrattii Moshkov, and others.

The Great Northern Expedition at first consisted of seven sections, and included such renowned explorers as Dmitrii L. Ovtsyn, Vasilii Pronchishchev, Mariia Pronchishcheva (wife of Vasilii and the first woman polar explorer), Semen I. Cheliuskin, Khariton P. Laptev, and Stepan P. Krasheninnikov. Exploration extended over almost the entire northern coastline of the country from Arkhangel to the Pacific and the shores of North America, as well as to the east of Kamchatka and along the Kuril and Japanese islands. In addition, a group of professors and adjuncts took part in the expedition: historians, botanists, chemists, astronomers, and medical personnel, including Gerhard F. Müller, Johann G. Gmelin, Georg W. Steller, and Louis Delisle de la Croyère. There were also painters and graphic artists.

The Senate and Admiralty College exercised overall leadership for the expedition, and the Academy of Sciences played an active role both in drawing up the instructions and in the actual work of the expedition.

The results of this Second Expedition were tremendous. The expedition discovered North America (southern Alaska), the Aleutian Islands, and other islands near America; found a sea route to Japan; charted the Kuril Islands; and mapped the northern coastline of Russia and many of the rivers that empty into the Arctic Ocean.

What did the future hold for the principal participants of the First Kamchatka Expedition?

The life of Vitus Bering came to a tragic end. On his return voyage from America aboard the *Sv. Petr*, he went off course and instead of reaching Kamchatka, came to one of the Komandorskie Islands. His ship was wrecked and the men had to spend the winter on the island. It was here that Bering died of scurvy on 8 December 1741, along with nineteen members of his crew who also died of the same disease. In memory of Bering this island now bears his name.

Bering served Russia for thirty-eight years and devoted to his geographical explorations and discoveries not only his skill and his strength, but indeed his life.

No less unfortunate was the fate of Aleksei Ilich Chirikov, who also gave his life to science. After the discovery of the northwest coast of America, he managed to reach the shores of Kamchatka and remained in the Far East for another five years. It was not until 1746 that he was ordered to return to St. Petersburg and the following year was promoted to Captain-Commander. But his health was undermined by scurvy and tuberculosis, and he died in December 1748, outliving Bering by only seven years although he was twenty-two years his junior.

Martyn Petrovich Spanberg's life took a different turn. He was demoted to lieutenant for his unauthorized return from Siberia to St. Petersburg (1745). In 1749 he was again prosecuted, this time for wrecking a ship and causing the death of twenty-eight men, but the court acquitted him. In 1751 he was made Captain first rank, and ten years later, in 1761, he died.

The youngest member of the expedition, Petr Avraamovich Chaplin, lived longest of all. In 1751 he was promoted to Captain third rank. Between 1755 and 1760 he became Captain second rank and served in the Baltic Fleet and took part in the Kolberg operation during the seven-year war with Prussia. In 1762 "by reason of old age and illness" he was named "Captain of the Port of Arkhangel," where he died in 1765.

Fortunately, descendants have carefully preserved the memory of these remarkable Russian seafarers. The finest memorials to them are the names given to many geographical points on the maps of the world. A large number of such points bear the name of the leader of the expedition.

In the last quarter of the eighteenth century there appeared on maps the names Bering Sea and Bering Strait in the northern part of the Pacific Ocean. Bering Bay in Alaska was named by Iurii F. Lisianskii in 1805; Cape Bering in Anadyr Bay was named by Fedor P. Lütke in 1828 (there is also a Cape Bering in the Sea of Okhotsk); Bering Island in the Komandorskie group was named by Sven Waxell, and the entire group of the Komandorskie Islands was named in the mid-eighteenth century by Russian promyshlenniks after Bering's naval rank.

Three capes bear the name of Chirikov: on the southern coast of the Chukotsk peninsula, named by Lütke in 1828; on Attu Island in the Near Aleutian group, named in the first half of the nineteenth century by the Russian American Company; and on

A reasonably accurate model of Bering's brig, the Sv. Petr, *constructed from a timber from the 1741 wreck of Bering's ship on the Second Kamchatka Expedition. (Photograph courtesy of the City Museum of Horsens, Denmark, the birthplace of Vitus Bering.)*

the Staritskii peninsula in the Sea of Okhotsk. There is also an island in the Gulf of Alaska named for Chirikov by the British
navigator George Vancouver in the late eighteenth century. Spanberg Island (Shikotan) in the Kuril chain was named by a Soviet
scientific exploring expedition in 1946. Cape Chaplin in the
southeastern part of the Chukotsk peninsula was named by Lütke
in 1828.

In addition to these geographic commemorations there are
many monuments and memorial exhibits in the Soviet Union.
Memorials to Vitus Bering have been erected at his grave site and
in Kamchatka. Memorial exhibitions devoted to the two Kamchatka expeditions are on display in the Central Naval Museum
in Leningrad and in the Museum of the Red Banner Pacific Fleet.
In 1944 the latter museum organized an expedition to Bering Island where the seafarer perished. On the mainland they presented

a display of furs and other items from the *Sv. Petr* on which Bering had sailed during the Second Kamchatka Expedition.

The memory of Vitus Bering is also deeply revered in Denmark, especially in his birthplace, the town of Horsens, where citizens have brought together a memorial exhibit consisting of a relief map with the routes of both expeditions and two cannon from the *Sv. Petr*, given to Denmark by the Soviet Union and presented by the sailors of the cruiser *Ordzhonikidze*, which paid a friendship visit to Denmark in 1956. In Horsens there is also a model of the *Sv. Petr*, which was made from the debris of the 1741 shipwreck, as well as a commemorative medal honoring Bering.

The importance of the famous Dane and the appreciation of the Russian people are evident in the making of two films about the brave deeds of the seamen under the command of Bering and Chirikov: *The Commander's Exploit* and *The Ballad of Bering and His Friends*.

The First Kamchatka Expedition always arouses great interest among seafarers and scholars, who have been studying it almost since the expedition took place. Many have turned to this subject although it is true that they have given their primary attention to the Second Kamchatka Expedition. The majority of researchers have contented themselves with using the documents that were introduced into circulation among scholars in the eighteenth and nineteenth centuries, rather than searching for new archival materials, feeling that the expedition had been sufficiently studied. In actual fact, as Academician Lev S. Berg observed, "we have very meager information about the course of the First Expedition." If one does not count periodical articles and separate chapters in books, only one publication has been devoted exclusively to this expedition, and that was a brochure published about 160 years ago.

Let us dwell briefly on the basic stages of the study of the history of the expedition.

The first news item appeared in print not in 1730 as has long been generally accepted, but in 1725, in an Amsterdam newspaper. We learn of this through the report of the Dutch envoy to St. Petersburg, Wilde, who wrote that on 20 February the newspaper reported that Bering had been sent to Kamchatka to determine whether "the extremity of Great Tartary is contiguous with the American continent" |101, l. 25|. The first mention of this in

Russia was an article in the *Sankt-Peterburgskaia Vedomost* of 16 March 1730. There is some reason to suppose that the author was the historian and future academician G.F. Müller.[109] In the same year news of the expedition was published in Denmark, and in 1740 in Germany. But all these early notices were brief and merely informational in nature. More penetrating study was hindered by the fact that the materials of the expedition were considered secret. It is interesting that in 1741 when the Academy of Sciences tried to publish maps from the information gathered during Bering's expeditions, they were warned that such a step would be inopportune, and Stellar's description of the voyage to the coast of America was removed from the Academy and deposited in the study of the Empress.

Detailed study of the expedition and publication of its material were stimulated by the falsified map of the French scholar Delisle (1752), disclaiming the merits of the Russians |35, ll. 1–36|.[110]

Delisle's *Trudy* was rebuked by scholars in France, England, Spain, and America. The American cartographer Henry R. Wagner found in Delisle's map "amazing absurdities" that reduced it to "a most interesting episode in the imaginary geography of the northwest coast of America" |91, I, p.162|. John Green in London (1753), P. Andres Marco Burriel in Madrid (1757), and G.N. Bolen in Paris also took a stand against Delisle. The Russian government attached political significance to Delisle's writings and decided that it was more important to publish the materials of the Kamchatka expeditions than to keep them secret. The Academy of Sciences was charged with responding to Delisle, a task Müller carried out. Müller's composite map,[111] compiled in 1758, and the description of the Russian discoveries in the Arctic and Pacific oceans appeared not only as a fitting response to Delisle, but as the first research in Russia into the history of northern voyages |68|. Both documents and the private papers of members of the expedition were used in this work.[112] Müller was the first scholar to declare that Bering had not proved the existence of a strait, and that in order to do so he would have had to proceed as far as the 72nd parallel, for only there "could he find a basis for declaring that the two parts of the world were not joined together" |68, T. VIII, pp.394,410|.

In the future, after the voyages of Vasilii I. Chichagov, Nikita Shalaurov, James Cook, and Billings-Sarychev, who did not manage to penetrate the arctic ice, scholars paid less attention to the expedition.

A rebirth of interest in the First Kamchakta Expedition was observed in the second decade of the nineteenth century when Russian circumnavigations were undertaken, including the scientific circumnavigation of Otto E. Kotsebue (1815), Mikhail N. Vasilev, and Gleb S. Shishmarev in the Arctic (1819), and Faddei F. Bellingshausen and Mikhail P. Lazerev in the Antarctic,[113] and also the sled expedition of Ferdinand P. Wrangell (1820–24), which had the aim of "determining the position of the Shelagsk Cape and describing the coast lying to the east of it, thus resolving for all time the hypothesis concerning the joining of Asia and America." The most important of all the activities that took place at this time were the search for and publication of the documents. The Russian naval historian V. N. Berkh in 1823 authored a brochure in which he set forth in a factual manner the content of the watch journal from the First Bering Expedition, which he had discovered in the archives. In the brochure there are admittedly distortions and mistakes, but it drew attention to the expedition |73|. A year later the "Brief Relation ... " |103|, which Bering had presented to the Tsaritsa, was published. Most later descriptions of the expedition were based on this publication.

One result of the interest in Bering's expedition was the circumnavigation by the sloop *Seniavin* under the command of F.P. Lütke, who exactly one hundred years later followed Bering's route. His instructions were to describe the land of the Chukchi and the Koriaks and the Kamchatka peninsula, which at that time were described and known only through Bering's voyage |59|.

Interest in the First Kamchatka Expedition was revived in the middle of the century in response to the overall increased development of Russian science, and especially the founding of the Russian Geographical Society, which brought about the creation of such splendid periodicals as *Zapiski Russkogo Geograficheskogo Obshchestva, Morskoi Sbornik*, and others. The immediate cause for the revival of this interest was related to the discussions between the naturalist K.M. Baer, and the historian A.P. Sokolov. Baer was the first to try to evaluate the goals and accomplishments of the expedition, declaring that Russian geographical discoveries had been stimulated not through the urging of foreigners and the desires of individual persons, but through "the circumstances of the moment." Baer exaggerated Bering's efforts |74, p.237|. Sokolov felt that Bering had not presented convincing proof of the discovery of a strait and was in too much of a hurry to turn back from the north before there was even a sign of ice |94, pp.104–6|. His contemporaries, the Laptevs, sailed in these same waters and "proved that with a firm will, devotion to duty, and obedience to obligation, one could accomplish exploits such as our philosophers had never dreamed of!" |106|. Then A.S. Polonskii published an article |46| using several new archival materials but making a series of mistakes, the chief one being the misrepresentation of an important document. This deception was widely disseminated and has endured to the present time |107|.

The publication of the documents of the expedition was very significant, especially the excerpts from the watch journal |53|, undertaken in the second half of the nineteenth century.

Foreign scholars, limited to the use of published Russian source materials, did not add anything new to the factual aspect of the history of the expedition. Their works are interesting in their overall appraisal of the expedition and its participants. Herbert Bancroft |108, pp.36,37,38,50| felt that the expedition appeared to be a serious test of Russian shipbuilding and the development of a cadre, and that it did discover the strait, since it established the Asiatic shore on the northeast of the mainland as "sharply turning to the west." The American scholar noted the extreme caution and indecisiveness of Bering; he characterized Spanberg as a cruel and egotistical man, but called Chirikov the pride and hope of the Russian Fleet. Bancroft's work was very important in popularizing this expedition in America. The book of Lauridsen, the Danish geographer |75, pp.19,20| is tendentious. He not only belittles the work of the Russian participants in the expedition, but scarcely even mentions them. He speaks out sharply against those who are critical of Bering's activity.[114] Lauridsen presented certain new biographical details of the seafarer. William H. Dall speaks with exceptional warmth of the Russian overlanders: "Whatever praise we may feel due to Bering and his companions, and it is certainly no stinted allowance, the appreciation of their struggles cannot fail to include with justice, the still more remarkable and nearly forgotten pioneer labors of the undaunted Siberiaks, who paved the way, not only for Bering's weary journey, but for the slow yet never ceasing march of civilization" |70, p.162|. Dall's research stands first and foremost among works in foreign literature about the First Kamchatka Expedition. He analyzed the instruments and methods of observation of that time, condemned Bering's precipitous departure from the North, and was the first foreigner to maintain that the expedition did not present indisputable proof of the existence of a strait.

In 1914, Frank A. Golder|31|[115] wrote that the expedition had not proved the existence of a strait. He considered Bering a good navigator but did not feel he was suited to leading a scientific expedition. He stated that "it was hardly worth sending him to Kamchatka in order to bring back the opinion of Chukchi and hunters," and he condemned Bering's hasty departure from the exploring arena. Golder gave high marks to the achievements of the Russians in the realm of geographical discoveries. As he wrote, "Bering Strait had been discovered, the Arctic coast of Asia from the White Sea to the Kolyma River had been charted, and the North Pacific coast of America from Cape Addington and Bering Island had been placed on the map. This was Russia's share in the work of discovery and exploration, and a very important contribution to geographical knowledge it was"|109, p.5|.

And finally, on the 200th anniversary of the expedition, the work of L.S. Berg|110| appeared, and with that began a new period in the study of the expedition—the stage of its investigation by Soviet scholars.

Berg devoted his primary attention to the Second Kamchatka Expedition, setting forth the history of the First Expedition more briefly than had been done previously. He rightly suggests that the expedition did not resolve its basic goal "with unquestionable evidence." He characterizes Bering as an indecisive person, ill-suited for the command of an expedition, and as a seafarer "who manifested no interest in scientific questions."

In 1941 Pokrovskii compiled a collection of materials |7| that included only one previously unknown document on the First Kamchatka Expedition—Apraksin's Instruction to Bering. He mistakenly proclaimed that the watch journals, Bering's reports, and reports of other members of the expedition had been lost. Andreev |17| made a step forward in widening the documentary base by finding several of Bering's reports.

The history of the First Kamchatka Expedition is also touched upon in the works of A.V. Efimov, M.I. Belov, N.N. Zubov |111|,

D.M. Lebedev, V.I. Grekov, and other Soviet scholars. Not having new materials at their disposal, with a few exceptions, they did not go into details of factual history, but rather devoted their primary attention to general questions.

In recent years, both in the Soviet Union and elsewhere, interest in research on the First Kamchatka Expedition has grown in connection with the implementation of a joint Soviet-American polar experiment called "Bering," and also in conjunction with the 250th anniversary jubilee of the expedition itself, and the 300th anniversary of the birth of Bering. The seafarer's route across Siberia has been marked on the map of post-war five-year plans with numerous grandiose structures transforming the face of this once wild land.

Notes

INTRODUCTION

1. One can hardly accept A.V. Efimov's statement that the Great Kamchatka Expedition was the turning point in the exploration of Siberia, "the prototype for both Bering expeditions . . . a school for seafarers" |5, p.194|.

REASONS FOR ORGANIZING THE EXPEDITION

2. Andreev also exaggerates Leibnitz' work in maintaining that "the famous scholar Leibnitz played the important role of initiator of the exploration of the northern part of the Pacific Ocean" |9, p.15|. M.V. Lomonosov did not consider Leibnitz the initiator |10, p.270|.
3. Spain, desiring to profit as much as possible from its Mexican possessions, controlled the import and export of all goods. For this purpose it maintained an entire flotilla of antiquated warships that it had purchased from England and Holland |16, l. 30|.
4. He wrote, "The first Bering expedition also pursued a trade goal—

179

the establishment of relations with Spanish Mexico, from whence came precious gold for the country" |17, p.31|.

5. Agreeing with Pokrovskii as far as the facts were concerned, he believed that the destination of the voyage at that time (1724–32) was acknowledged to be Mexico |18, p.94|.

6. For example, in the report given to Peter's daughter, Tsaritsa Elizabeth Petrovna, Bering wrote, "The most important part of this expedition, on the basis of His Highness' instruction, is to observe from Kamchatka the configuration of the coast between north and east, as far as the next cape which is called Chukchenskii Nos, to see whether that coast is in any way connected to the west coast of America" |7, p.368|.

7. Lomonosov's opinion is interesting; in speaking of the difficulties of invading the Siberian Far East he wrote, "No European power can wage battle in the Far East either in the north or in the south, and even if they did manage to invade, the strong would become exhausted from transporting rotting provisions to supply their men, with no hope of aid from neighboring peoples—in a place where we would have an inexhaustible supply of assistance" |23, p.49|.

8. We know that it was not until fifty years after the First Kamchatka Expedition that the first peaceful foreign ships appeared along the shores of Kamchatka. The only time in history there has been an armed attack (and even that was of insignificant strength and did not aim at capturing Kamchatka) was during the Crimean War. Finally, there is not a single reference to the defense of the eastern borders in any of the documents of the expedition. The words of G.I. Nevelskoi, the seafarer and explorer of the Far East, are almost prophetic: "On the barren Kamchatka peninsula, covered with mountain ranges, with sparse settlements in between, not a single foreign power will be able to gain a foothold because of the unfavorable climatic conditions" |24, pp.100–111|.

9. Both Divin and Raymond H. Fisher |113, pp.11,22| use testimony of Peter's contemporary, Andrei Nartov, although historical studies have proved that *Nartov's Account of Peter The Great* is a very free treatment made by his son in the 1870s. I also note that Divin attributes to [E.G. Kushnarev], without foundation, a purely geographical method of resolving the question of the objects of the First Kamchatka Expedition and a complete denial of the problem of security for the Far East |25, p.46|.

10. It was not by chance that I.F. Kruzenstern wrote in the plan for his project of circumnavigation (1799), "The costs in Okhotsk for everything are astronomical, since it all has to be brought in from Iakutsk on pack horses" |26, p.344|.

11. In the Senate report we read:

> [We recommend] taking possession of such peoples and lands for the following reasons:
> 1. These lands are adjacent to the Russian domain and are not

subject to any other powers. It will not be difficult to bring
them under the authority of the Russian State.

2. [They will bring] profits to the state, because there are sable
and other fur-bearing animals in these places ...

3. [We will gain] knowledge of a sea route along the Eastern
Sea [Pacific Ocean], which might in the future lead to com-
merce with Japan ...

4. This is particularly desirable for the undeveloped lands, so
that no one from other lands ... will come and lay claim to
these newly discovered lands.

Further along there is an underlined passage, "First lay claim to
these lands to which Russian possession has already been extended; and until this has been done do not proceed to the islands
in the sea or build ostrogs" |27, ll. 6–17|.

12. Soimonov wrote that when persons spoke to Peter "about Siberia,
the eastern coastal areas and about Kamchatka," he would reply,
"Yes, I know all about that, but now is not the time, it is far away"
|30, pp.551–2|.

13. Where this map was made is not known. Kirilov saw it later in the
possession of General Ia. V. Bruce, and after that it was published in
Homann's atlas. Kirilov later made changes in the map on the basis
of information he had received from Shestakov. The changes in the
map are known through Delisle's copy, which Golder published |31,
p.111|, and also through the copy made by LeRua, which is
preserved in the Manuscript Division of the Library of the Academy of Sciences of the USSR and was published by L.S. Berg as the
Shestakov map |32, pp.96–7|.

14. For example, Berg maintained that there were sixty sailors, soldiers,
and artisans. Pokrovskii counts more than sixty sailors alone. I.P.
Magidovich wrote that between seventy and seventy-five men
went from St. Petersburg to Okhotsk.

15. Everything that pertains to Bering's being put on the retired list and
his return to service is set forth here on the basis of archival ac-
counts |34, l. 81–93|.

16. In historical literature one may find the assertion that the Tsar remembered this, and upon Bering's return to the fleet he was named
"commander-in-chief" of the ship *Marlborough* |25, p.46|.

17. Bering wrote to Apraksin from Tobolsk in March of 1725. "I thank
Your Excellency for the generosity that my father, the Sovereign,
has extended to me. ... I ask that in the future Your Excellency's
concern may also be extended to my family who remain in St.
Petersburg" |36, l. 265|.

18. The author deems it necessary to name all the sailors and artisans
who have until now remained unknown. The list of names follows
|37, l. 29|: Quartermaster Ivan Borisov from the ship *Shliutelburkh*;
seamen first class Grigorii Barbashevskii, Nikifor Lopukhin,
Grigorii Shiriaev, Afansii Osipov, Nikita Efimov, and Prokopii El-

fimov, all from the ship *Lesnoe*, men whom Bering had previously commanded; Dmitrii Kazachinin and Vasilii Feofanov from the ship *Frende Molera*; Savelii Ganiukov and Elisei Selivanov from the *Ingermanland*; Afanasii Krasov from the *Sv. Ekaterina*; Ivan Belyi from the *Rafail* and Aleksei Kozyrev from the *Sv. Petr*. Admiralty seamen: carpenter-desiatnik Ivan Vavilov; carpenters Aleksei Ivanov, Nikifor Khleskov, and Gavrilo Mitrofanov; sailmakers Semen Danilov and Ignatii Petrov; caulkers Vasilii Ganin and Akim Matveev; blacksmith Evdokim Ermolaev.

19. An entry for 1724 in the Admiralty College journal reads, "One Bering is given leave to Vyborg to attend to his affairs as of 7 January 1725" |38, l. 302|.

    According to information from a kind colleague in the National Archives of Finland, Elias Orrman, the notes in parish books from a Swedish community in Vyborg indicate that in 1713 Bering and Anna Charlotte Piulse, the daughter of a local merchant, were married. There is no mention of the baptism in October 1725, and funeral in November of the same year, of their son. Apparently during Bering's absence his family lived in Vyborg with his wife's family.

20. It is interesting to note the monthly salaries of the expedition members. Bering received forty rubles per month plus fifty kopecks each for four batmen; Chirikov and Spanberg each received fifteen rubles plus fifty kopecks for a batman; the doctor, ten rubles plus fifty kopecks for a batman; the navigator, twelve rubles; the geodesist, six rubles; Chaplin, one ruble; the apprentice Kozlov, three rubles; the apprentice artisans, one ruble; quartermaster, two rubles; seamen one ruble, fifty kopecks; master craftsmen, one ruble. They also received one-half *osmin* (about 105 liters) of flour and about a *chetvert* of groats.

FROM ST. PETERSBURG TO TOBOLSK

21. Divin mistakenly states that twenty-six men left the capital and that "five servitors" *(piat sluzhilykh liudei)* went with Bering. (Military line servitors, *riadovykh voennosluzhashchikh*, at that time, as distinguished from servitors in state service, were referred to as *sluzhitelyi* |25, p.49|.)

22. This apparently refers to the map drawn up by I.K. Kirilov and dated here according to the time of the compiling of the originals—the Evreinov-Luzhin map and a foreign map.

23. The author feels compelled to give the names of all the soldiers for the first time. They were detached from Siberian regiments as noted. From St. Petersburg: Dmitrii Sazhin, Mikhailo Shorokhov, Vasilii Lykov, Aleksei Kistenev, Abrosim Kalinin, Prokofii Iudin, Lavrentii Solovev, Semen Arapov, Semen Kiprianov, Andrei Kirsanov, Grigorii Vologodskii, Semen Trifonov, and Avram Iakushev; from Moscow: Corporal Ivan Anashkin, Aleksei Shchepetkin,

Iakim Sharoglazov, Ivan Kononvalov, Fedor Vorotnikov, Petr Kapotilov, Ivan Shalaev, Makhailo Miasnikov, and Ivan Pletnev. From Tobolsk: Sergeant Ivan Liubimskii, Kozma Kurochkin, Ivan Kozlov, Foma Morokov, Boris Vyrodov, Dmitrii Zolotukhin, Aleksei Popadenkin, Andrei Khrushkov, Aleksandr Korkin, Timofei Talankin, Matvei Bragin, Stepan Lomonosov, and Nefed Erlagin |39, ll. 21–22|.

FROM TOBOLSK TO ILIMSK
VIA THE IRTYSH, OB, AND KET RIVERS

24. Grekov states that from Surgut to Makovsk there were only three such setbacks |42, p.24|. This estmate is made on the basis of published watch journal entries just for the 6th and 49th days.
25. Andreev mistakenly writes that since appropriate ukazes had been sent throughout Siberia "the necessary carpenters, blacksmiths and others were already there, for which reason there were no delays" |17, p.8|.
26. An example of the text of one such entry: the Eniseisk carpenter Denis Borisov vouched, "for my son Iakov, so that he, Iakov, might be hired to work with the Eniseisk carpenter Vasilii Kasiakov in Kamchatka for shipbuilding; for Captain Bering ... he does not gamble or play cards ... and he will never take leave without permission from his captain nor will he desert." Posting twenty rubles bond in advance for his son, the father pledges himself, in case his son should desert, to go personally to perform the "work of shipbuilding" |39, l. 32|.

WINTER IN ILIMSK

27. As testimony to Tatarinov's zealous aid, there is a lengthy list of inhabitants of Ilimsk from whom he temporarily confiscated lodkas for the expedition. The list includes the town warrant officer, the priest, several *syn boiarskii* and others |44, l. 25–26.| Berg and Efimov regard Tatarinov only as the prikaschik of Anadyrsk ostrog. However, the instructions that he received read, "Go from Tobolsk to Kamchatka and also take charge at Anadyrsk ostrog ... help find a route to Kamchatka by sea" |45, p.86|.
28. At that time navigators were using the Davis quadrant, an instrument without an optical device. The astrolabe was even more primitive. Not only did they have no chronometer, but not even ordinary spring watches; they used sand glasses. The improvement in timepieces did not come about until the early nineteenth century.
29. There can be no doubt of the fact that Bering sent only one report from Eniseisk, since he began every report with a note on the date, the place from which it was sent, and a brief summary of the previous report.

30. Prior to the First Kamchatka Expedition, Elchin said that the former routing to Kamchatka was "from Iakutsk by way of the Verkhoiansk, Indigirsk, Alazeisk, and Kolymsk ostrogs, through barren distant places with great difficulty." By his time a river route from Iakutsk to Okhotsk and then across the Sea of Okhotsk was also being used |27, ll. 13–14|.

FROM ILIMSK TO IAKUTSK

31. Grekov is mistaken in asserting that Bering and Vladislavich Raguzinskii met in Ilimsk. Raguzinskii did not reach Ilimsk until 31 March; Bering was already in Ust-Kut by 28 March.
32. Divin suggests that prior to Bering's arrival Chaplin had been engaged in "large-scale preparations" in Iakutsk, that he had made the decision to send the expedition's cargo to Okhotsk by horses and had carried this out. But, in actual fact, it was Bering who did this. Likewise puzzling is Divin's assertion that Chaplin was to build ships and convey them to Okhotsk over portages. Portages are used to haul vessels over dry land from one river to another at a relatively short distance from the first. Here, according to information from the expedition itself, the distance was 1,177 versts, there were no roads at all, and men on foot could traverse the terrain only with great difficulty. The ships for the expedition were built not in Iakutsk but in Ust-Kut, in the spring of 1726, under the supervision of Spanberg who was sent for that purpose with the cargo from Iakutsk via the rivers Aldan, Maia, and Iudoma |25, p.50|.
33. On 14 November the Siberian governor even reported to the Senate on Kozyrevskii and the proposal to use him in the expedition |27, l. 6|. Several writers (Berkh, Polonskii, Golder, and others) mistakenly thought Kozyrevskii was a member of the expedition.

BY RIVER AND OVERLAND TO OKHOTSK

34. Bering also envisaged the arrangements for this return: "If anyone dies, examine his baggage, sell it, and take back any unearned money."
35. A brief table drawn up by Chaplin gives an idea of the number of horses that were lost in each detachment (listed with the detachment leader):

Packs taken from Iaktusk	Bering	Kozlov	The doctor	The sergeant	The desiatnik	TOTAL
With flour	—	270	88	174	64	596
With groats	—	38	32	—	—	70

Number of horses	Bering	Kozlov	The doctor	The sergeant	The desiatnik	TOTAL
Started out from Lena River	77	223	103	124	133	660
Left at Iudoma Cross	27	24	—	—	—	51
Abandoned on the way	14	24	42	25	71	176
Fell	4	19	4	4	—	31
Ran off	—	—	1	—	8	9
Total dead	45	67	47	29	79	267
On hand at present	32	156	56	95	54	393

36. After the conclusion of the expedition Chirikov wrote that it was especially important to prepare enough heavy felt for sweat cloths for the packhorses, "because it is quite useless for the Iakuts to send ... provisions and the like to Okhotsk on packhorses, for the horses die not as a result of their burdens, but for want of good sweat cloths. With these, a horse could survive ten trips, but with covers of reindeer hide many cannot withstand even one trip" |47, l. 129|.

37. In historical literature one sometimes encounters a distorted picture of this detachment. For example this is how N.K. Chukovskii |48, pp.20–21| describes it: "The lieutenant asked the Iakuts and the Tungus who lived along the banks of the Iudoma ... for sled dogs and sleds. ... And he used the knout and the gallows as strong enforcers. He managed to bring together one hundred teams and sleds." This is completely wrong. No one lived along the Iudoma; the men themselves pulled the sleds they had made; and gallows could not have been used on the expedition. Grekov is mistaken in supposing that this trip was no more difficult than the overland trail, that the men who traveled with Bering carried provisions on sleds drawn by dogs, and that in this detachment the geodesist F. Luzhin died. In actual fact, the provisions were carried on horses, and Luzhin was in Spanberg's detachment.

WINTER IN OKHOTSK

38. In regard to the question of the expedition's route from Okhotsk to Kamchatka, some scholars have suggested the Bering wanted to set

out for there by an overland route in that same year, 1726. Andreev, for example, commented, "It was extremely difficult to go on to Kamchatka, even if they could replace the horses with dogs. But Bering nevertheless hoped to reach Kamchatka in that same year" |17, p.8|. Actually, from the time of the very beginning of the expedition, Bering intended to sail to Kamchatka on the Sea of Okhotsk and never departed from this decision. Otherwise why would they have had to build a ship in Okhotsk? The sea route to Kamchatka, discovered in 1716, was significantly shorter, more convenient, and safer than the overland route, which lay through a land populated by hostile natives. Furthermore, it was not possible to use horses for winter travel there, and dogs were not to be considered, since several thousand would be needed. The statement that Bering wanted to be in Kamchatka in 1726 is also erroneous: there had been no news from Spanberg's detachment for a long time, and there was no idea of setting out without him, since he was transporting the items that were necessary for building a ship in Kamchatka. And finally, the ship had not yet been built in Okhotsk.

39. Among Morrison's private effects that he intended to trade for furs were more than one thousand glass buttons and more than two puds of Chinese tobacco |39, l. 167|.

40. The Iakut servitors received two puds of flour for a three-month period, only half as much as the sailors and soldiers. We have mentioned the time when Spanberg shared his own provisions with the Iakuts. Later he asked them to return them, and drew up a list of ninety-three names. Where had he acquired such a stock of provisions? It appears that in Iakutsk he, Bering, and Morrison bought flour with their own money: Bering one hundred puds and Spanberg and Morrison eighty puds each |39, l. 181|. A large part of this flour was sold and exchanged for furs in Okhotsk.

41. In a report to Bering, Spanberg wrote that the scribe had declared that "he has important information about you personally, pertaining to the first point" |39, l. 177|. This referred to the so-called "word and deed," that is, an accusation of an important state offense. In the archives we have managed to find only a few notations written by the expedition's scribe, Turchaninov. A certain Petr Merovich, a participant in the Second Kamchatka Expedition, testified that Bering had boasted to him that Semen Turchaninov and others, during the Second Kamchatka Expedition "had cried ... the word and deed, but that no one believed them." From the documents it also appears that Turchaninov died soon after, and all the others who later made complaints about Bering (Fridrikh, the hieromonk) were declared insane |51, ll. 150,203|.

42. Grekov suggests that Spanberg made the first run from Okhotsk to Kamchatka in 1726. Actually, however, he did not reach there until January of 1727. Berkh's version is likewise incorrect in stating that

thirteen merchants were sent to Kamchatka with Spanberg.

43. This is how Chaplin described "hunting" in his journal: "In the evening twenty or more boats set out, with five or six men in each, and they go six or seven versts and spend the night on shore. The next morning at dawn, if the sea is calm, they go four or five versts out to sea; the ducks at that time are idle and they do not have large wings. They scurry along the incoming tide to the mouth of the Okhota River ... which pulls the ducks forcibly into the river. The men pull out about three versts into the bay ... and post a guard in an arc of boats and do not go back out to sea. When the water begins to ebb ... they get out of the boats, and then from shore a large number of men skewer the ducks or take them alive." With such barbaric methods they took three thousand ducks in one day, 7 August.

44. Müller mistakenly believed that this ship came from Kamchatka together with the *Fortuna* on 10 August. If this had been so, the expedition to Okhotsk would have lasted another month, since the old vessel was completely decrepit, and it took more than twenty-five days to repair.

ACROSS THE SEA OF OKHOTSK TO KAMCHATKA

45. However, it is impossible to agree with Grekov that in this case the seafarers could have launched a ship in the fall in Kamchatka. He does not take into account the fact that they had to prepare lumber and bring it to the construction site. Berkh is even more mistaken in thinking that if they had been sent around Kamchatka by sea the seafarers would have gained two years. Lebedev and Esakov |52, p.194| are also wrong in thinking that the cargo was transported across Kamchatka only on dogs, and that this delayed construction of the ship by nearly a year. A significant part of the cargo, including the heaviest and most cumbersome items, was transported by river and on the *Fortuna* around Kamchatka.

46. Berkh wrote, "... 6 October the above-mentioned boats arrived from Nizhnekamchatsk." This is impossible. The boats could not have come from Nizhnekamchatsk because a watershed lay between the Bystraia and Kamchatka rivers, across which it was difficult to transport even bales, let alone boats. They carried the transferred cargo farther on other vessels.

47. The members of the expedition usually gave a rough estimate of the numerical makeup of the population. According to Senate documents, in 1724 the following lived on the Kamchatka peninsula: 134 in Verkhnekamchatsk of whom twenty-seven were *razno-chintsy* [intellectuals not belonging to the gentry], 101 were slaves, four were registered in the settlement, and two were fort laborers; 143 in Bolsheretsk of whom thirty-four were raznochintsy, 108 were slaves and one was registered to the settlement; and fifty-

eight in Andyrsk ostrog of whom twenty-six were raznochintsy, twenty-seven were slaves, and five were registered |37, l. 28|.

48. As was also the case on a previous occasion, the doctor was with Bering in spite of the fact that Spanberg was ill in Nizhnekamchatsk and had been confined to his bed for some months.

49. It is interesting that in 1726 the local inhabitants wrote to Iakutsk: "We live in Nizhnekamchatsk, some distance up the Kamchatka [River] beyond the church ... where there are presently an ostrog, a iasak zimov'e, and our households—the place is low and is flooded in the spring, so the households stand in water for six weeks. But at the springs at Nikolskii church there is high land. Therefore, we have been ordered to move the ostrog, iasak izba, and our homes there on rafts" |45, pp.110–11|.

50. Kruzenstern wrote, "The population of Kamchatka is so small that we must take all measures to prevent the disappearance of this race, an event which appears certain if we do not treat them more humanely and if we do not guarantee them all the necessities of life" |26, p.345|.

51. In historical literature one finds incorrect data on the dimensions of the boat. Grekov gives the width as 16.1 meters. With such a width the vessel would have had to be almost square. The Sv. Gavriil is sometimes referred to as a galiot. This is incorrect. The builder, F. Kozlov, wrote, "I do not know how to build galiots, I did not learn any specialty beyond boat-making" |39, l. 205|. In the List of Russian war ships |56, p.722| the ship launching is erroneously given as 1729, and the builder is not named.

52. According to Divin the ship was put in the water and launched on 8 June 1728 in Okhotsk |25, p.52|. However, it is not clear who built it and launched it in Okhotsk, if, as this author suggests, during the summer of the previous year the expedition went from Okhotsk to Kamchatka on the Fortuna. (Actually it was not on the Fortuna but on an old local vessel.) Nor is it clear how the Sv. Gavriil happened to be in Nizhnekamchatsk.

53. The fact that Chirikov proposed taking interpreters (who were in fact taken) who could converse with the Chukchi and other natives living beyond the Anadyr, is one more documentary refutation of Polevoi's contention that the expedition was supposed to sail east to America. Incidentally, Bering was not receptive to all of Chirikov's wise suggestions, and he even resented some of them. In 1739 Chirikov proposed that they put the conveyances along the rivers to Okhotsk in better condition. Bering assigned him to raft the provisions, as Chirikov wrote to the [Admiralty] College, "... not so much to improve the situation as to spite me for having made the proposal. Previously a lieutenant had been temporarily assigned to the rafts of provisions and material, or sometimes an under-officer ... so by doing this, the Captain-Commander apparently intended to insult me" |83, l. 12|. In a letter to N.F. Golovin,

which was sent the same day, Chirikov added, "... and for previous proposals that I had made ... he threatened to send me on journeys, but I never asked to be excused from them" |83, 1. 13|.

TO THE HIGH NORTHERN LATITUDES

54. There is no direct evidence as to the number of watches. Only in Chirikov's journal for 6 August is there an indirect mention of this: "We were under full sail *for both watches* ... " [italics added]. This could indicate that each officer stood two watches per day and that in this instance he was writing about his own watches.

55. One such occurrence, we will recall, took place in Ilimsk when Chirikov "kept in his special notation" all the details of the observations of the lunar eclipse, which, as with the "certain sketch map," have never been found.

56. In this matter the documents do not support Berkh's statement that the expedition to Krest Bay was searching for fresh water and an anchorage. He is also mistaken in referring to Krest Bay as Nochek Inlet, in not showing Meechken Spit, and in identifying Krest Bay as the northern part of Anadyr Bay.

57. Berkh again adds up the hourly indications of speed and concludes that they made sixty-two miles. He makes this mistake several times. He also incorrectly states the daily variation of longitude as 8', whereas it was actually 12'.

58. Alekseev |60, p.292| suggests that since "in the strait the American shore was not observed, they had to make a decision about the further plans of the expedition." Actually, Bering did not know anything of the location of America in this region and asked the officers to express their opinion, because the shore of Asia had disappeared from view. Further, in historical literature we often find the assertion that Bering convened a meeting *(konsiliiu)* of the officers during which an argument supposedly flared up. In actual fact there was neither a meeting nor an argument. Furthermore, arguments with the commander of a military vessel are not to be tolerated.

59. Chirikov is here referring to some other latitude. The longitude of 65°30' seems more likely, as Bering and Spanberg identified it. It is possible that Chirikov did not enter the minutes, and rounded off the latitude.

60. It has been noted that Berg and other scholars came to the unfounded conclusion that Chirikov had confused surnames, and that when he referred to Petr Tatarinov he really meant Petr Popov, who in 1711 had drawn up the description of Alaska from Chukchi accounts that Müller discovered in 1736 in the Iakutsk archives. Lebedev was one of those who accepted the substitution of Popov for Tatarinov as a fact and wrote, "Burdened with routine affairs of the expedition, Chirikov personally carried out scientific investiga-

tions ... " |18, p.97|. To all appearances, the author is referring to
the work in the archives, where Popov's *skazka* was later found.
But it is doubtful that Chirikov would have been concerned with
this. In any event, neither in his journal nor in other documents is
there any hint of such work. Lebedev does not change his opinion
even later |60, p.327; 52, pp.180,195|. Magidovich |63, p.403|
misinterprets Chirikov's proposal about wintering over when he
maintains that the seafarer proposed going north "as far as possible
until 5 September and halting there for the winter."

61. Grekov, speaking of the fact that Bering translated Spanberg's reply
in a none too grammatical fashion, cites Polonskii. Concerning the
fact that Bering did translate the document, testimony is found in a
note on the translation. We can judge the quality of the translation
only by the style, since Spanberg's original reply has not been preserved.

62. Alekseev maintains that Spanberg suggested sailing east |60,
p.292|.Lebedev |60, p.327| and Divin |25, p.55| erroneously suggested
that Spanberg advised sailing another three days.

63. In historical literature there are many improbable fictions. For example, N.K. Chukovskii writes, "Bering had a trait unexpected in
an eighteenth century man: he was democratic. In all difficult situ-
ations he loved to be advised, to consult, to hear the opinions of his
subordinates, giving them complete freedom to speak out.... And
not infrequently he had advice ... even from common sailors" |48,
p.26|. This is an obvious delusion. Naval regulations, not a trait of
character, obliged Bering to take counsel with Spanberg and
Chirikov. During the expedition he turned to them four times, but
there was not a single occasion when he took counsel with the
sailors, or even with the midshipman Chaplin.

64. Some scholars believe that Bering lost sight of land only at the
northernmost point of his voyage. For example, Magidovich wrote,
"26 August [new style] they reached 67°18' northern latitude where
land was lost from view" |63, p.403|.

65. Chaplin indicates a different longitude—30°17'04". Berkh mistak-
enly thinks that the longitude was taken by the seafarers east of
Nizhnekamchatsk, rather than from the mouth of the Kamchatka
River. The same mistake was subsequently made by Lauridsen,
Dall, and others.

66. M.A. Ratmanov was a fellow voyager with I.F. Kruzenstern. Grekov
for some reason refers not to the island, but to "the Diomede Islands, discovered on the return voyage." Efimov suggests that it has
not been determined which of the islands the expedition discovered.

MAPPING BERING'S 1728 VOYAGE

67. Dall specifically emphasized that the historical researchers on the
expedition did not know that the *Sv. Gavriil* was sailing far from

shore and that they had no information on the depth and color of the water, the weather condition, and the fog. However, Dall says that he had spent three years on the same coast that the Bering Expedition visited and placed on the map. "If the interest in the subject," wrote Dall, "were to be stimulated by discussion from these opposing points of view, so as to result in the publication of some of the material still hidden in Russian archives, I shall be more than repaid for the time I have devoted to the question, even if publication of the original data should show some of my conclusions to be ill founded or erroneous" |70, p.166|. This was a justified reproach to Russian scholars who were not devoting themselves to a painstaking study of the archival material of the expedition.

68. Grekov made a similar attempt |42, p.341|. Comparing only two sources, the "Brief Relation ... " and the first account by the Chukchi, he came to the conclusion that Bering "changed their words considerably."

69. It is interesting to introduce the opinion of Lütke, who sailed there one hundred years later, about the Chukchi and the interpreters. He wrote, "The interpreter, not having the remotest comprehension of the matter being questioned, would refer the question to the native, who often for a long time could not understand what was wanted of him; what should be the clarity of the answer that is given to the questioner by this means? Add to this the natural suspicion the natives would have in regard to such questioning, and even more the vast difference between their comprehension and ours, even on the most basic concepts: large and small, near and far, and the like. . . . Such interpreters were of little help when the subject under inquiry was beyond the narrow range of their comprehension" |72, p.195|.

70. In this instance Bering cites the longitude as entered by Chirikov (Chaplin gives it as 30°17′). This indicates that the leader evidently placed greater reliance on Chirikov's data.

71. He wrote, "We must suppose that Captain Bering turned back because having sailed more than two hundred miles north from Chukotskii Nos, he did not see land either to the east or to the west" |73, p.56|. Berkh is mistaken here, which is all the more unfortunate since he had the watch journal at his disposal. The *Sv. Gavriil*, as noted earlier, was out of view of the coast of Chukotka less than a third of the time.

72. Baer observed that Bering "decided on 16 August to turn back from 67°18′ latitude, first in order not to be stranded by the ice, and second in order to reach Petropavlovsk harbor on Kamchatka before winter set in" |74, p.237|. But the fact was that in August the ship was only at the polar circle and the seafarers still had not seen any ice. Petropavlovsk harbor was not named until later.

73. Dall first wrote about this in a book on Alaska |76|. "Being naturally timid, hesitating, and indolent, [Bering] determined to go no farther for fear of being frozen in, and returned through the strait—strange

to say—without seeing the Diomedes [he did see one of them], or the American coast. . . . "

74. Here are several episodes from Cook's voyage in this region in 1778. 17 August: "At 1:00 P.M. the sight of a large field of ice left us no longer in doubt about the cause of the brightness of the Horizon we had observed. At half past two we tacked close to the edge of it in 22 fathoms Water being then in the latitude of 70°14′. . . . " 28 August: "We spent the night Standing off and on amongst the drift ice. . . . " On 1 September the English navigator was still located beyond 67° northern latitude |71, pp.417,425–6,429|.

75. For example, Berg wrote, "The cautious commander joined his voice to Spanberg's opinion" |32, p.89|. (Bering received the rank of commander after the expedition, in 1730.)

76. Apparently Chirikov proposed this, knowing that Bering would not agree to repeat his voyage to the north the following year.

77. According to Dall's data, the eclipse was on 14 February 1729 (new style). Dall expressed doubt that the members of the expedition actually observed the eclipse on Kamchatka itself |70, pp.115–16|.

THE VOYAGE OF 1729 AND THE RETURN TO THE CAPITAL

78. Of course they were not describing a direct sighting here, since the distance to the Komandorskie Islands is at least 185 kilometers; rather, they are describing a mirage, the same kind of phenomenon that for example, enables people on the Cote d'Azur in southern France to see the hills of Corsica two hundred kilometers away, early on a clear morning.

79. His precise words were, "In 1729 we went back to sea in the vicinity of the southern part of Kamchatka, but the entire expedition was uneventful" |49, 1. 104|.

80. The ukaz directs, ". . . Send a detailed account to the [Admiralty] College from the beginning of your appointment to the expedition, detailing what your income was and how much you spent on provisions and supplies and other things each year and each day, and where you spent the money. Until this account is received, your wife will receive no more of your salary from the Admiralty. 20 January 1729" |49, 1. 259|.

THE SCIENTIFIC RESULTS AND
THE SIGNIFICANCE OF THE EXPEDITION

81. In historical literature one may encounter the notion that Spanberg supposedly found the information about the earlier voyage around Chukotka in the Iakutsk archives at the time the expedition returned. This is obviously a mistake. Spanberg was ill; he reached Iakutsk later than the others; and he spent less than a week there and could not have worked in the archives.

82. An analogous evaluation of the scientific results of the expedition is also given in the Senate ukaz of 16 February 1733.

83. This is no less clearly expressed in another ukaz from the Admiralty College: "For first-hand information ... as to whether there is a passage by way of the Arctic Ocean, build double-sloops with decks and 24 oars ... and go around the point that is indicated on the map in 73°" |78, l. 1059|.

84. True, Kirilov noted in brackets, "I hope that ultimately they will be able to accomplish this through various investigations." Divin took this out of context and concluded that apparently Kirilov "was certain that Asia was separated from America by a strait, and steadfastly expressed the idea of the possibility of sailing from the northern Arctic Ocean to the Pacific Ocean" |61, p.76|. But how can one equate "hope" and "certainty"?

85. It is impossible to understand Andreev's contention |80, p.41| that the longitudes of Kamchatka and Tobolsk were first established by Delisle. This was done by the First Kamchatka Expedition.

86. The French scholar Gustave Cahen feels that Homann's 1722 map was copied. The Russian traveler Daniel Messerschmidt, who met the voyagers in Eniseisk, attested to the fact that Bering had possession of this map.

87. Bering reported to the Iakutsk chancellery, "3 April 1726 His Excellency Count Savva Vladislavich wrote to me and asked me for a sketch map of this region and of the Ud and Amur rivers, on which we do not have detailed information, so I have been searching for an old map in Irkutsk, which I want to have copied to send to His Excellency; and for this purpose we are requesting the help of the syn boiarskii Ivan L'vov" |41, l. 85|.

88. Andreev |17, p.9| and Grekov |42, p.39| maintain that this map was sent to the College in June 1727. However, that is incorrect. It is definitely known that Bering sent the map, together with the report, from Okhotsk the day before he put out to sea, 21 August.

89. The final map, called the map "of our entire trip from Tobolsk by rivers and by sea until our return," was made in the winter of 1728–1729, between the two voyages, and not in 1730, as Andreev supposes |81, p.5|. At the beginning of 1730 the scientists of the expedition set out on their way, and when they reached the capital they delivered the prepared map.

90. Grekov states that the final map was appended to two reports: the report of 10 February 1730, and the "Brief Relation.... " In actuality, as mentioned above, the report of 10 February did not exist, and the suggestion that the map was appended to the "Relation" is not confirmed by the documents. On the other hand, in his report to the Senate of 4 August 1730 Bering wrote in regard to the map, "I hope that it will be forwarded ... to the Senate from the State Admiralty College" |27, l. 4|.

91. B.G. Ostrovskii maintains that "neither Bering's expense book nor

his map ... have ever turned up, in either the original or copies"
|82, p.125|. However, the journals, as we have seen, were used in
part by Nagaev, Berkh, and Vakhtin; they have not been lost, but
neither have they been studied by present-day scholars. Andreev
|81, p.46| writes that all the original journals were sent to Tobolsk
where they were burned in 1787. This is not accurate in regard to
Chirikov's journal and to a group of other documents that were
saved. Grekov found it possible to state |42, p.339| that "V.N. Berkh
attributes to A.I. Chirikov the keeping of the ship's log, which was
sewn to the journal of P.A. Chaplin." And in M.I. Belov |65, p.156|
we find indications that "the log of the *Sv. Gavriil* has not to the
present time come to light, it not being known whether it was regu-
larly kept." The scholar conjectures about a fact that we consider
indisputable—that Chaplin's journal (as well as Chirikov's) com-
prises the journal of the *Sv. Gavriil.*

92. It is known that as early as 1760, in comments on Voltaire's book
on the history of Russia under Peter I, Lomonosov, in speaking of
the Second Kamchatka Expedition, announced in no uncertain
terms that Chirikov "was the principal, and penetrated farther,
which was necessary for our honor" |23, p.363|.

93. There are documentary testimonials to Chirikov's outstanding
abilities. In the journal of protocols from the Admiralty College 20
January 1725 it is written, "... Under-Lieutenant Aleksei
Chirikov, although he had not yet reached line position, is to be advanced to the rank of lieutenant. Rear-Admiral Sanders has stated
that insofar as training the naval cadets is concerned, the most brilliant of the navy officers is one named Chirikov; according to the
professor, Chirikov is learned in science. And Guards Captain
Kazinskii pointed to 142 naval cadets whom Chirikov had instructed in science and said that for this reason Chirikov should
now be appointed to this expedition. The Admiralty College knows
about Chirikov's scientific knowledge and his ability to teach his
fellows other naval arts; and he is worthy of this promotion ...
thus it is necessary to observe other servitors in the Navy in regard
to their practical knowledge and service, those who have demon-
strated their zeal, so that ... like Chirikov they will be promoted
in rank" |15, Part IV, p.698|. The College decided to find as replace-
ment for Chirikov for the Naval Academy "navigators of the highest standing." But by 26 January 1725 at the session of the College a
report from the Head of the Academy was read, in which he said
"... there are no navigators [who can] oversee the naval cadets and
teach them ... " to replace Chirikov |38, l. 326|.

94. There is convincing evidence that Chirikov was a bold and enter-
prising explorer. In the spring of 1740, not realizing that Laptev had
succeeded in rounding Chukotka by sea from west to east, Chirikov wrote that he had "suggested in a discussion with the captain-
commander that he [Bering] might send me in the brigantine ... to

observe the area located north and east of Kamchatka opposite Chukotsk Nos and [other places on] the west coast of America." Bering refused. This is an eloquent reply to those who feel that it was easy for Chirikov to make his suggestion at the time they were sailing in the strait in 1728, since he was not the commander and was not responsible for the men and the ship. And incidentally, in 1733 Chirikov had already determined "that America is not very far from the eastern point of Chukotka, which is in 64 degrees ... [let us] proceed to the land of Chukotka, to 65 degrees and ... east, beyond the small island which we saw on our first voyage, even on to America ... " (Chirikov's opinion on 12 February 1733) |27, ll. 436–37|.

95. Although Chaplin's signature appears on copies of the map, and although he kept more than one sailing journal, nevertheless he never wrote up the "reports of the expedition." Bering did not entrust this task to anyone but himself.

96. The fact that Chaplin did not immediately master the ability even to copy maps is attested to indirectly by Bering's having to enlist the services of Ivan L'vov in 1726 for copying.

97. An ukaz from the Senate directs, "The journals of Captain-Commander Bering and of the then Lieutenant Chirikov are to be sent to the Senate and returned to the College" |84, l. 109|.

98. It may be surmised that on shore a fair copy was made of the original map, compiled on the *Sv. Gavriil* during the voyage, which Chirikov called a "drawing" and a "sketch map." The originals that were made during the voyage have not been found.

99. An enumeration of mistakes does not diminish the general high esteem in which the results of the cartographic work of the expedition are held, but it may rather completely negate Lauridsen's extravagant claims that Bering made "precise maps, in which there was nothing imaginary."

100. The 1733 map was published in Sven Waxell's book |9|, and Golder published the 1731 map |109|. These are similar but not identical. Müller |35, l. 10|, and in the present time Andreev |80, p.39| mistakenly believed that Delisle drew up only one of these, the 1733 map. Delisle's maps refute Berg's assertion |32, p.347| that the results of the cartographic work of the expedition were first reflected on Kirilov's 1734 map.

101. Efimov notes that the Russian Academy professor Bernulli publicly accused Delisle of having sent that copy of the map to France. The uproar over the documents of the First Kamchatka Expedition among foreigners in St. Petersburg did not quickly subside. In "The Protocols of the Sessions of the Conference of the Academy of Sciences" |88, pp.166,180|, in 1735 there are the following notes: "Your Excellency, have a copy made for the notary, of the description of the journey to Kamchatka undertaken in 1725, written in German and translated into French" (7 March). "Your Excellency

gave to the notary the three copies of Bering's journal of the expedition to Kamchatka. Delisle is to receive the old French copy since it belongs to him. You are to receive the other two copies, transcribed into French and German. Professor Windsheim took the original of the German copy" (31 March).

102. Bering's proposals are often mistakenly considered as drawn up by him on his own initiative.

103. Following Berkh's example the erroneous notion came about that Bering worked out his proposals in April of 1730 and presented them to the Admiralty College. The Senate transactions provide documentary refutation of this. We cite Bering's proposals in the original version, preserved in the Senate fond |27, ll. 77–82| (the note under 4 December 1730). They were initially published by Berkh, but only the first part of each point. Sokolov gives the proposals in full, but he has a number of errata and a confused sequence of accounts, such as in number 15 |94, pp.427–33|.

104. Andreev wrote, "Immediately upon his return from the expedition Bering likewise began to *persistently seek* to take various measures to develop the far reaches of the realm ... " |17, p.12|.

105. The financial documents of the expedition were evidently in complete disarray. Bering did not like to bother with them. This trait had become apparent earlier, as is apparent from a document preserved in the archives concerning the time of his suspension in 1716 from command of a ship "until presentation of accounts of treasury funds expended during his voyage" |96, l. 197|.

106. Golovin's proposal included a brief introduction, three fundamental points, and ten points indicating "benefits to the state" of a circumnavigation. It was drawn up on 21 October, not on 1 October as Divin wrote |61, p.66|. It appears that Sarychev in 1820 was the first to report about this project in print.

107. This proposal consisted of nine paragraphs, of which the last contained fifteen separate points demonstrating the advantages of a circumnavigation. This is written in old German, which is very difficult to read.

108. The sixth point of the instructions of 16 March 1733 reads, "To search for the shortest route to the Sea of Kamchatka that does not go by way of Iakutsk ... send two geodesists on the mission with experienced local Siberian men." In the report signed by Bering, Chirikov, and the other officers, they advised that since 1734 they had twice sent out from Irkutsk via Nerchinsk the renowned geodesists Petr Skobeltsyn and Vasilii Shatilov to search for a good route, but without success.

EPILOGUE

109. We cannot agree with the opinion that Bering was the author |52, p.196|. In the first place the article contains absurd mistakes, which

he could never have made: that there were "a great many officers" in the expedition, that two ships sailed north, that Kamchatka extended to 67° northern latitude. And secondly, Bering was ordered to learn from the Siberians about a certain ship that fifty to sixty years before had sailed from the Lena to Kamchatka. (Both Grekov and Fisher, despite many discrepancies in the data, consider the report of this vessel as the first mention in print of Dezhnev's voyage.) The authorship of Müller is indirectly corroborated by the fact that he was later the editor of the *Sankt Peterburgskaia Vedomost* and naturally, knowing who had written the article, Müller later (in a reply to Delisle) did not give the name of the author, observing, "Bering in Kamchatka perhaps had not heard about the arrival of a vessel on the Lena, for even in the record of his voyage there was no mention of it" |35, 1. 8|.

110. This scholar, who was in service in Russia, sent sealed cases of secret Russian maps to France by diplomatic post. He was an undercover agent for the French Naval Ministry and received a salary of three thousand francs per year and a lifetime annuity of two thousand francs. He was subsequently expelled from Russia.

111. He first anonymously published in Berlin in 1753 "Letter from Russia from a naval officer to a certain distinguished person . . . " (soon also published in Amsterdam and London) |102|, in which he exposed the Delisle falsification.

112. The great M.V. Lomonosov gave it a favorable review, using it to further his own proposal for discovering a northeastern passage |23, p.604|. Many western scholars also valued it highly. For example, Golder wrote, "The most important book on this field is, after all, Volume Three of Müller's *Sammlung Russicher Geschichte*, published in 1758. Soon after its appearance this work was translated into Russian, English, and French. Although since that time much paper and ink have been used up in telling this story, yet very little that is new has been added to our knowledge of the subject" |31, p.339|.

113. It is characteristic of Kotsebue that even while he was promoting the project for an Antarctic expedition, he was thinking about exploring the Arctic. He recommended sailing in the southern latitudes only until the middle of February and then moving north in order to explore the Bering Strait |112, p.78|.

114. Dall remarked that Lauridsen was narrow and nationalistic, traits sometimes taken for patriotism. Lauridsen tried to find documents in Russian archives but had to give it up because of difficulty with the language.

115. Golder also worked in archives in Russia and even authored *Guide to Materials for American History in Russian Archives*, two volumes published in 1917 and 1922 in Washington, D.C. However, he did not find new materials on the First Kamchatka Expedition. In his second book |109| he basically repeats material from the first.

Archival Materials and Other Sources Consulted

1. *Atlas geograficheskikh otkrytii v Sibiri i v severo-zapadnoi Amerike, XVII-XVIII vv.* [Atlas of geographical discoveries in Siberia and in northwestern America, 17th-18th centuries]. Compiled by A.V. Efimov, M.I. Belov, O.M. Medushevskaia; edited by Corresponding Member of the Academy of Sciences of the USSR, A.V. Efimov. Moscow, 1964.
2. Belov, M.I. *Podvig Semena Dezhneva* [The exploit of Semen Dezhnev]. Moscow, 1973.
3. Navrot, M.I. "Predvaritelnoe soobrazhenie o rukopisnoi karte Sibiri nachala XVIII veka" [A preliminary consideration of the manuscript map of Siberia from the early 18th century] in *Ezhegodnik Gos. istor. muzeia za 1958 g.* Moscow, 1952.
4. *Russkie morekhody v Ledovitom i Tikhom okeanakh* [Russian seafarers in the Arctic and Pacific oceans]. *Sbornik dokumentov.* Leningrad-Moscow, 1952.
5. Efimov, A.V. *Iz istorii velikikh russkikh geograficheskikh otkrytii* [The history of great Russian geographical discoveries]. Moscow, 1971.

6. Kushnarev, E.G. "Nereshennye voprosy istorii Pervoi Kamchatkskoi Ekspeditsii" [Unresolved questions on the history of the First Kamchatka Expedition]. In *Russkie arkticheskie ekspeditsii XVIII-XX vv.* Leningrad, 1964.

7. *Ekspeditsiia Beringa* [The Bering expeditions]. *Sbornik dokumentov.* Edited by A. Pokrovskii. Moscow, 1941.

8. Berg, L.S. *Otkrytie Kamchatki i ekspeditsiia Beringa* [The discovery of Kamchatka and the Bering expeditions]. Leningrad, 1935.

9. Waksell [Waxell], Sven. *Vtoraia Kamchatskaia ekspeditsiia Vitusa Beringa* [The Second Kamchatka Expedition of Vitus Bering]. Leningrad-Moscow, 1940.

10. Perevalov, V.A. "Trudy Lomonosova po geografii severnykh poliarnykh stran" [The works of Lomonosov on the geography of the northern polar lands] in Lomonosov: *Sbornik statei i materialov.* Moscow-Leningrad, 1940.

11. *Sbornik pisem i memorialov Leibnitsa, otnosiashchikhsia k Rossii i Petru Velikomu* [Collection of letters and memoranda of Leibnitz pertaining to Russia and Peter the Great]. St. Petersburg, 1873.

12. Gere, V. *Otnoshenie Leibnitsa k Rossii i Petru Velikomu, po neizdannym bumagam Leibnitsa v Gannoverskoi biblioteke* [The relationship of Leibnitz to Russia and Peter the Great, according to unpublished papers of Leibnitz in the Hannover Library]. St. Petersburg, 1871.

13. Perri, D. *Sostoianie Rossii pri nyneshnem tsare* [The condition of Russia in the time of the present Tsar]. Moscow, 1871.

14. Pokrovskii, A.A. "Bering i ego ekspeditsiia (1725–1743 gg)" [Bering and his expeditions, 1725–1743], in *Ekspeditsiia Beringa.* Moscow, 1941.

15. *Materialy dlia istorii russkogo flota* [Materials for a history of the Russian Navy]. St. Petersburg: part 4, 1867; part 5, 1875; part 7, 1879.

16. Tsentralnyi gos. arkhiv drevnikh aktov (TSGADA), [Central State Archive of Ancient Acts], f. 397, op. 1, d. 265.

17. Andreev, A.I. "Ekspeditsiia Beringa" [The Bering Expeditions] in *Izvestiia Vsesoiuznogo geograficheskogo obshchestva,* 1943, T. 75, vyp. 2.

18. Lebedev, D.M. *Geografiia v Rossii petrovskogo vremeni* [Geography in Russia in the time of Peter the Great]. Moscow-Leningrad, 1950.

19. Belov, M.I. "Daniia i Vitus Bering" [Daniia and Vitus Bering] in *Puteshestviia i geograficheskie otkrytiia v XV-XIX vv.* Moscow-Leningrad, 1965.

20. Zubov, N.N. "Russkie moreplavateli—issledovateli morei i okeanov" [Russian seafarers—discoverers of seas and oceans] in *Russkie moreplaveteli.* Moscow, 1953.

21. Polevoi, B.P. "Glavnaia zadacha Pervoi Kamchatkskoi ekspeditsii

po zamyslu Petra I (O novoi interpretatsii instruktsii Vitusu Beringu 1725 g.)" [The main purpose of the First Kamchatka Expedition according to the intention of Peter I (Concerning a new interpretation of his instructions to Vitus Bering of 1725) in *Voprosy geografii Kamchatki*, 1964, vyp. 2.

22. *Istoriia Sibiri s drevneishikh vremen do nashikh dnei* [The history of Siberia from ancient times to the present], tom 2, 1968.

23. Lomonosov, M.V. *Polnoe sobranie sochinenie* [Complete Collection of Works]. Moscow-Leningrad, tom VI, 1952.

24. Nevelskoi, G.I. *Podvigi russkikh morskikh ofitserov na krainem vostoke Rossii, 1849–55 gg.* [The exploits of Russian naval officers in the Russian Far East, 1849–55]. Moscow-Leningrad, 1947.

25. Divin, V.A. *Russkie moreplavateli na Tikhom okeane v XVIII veke* [Russian seafarers on the Pacific Ocean in the 18th century]. Moscow-Leningrad, 1971.

26. Kushnarev, E.G. "Proekt krugosvetnogo plavaniia Kruzenshterna" [Kruzenstern's project for a circumnavigation] in *Izvestiia Vsesoiuznogo geograficheskogo obshchestva*, 1963, T. 95, vyp. 4.

27. TSGADA,f. 248, d. 666.

28. Gnucheva, V.F. *Materialy dlia istorii ekspeditsii Akademii nauk v XIX vv.* [Materials for a history of the expeditions of the Academy of Sciences in the 19th century]. Moscow-Leningrad, 1940.

29. Efimov, A.V. *Iz istorii velikikh russkikh geograficheskikh otkrytii v Severnom Ledovitom i Tikhom okeanakh, XVII-pervaia polovina XVIII v* [From the history of great Russian geographical discoveries in the northern Arctic and Pacific oceans, 17th century to the first half of the 18th century]. Moscow, 1950.

30. *Zapiski Gidrograficheskogo departamenta Morskogo ministerstva* [Notes of the Hydrographic Department of the Naval Ministry]. 1852, Ch. x.

31. Golder, F.A. *Russian Expansion on the Pacific, 1641–1850*. Cleveland, 1914.

32. Berg, L.S. *Otkrytie Kamchatki i ekspeditsii Beringa 1725–1742* [The Discovery of Kamchatka and the Bering Expeditions, 1725–1742]. Moscow-Leningrad, 1946.

33. Tsentralnyi gosudarstvennyi arkhiv voenno-morskogo flota [Central State Archive of the Navy] (TSGAVMF), f.223, op.1, d. 29.

34. TSGAVMF, f.212, d.30.

35. Arkhiv AN SSSR [Academy of Sciences of the USSR], r. IV, op.1, d.99.

36. TSGAVMF, f.233, op.1, d.235.

37. TSGAVMF, F.186, op.1, d.47.

38. TSGAVMF, f.212, op.7, d.48.

39. TSGAVMF, f.216, op.1, d.87.

40. TSGAVMF, f.186, op.1, d.43.

41. TSGAVMF, f.216, d.88.

42. Grekov, V.I. *Ocherki iz istorii russkikh geograficheskikh issledovanii v 1725–1765 gg.* Moscow, 1960.

43. Novlianskaia, M.G. "D.G. Messershmidt i ego dnevnik puteshestviia po Sibiri" [D.G. Messerschmidt and his journal of his travels in Siberia] in *Izvestiia Vsesoiuznogo geograficheskogo obshchestva*, 1962, T. 94, vyp. 3.
44. TSGADA, f. Ilimskaia voevodskaia kantselariia, d.192.
45. *Morskoi sbornik*, 1869, No. 4.
46. Polonskii, A.S. "Pervaia Kamchatskaia ekspeditsiia Beringa 1725–1729 gg" [The First Kamchatka Expedition of Bering, 1725–1729] in *Zapiski Gidrograficheskogo departamenta*, 1850, Ch. VIII.
47. TSGAVMF, f.408, Ch. 1.
48. Chukovskii, N.K. *Bering*. Moscow, 1961.
49. TSGAVMF, f.216, d.110.
50. *Zapiski Gidrograficheskogo departamenta*, 1850, Ch. VIII.
51. TSGADA, f.7 (Gosarkhiv), d.477.
52. Lebedev, D.M., Esakov, V.A. *Russkie geograficheskie otkrytiia i issledovaniia s drevnikh vremen do 1917 goda*. Moscow, 1971.
53. Vakhtin, V.V. *Russki truzheniki moria. Pervaia morskaia ekspeditsiia dlia resheniia voprosa, coediniaetsia li Aziia s Amerikoi* [Russian toilers of the sea. The first maritime expedition to resolve the question of whether Asia is joined to America]. St. Petersburg, 1890.
54. Arkhiv Leningradskogo otdeleniia Instituta istorii [LOII] Akademii nauk SSSR, f.209, op.1, d.1.
55. *Morskoi sbornik*, 1869, T. CI, No. 4.
56. *Spisok russkikh voennykh sudov*. St. Petersburg, 1872.
57. TSGAVMF, f.216, d.3.
58. TSGAVMF, f.913, op.1, d.2.
59. Lütke, F.P. *Puteshestvie vokrug sveta na voennom shliupe Seniavin v 1826–29 godakh* [Voyage around the world on the sloop-of-war *Seniavin*, 1826–29]. St. Petersburg, 1835.
60. *Liudi russkoi nauki* [Men of Russian Science], kn. 2, Moscow, 1962.
61. Divin, V.A. *Velikii russkii moreplavatel A.I. Chirikov* [The great Russian seafarer A.I. Chirikov]. Moscow, 1953.
62. *Istoriia otkrytiia i issledovaniia Sovetskoi Azii* [The history of the discovery and exploration of Soviet Asia]. Moscow, 1969.
63. Magidovich, I.P. *Ocherki po istorii geograficheskikh otkrytii* [Essays on the history of geographical discoveries]. Moscow, 1957.
64. *Russkie moreplavateli* [Russian seafarers]. Moscow, 1953.
65. Belov, M.I. *Arkticheskoe moreplavanie s drevneishikh vremen do serediny XIX veka* [Arctic voyages from ancient times to the mid-19th century]. Edited by Ia. Ia. Gakkel et al. Moscow, 1956.
66. TSGADA, f.192.
67. TSGAVMF, f.1331, op.4.
68. Müller, G.F. "Opisanie morskikh puteshestvii po Ledovitomy i Vostochnomy moriu, s rossiiskoi storony uchinennykh" [Description of sea voyages in the Arctic and Pacific oceans, undertaken from the Russian side] in *Soch. i perevody, k polze i*

uveselen. sluzhashchie, 1758, T. VII, genvar-mai; T. VIII, iiul-sentiabr, noiabr.

69. [Du Halde, J.B.] *Description geographique, historique, chronologique, politique et physique de l'Empire de la Chine, et de la Tartarie Chinoise*. Vol. IV. Paris, 1735.

70. Dall, W.H. "Critical review of Bering's first expedition, 1725–30." *National Geographic*, 1890, vol. 11, no. 2.

71. Cook, James. *The Journals of Captain James Cook on His Voyages of Discovery*. Four volumes and a portfolio. Edited from the original manuscripts by J.C. Beaglehole. Hakluyt Society, Extra Series No. XXXVI. Vol. III: The Voyage of the *Resolution* and *Discovery* 1776–1780.

72. Lütke, F.P. *Puteshestvie vokrug sveta* Seniavin *v 1826–29 godakh*. [Voyage Around the World of the Seniavin in 1826–29]. Moscow, 1948.

73. Berkh, V.N. *Pervoe morskoe puteshestvie rossiian, predpriniatoe dlia resheniia geograficheskoi zadachi: coediniaetsia li Aziia s Amerikoi i sovershennoe v 1727, 28 i 29 godakh pod nachalstvom flota kapitana I ranga Vitusa Beringa* [The first sea voyage of the Russians undertaken to resolve the geographical question of whether Asia is joined to America, accomplished in 1727, '28 and '29 under the leadership of Navy Captain First Class Vitus Bering]. St. Petersburg, 1823.

74. Baer, K.M. "Zaslugi Petra Velikogo po chasti rasprostraneniia geograficheskikh poznanii" [Peter the Great's service in spreading geographic knowledge] in *Zapiski Russkogo geographicheskogo obshchestva*, 1849, kn. 3; 1850, kn. 4.

75. Lauridsen, P. *Russian exploration, 1725–1743. Vitus Bering: The Discoverer of Bering Strait*. Chicago, 1889.

76. Dall, W.H. *Alaska and its Resources*. Boston, 1870.

77. Dobrovolskii, A.D., Zalogin, B.S. *Moria SSSR* [The seas of the USSR]. Moscow, 1965.

78. TSGAVMF, f.216, d.4.

79. *Polnoe sobranie zakonov Rossiiskoi imperii* [Complete collection of laws of the Russian Empire]. St. Petersburg, T. VIII, 1830.

80. Andreev, A.I. "Russkie otkrytiia v Tikhom okeane v pervoi chetverti XVIII v" [Russian discoveries in the Pacific Ocean in the first quarter of the 18th century] in *Izvestiia Vsesoiuznogo geograficheskogo obshchestva*, 1943, T. 75, vyp. 3.

81. Andreev, A.I. *Ocherki po istochnikovedeniiu Sibiri XVIII v (pervaia polovina)* [Essays on source materials for Siberia, first quarter of the 18th century]. Moscow-Leningrad, vyp. 2, 1965.

82. Ostrovskii, B.G. *Bering*. Leningrad, 1939.

83. TSGAVMF, f.315, op.1, d.340.

84. TSGADA, f.248, d.664.

85. Cook, James and J. King. *A Voyage to the Pacific Ocean*. Vol. II, London, 1785.

86. TSGADA, f.192 (Karty Irkutskoi gubernii) [Map of the Irkutsk gubernia].
87. *Materialy dlia istorii Akademii nauk* [Materials for a history of the Academy of Sciences], T.V, 1742–1743. St. Petersburg, 1889.
88. *Protokoly Zasedanii Konferentsii Akademii Nauk* [Protocols of the session of the conference of the Academy of Sciences], T. 1. St. Petersburg, 1897.
89. Bagrov, L.S. *Karty Aziatskoi Rossii* [Maps of Asiatic Russia]. Petrograd, 1914.
90. Müller, G.F. *Istoriia Sibiri* [History of Siberia]. T. 1. Moscow-Leningrad, 1937.
91. Wagner, H.R. *The Cartography of the Northwest Coast of America to the Year 1800*. Berkeley, 1937.
92. Fel, S. E. *Kartografiia Rossii XVIII v* [Cartography of Russia in the 18th century]. Moscow, 1960.
93. TSGAVMF, f.212, op.3, d.906.
94. Sokolov, A.P. "Severnaia ekspeditsiia 1733–43 gg" [The Northern Expedition 1733–43]. In: *Zapiski Gidrograficheskogo departamenta*, 1851, Ch. IX.
95. TSGAVMF, f.212, otd.II, d.2.
96. TSGAVMF, f.233, d.246.
97. TSGADA, f.248, d.159/2030.
98. TSGADA, f. Gosarkhiv, razr. XXIV, d.8, 1732.
99. TSGADA, f. Gosarkhiv, razr. XXI, d.9 (dop.).
100. Pikul, V. *Slovo i delo* [Word and Deed], Kn. 2. Leningrad, 1975.
101. Arkhiv LOII, AN SSSR, f.36 (Vorontsovykh), kollekts, 40. op.1, d.70.
102. Arkhiv Akademii nauk SSSR, f.21, op.5, d.159.
103. *Kratkaia reliatsiia o Sibirskoi ekspeditsii flota kapitana Beringa* [The Brief Account of the Siberian Expedition of Navy Captain Bering]. St. Petersburg, 1824.
104. Sokolov, A.P. "Naznachenie Pervoi Beringovoi ekspeditsii" [The purpose of the First Bering expedition]. In: *Zapiski Gidrograficheskogo departamenta*, 1851, Ch. IX.
105. *Severnaia pchela*, 1849, Nos. 93, 133.
106. *Russkii invalid*, 1849, Nos. 121–123.
107. Kushnarev, E.G. "Reis cherez Sibir Pervoi Kamchatskoi ekspeditsii" [The journey across Siberia of the First Kamchatka Expedition]. In: *Sibirskie ogni*, 1962, No. 9.
108. Bancroft, H.H. *Works*, Vol. 33. *History of Alaska, 1730–1885*. San Francisco, 1886.
109. Golder, F.A. *Bering's Voyages*, Vol. 1. New York, 1922.
110. Berg, L.S. *Otkrytie Kamchatki i ekspeditsiia Beringa, 1725–1742* [The discovery of Kamchatka and the Bering Expeditions, 1725–1742]. Moscow-Leningrad, 1924.
111. Zubov, N.N. *Otechestvennye moreplavateli-issledovateli morei i okeanov* [Native (Russian) Seafarer-explorers of the seas and oceans]. Moscow, 1954.

112. Sokolov, A.V. and E.G. Kushnarev, *Tri krugosvetnykh plavaniia M. P. Lazareva* [The three circumnavigations of M.P. Lazarev]. Moscow, 1951.

113. Fisher, R.H. *Bering's Voyages: Whither and Why*. Seattle and London, 1977.

114. Polevoi, B.P. "Iz istorii otkrytiia severo-zapadnoi chasti Ameriki" [History of the discovery of the northwestern part of America]. In: *Ot Aliaski do Ognennoi zemle* [From Alaska to Tierra del Fuego]. Moscow, 1967.

115. Polevoi, B.P. "K istorii formirovaniia geograficheskikh prestavlenii o severo-vostochnoi okonechnosti Azii v XVII v" [History of geographical notions/representations of the northeastern extremity of Asia in the 17th century]. In: *Sibirskii geograficheskii sbornik*, No. 3, Moscow-Leningrad, 1964.

116. Pasetskii, V.M. *Vitus Bering*. Moscow, 1982.

117. Veselago, F. *Kratkaia istoriia russkogo flota* [Brief history of the Russian fleet]. Moscow-Leningrad, 1939.

118. Belov, M.I. *Po sledam poliarnykh ekspeditsii* [In the tracks of polar expeditions]. Leningrad, 1977.

119. Glushenkov, I.V. *Navstrechu neizvestnomu* [To meet the unknown]. Leningrad, 1980.

120. Alekseev, A.I. *Kolumby russkie* [Russian Columbuses]. Magadan, 1966.

Index

North
Pacific
Studies
Series

No. 4 *The End of Russian America: Captain P. N. Golovin's Last Report, 1862.*
Translated with introduction and notes by Basil Dmytryshyn and E.A.P. Crownhart-Vaughan.
1979

No. 5 *Civil and Savage Encounters: The Worldly Travel Letters of an Imperial Russian Navy Officer, 1860–61.*
By Pavel N. Golovin.
Translated and annotated by Basil Dmytryshyn and E.A.P. Crownhart-Vaughan, introduction by Thomas Vaughan.
1983

No. 6 *Log of the* Union: *John Boit's Remarkable Voyage to the Northwest Coast and Around the World, 1794–1796.*
Edited by Edmund Hayes, foreword by Thomas Vaughan.
1981

No. 7 *For Honor and Country: The Diary of Bruno de Hezeta.*
Translated and edited by Herbert K. Beals, foreword by Thomas Vaughan.
1985

No. 8 *The Wreck of the* Sv. Nikolai: *Two Narratives of the First Russian Expedition to the Oregon Country, 1808–1810.*
Edited with introduction and notes by Kenneth N. Owens. Translated by Alton S. Donnelly.
1985

No. 9 *Russia's Conquest of Siberia, 1558–1700: A Documentary Record.*
Edited and translated by Basil Dmytryshyn, E.A.P. Crownhart-Vaughan, and Thomas Vaughan.
To Siberia and Russian America: Three Centuries of Russian Eastward Expansion, 1558–1867.
VOLUME ONE.
1985

No. 10 *Russian Penetration of the North Pacific Ocean, 1700–1797: A Documentary Record.*
Edited and translated by Basil Dmytryshyn, E.A.P. Crownhart-Vaughan and Thomas Vaughan.
To Siberia and Russian America: Three Centuries of Russian Eastward Expansion, 1558–1867.
VOLUME TWO.
1988

No. 11 *The Russian American Colonies, 1798–1867: A Documentary Record.*
Edited and translated by Basil Dmytryshyn, E.A.P. Crownhart-Vaughan and Thomas Vaughan.
To Siberia and Russian America: Three Centuries of Russian Eastward Expansion, 1558–1867.
VOLUME THREE.
1989

No. 12 *Juan Pérez on the Northwest Coast: Six Documents of His Expedition in 1774.*
Translation and annotation by Herbert K. Beals, foreword by Donald Cutter.
1990

No. 13 *Voyages of the Columbia to the Northwest Coast 1787–1790 and 1790–1793.*
Edited by Frederic W. Howay, foreword by Bruce Taylor Hamilton.
Second Edition, revised
1990

No. 14 *Soft Gold: The Fur Trade & Cultural Exchange on the Northwest Coast of America.*
Historical introduction and annotation by Thomas Vaughan. Ethnographic annotation by Bill Holm.
Second Edition, revised
1990

No. 15 *Bering's Search for the Strait: The First Kamchatka Expedition, 1725–1730.*
[*V Poiskakh Proliva: Pervaia Kamchatskaia Ekspeditsiia, 1725–1730.*]
By Eugenii G. Kushnarev. Edited and translated by E.A.P. Crownhart-Vaughan.
1990

Colophon

THIS IS THE FIFTEENTH VOLUME in the Oregon Historical Society Press' North Pacific Studies Series.

The text and display were typeset in Trump Mediaeval
by The Typeworks, of Point Roberts, Washington. Trump
Mediaeval was designed in the mid-1950s by Stuttgart designer
Georg Trump. Nearing the end of his distinguished career, Trump
produced two other well-respected type designs (Delphin and
Jaguar), as well as his namesake face. Trump Mediaeval is characterized by type scholar Charles Bigelow as "lean and lank as a
greyhound, surefooted in its chiseled serifs, the fair curves of its
arches and bowls broken by nervous calligraphic flicks. Trump
ranges on the page with a restless energy."

Edwards Brothers, of Ann Arbor, Michigan, printed and bound
the book. The paper used was 55-lb. Glatfelter B-16, an archival
stock. Holliston Kingston in Navajo Red is the cover cloth.

Borders for the maps were provided by Harold Berliner's
Typefoundry, Nevada City, California. Christine Rains prepared
the maps.

Bering's Search for the Strait was designed and produced by the
Oregon Historical Society Press.

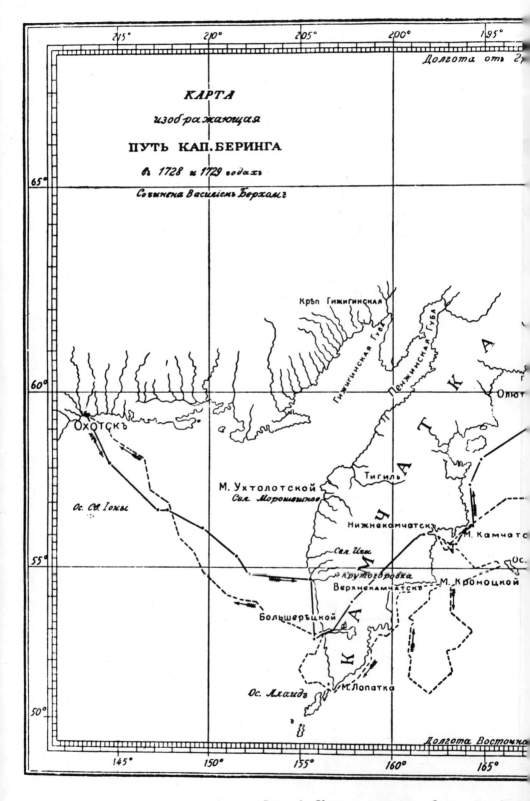

Фиг. 4. Карта плавания бота «Св. Гавр...